Grade Aid

for

Gerrig and Zimbardo

Psychology and Life

Eighteenth Edition

prepared by

Dale V. Doty
Monroe Community College

PEARSON

Boston   New York   San Francisco
Mexico City   Montreal   Toronto   London   Madrid   Munich   Paris
Hong Kong   Singapore   Tokyo   Cape Town   Sydney

ISBN-13: 978-0-205-54876-7
ISBN-10:   0-205-54876-8

Printed in the United States of America

10 9 8 7 6 5 4 3 2 1   11 10 09 08 07

Table of Contents

Preface

This Grade Aid is designed to help you understand the concepts presented in *Psychology and Life, Eighteenth Edition* by Richard Gerrig and Philip Zimbardo. The Grade Aid is an effective tool for studying, self-testing, conceptualizing, and remembering the important aspects of each chapter. At the end of the chapter, you will find an answer key to the practice tests as well as the page numbers where the correct responses can be found to help you study more efficiently.

In this Grade Aid, you will find:

- **Before You Read** sections designed to give you a brief overview of the chapter and introduce you to the major concepts that will be presented;

- **Chapter Objectives and Term Identifications** to guide your reading towards specific goals;

- **As You Read** sections composed of exercises and activities to help you comprehend the material using a variety of learning methods and strategies;

- **After You Read** sections with three practice tests, including a comprehensive exam, designed to help you review what you have learned and to give you test-taking experience; and

- **When You Have Finished** sections providing web links for further study and a crossword puzzle incorporating key words from the chapter.

We hope you will find this Grade Aid an effective study tool in your psychology course and that you enjoy delving further into the concepts presented in the text. Best of luck!

 **Chapter 1**

Psychology and Your Life

Before you read . . .

This chapter introduces you to the field of psychology. It begins with the definitions and goals of psychology then explains what makes psychology unique. You will be exposed to the history and evolution of modern psychology including its early schools and perspectives. You should gain a broader understanding of psychology's varied roots as well as current views in the field. You will learn about what psychologists do today, in what settings they are found, and in what type of work they are engaged. The chapter ends with techniques for studying psychology and other academic subjects. This first chapter lays the foundation for the perspectives of psychology which will reoccur in subsequent chapters. It also provides samples of critical thinking about psychology. It will be wise to learn about and to reflect on the early schools and perspectives so that you are well prepared for what is to come. Good luck in your quest.

Chapter Objectives

After reading this chapter you should be able to:

- Define psychology, scientific method, and behavior.

- List and describe the goals of psychology.

- Explain how structuralism and functionalism emerged, what they emphasized and how they differ.

- List and describe the seven contemporary approaches to psychology and how they differ in their view of human nature, determinants of behavior, focus of study, and research approach.

- Identify the different types of psychologists practicing today, what they do, and the settings in which they work.

- Describe effective study strategies for use in this and other courses.

As you read . . . Term Identification

Behavior	Evolutionary Perspective
Behavioral Data	Functionalism
Behavioral Neuroscience	Humanistic Perspective
Behaviorism	Psychodynamic Perspective
Behaviorist Perspective	Psychology
Biological Perspective	Scientific Method
Cognitive Neuroscience	Sociocultural Perspective
Cognitive Perspective	Scientific Method
	Structuralism

As you read . . . Questions and Answers

What Makes Psychology Unique

1. Give some examples of behavior.

2. What types of individuals do psychologists study?

3. Why is there a focus on mental processes?

4. Why is psychology considered to be a unique field?

The Goals of Psychology

1. Make sure that you understand how each of the goals is different from the others. Begin by listing the four goals of psychology:

_____   _____

_____   _____

2. Suppose you want to describe behavior. What choices must you make?

3. What does an explanation add to a description?

4. What types of factors do psychologists consider when forming explanations?

5. For what sorts of explanatory patterns do psychologists look?

6. What is the relationship between explanations and predictions?

7. Why are control and precision such important goals?

8. Give an example of how the findings of psychology can be used to help find a career.

The Evolution of Modern Psychology

1. What sorts of psychological questions have been posed by thinkers since ancient times?

2. Who were some of the figures that founded early psychological laboratories?

3. What debate arose from the emerging discipline of psychology?

4. What was the main focus of structuralism? What scholar is associated with this perspective?

5. What role did introspection play in structuralist research?

6. What were some of the important objections to structuralism?

7. Why was Gestalt psychology an alternative to structuralism?

8. What was the main focus of functionalism? What scholars are associated with this perspective?

9. Using this entire section on history, make a list of early psychologists and what they wished to study (include topics and methods):

Scholars	What they wished to study

Current Psychological Perspectives

1. List the seven perspectives that dominate contemporary psychology.

_____   _____   _____

_____   _____   _____

_____

2. What dimensions help define the unique approach of each perspective?

3. What is the importance of instinctual, biological drives in the psychodynamic perspective? What role did Freud play in the development of the psychodynamic perspective?

4. What is the main objective of behaviorist analysis, and how do behaviorists collect their data?

5. Why do humanistic psychologists focus on individual lives?

6. What determines behavior according to the cognitive perspective? Why does the cognitive perspective present a challenge to behaviorism?

7. At what levels do researchers who adopt the biological perspective try to understand behavior? What are the assumptions of the perspective?

8. How are behavioral neuroscience and cognitive neuroscience related to the biological perspective?

9. Why do researchers who adopt the evolutionary perspective analyze environmental conditions in the Pleistocene era? How does evolutionary psychology differ from other perspectives?

10. Why is cross-cultural research important for testing the universality of psychological theories?

11. How are multiple perspectives used to understand a particular domain of psychological research?

12. Describe how each perspective attempts to understand the nature of aggression and violence.

    Psychodynamic perspective

    Behaviorist perspective:

    Humanistic perspective:

    Cognitive perspective:

    Biological perspective:

    Evolutionary perspective:

    Sociocultural perspective:

What Psychologists Do

1. Why do psychologists have so many different areas of expertise?

2. Around the world, how many people are engaged in the research and practice of psychology?

3. How has the role of women changed across the history of psychology?

How to Use This Book

1. What strategies and techniques should you use to study any academic subject?

2. How will the special features included within this text help you acquire knowledge regarding psychology?

For Group Study

One of the best ways to prepare for an exam is to study with your classmates. This study guide can help you do that in many ways. For each chapter, we will also make specific suggestions of extra activities you can carry out in group study. Some of the exercises you could carry out on your own, but doing them with friends will enhance the experience. If you teach your friends and they teach you, you will end up with greater mastery of the material.

The Goals of Psychology

Choose a topic that is of interest to all the members of your group. Discuss how each of the five goals of psychology applies to an examination of that topic.

Current Psychological Perspectives

Your textbook describes how each of the seven different perspectives contributes to an analysis of aggressive behavior. Choose another aspect of human behavior that interests you, and discuss how each perspective may apply. You might consider dating and loving relationships, sports and competition, or child rearing practices.

What Psychologists Do

Try to formulate questions from your own life, and discuss what type of psychologist might answer them.

How To Use This Book

Formulate a workable plan to be successful in this psychology course.

Practice Test 1

1. Vicky and Amelia are talking about whether Rahul will be on time for an important meeting. They both say "no." Vicky thinks Rahul will be late because he is not a very conscientious person. Amelia thinks he will be late because the meeting room is hard to find. Vicky is using a(n) _____ variable; Amelia is using a(n) _____ variable.

a. internal; external
b. internal; organismic
c. stimulus; response
d. environmental; stimulus

2. Psychologists are most likely to study _____ in _____.

a. the scientific method; natural habitats
b. mental processes; individuals
c. the scientific method; individuals
d. limitations; mental processes

3. To what domain did John Dewey apply his functionalist perspective?

a. Politics
b. Physics
c. Education
d. Philosophy

4. Alberto is writing a research report on memory. In order to review the most recent information, he decides to interview a psychologist in the Psychology Department. The psychologist he will most likely interview will be a

a. clinical psychologist.
b. cognitive psychologist.
c. social psychologist.
d. personality psychologist.

5. You have been asked to represent the humanistic perspective in a panel discussion on dreaming. The title of your talk is most likely to be

a. "The Effects of Birth Order on Dream Onset."
b. "Brain Activity During Dreaming."
c. "Dreaming and Memory Enhancement."
d. "Dreaming and Creative Potential."

6. Sigmund Freud claimed that his theories of the mind were applicable to all humans. In order to test this claim, you would most likely select a researcher trained in the _____ perspective in psychology.

a. behavioral
b. biological
c. sociocultural
d. evolutionary

7. Your teacher has asked whether anyone in the class knows Wilhelm Wundt's significance to modern psychology. You should answer that Wundt

a. founded the first formal experimental psychology laboratory.
b. invented the scientific methods that ensure objectivity.
c. was one of the professors who trained Sigmund Freud.
d. originated the idea that mental processes control behavior.

8. Psychologists can be characterized as "a rather optimistic group" because they believe that

a. virtually any undesired behavior can be modified with an appropriate intervention.
b. the legal system will always follow the conclusions drawn by researchers.
c. mental processes can be understood without the use of inference.
d. ethical issues never interfere with the goal of controlling behavior.

9. Researchers who adopt the evolutionary perspective

a. explore the mechanisms that allow human brains to acquire new information.
b. view antecedents and consequences as the most important forces in the environment.
c. focus on environmental conditions in which the human brain was formed.
d. study the instinctual forces that give rise to modern behavior.

10. Which of the following might have been a book written by Edward Titchener?

a. Introspection Reveals the Contents of the Mind
b. The Triumph of Functionalism
c. The Multiple Purposes of Behavioral Acts
d. The Dangers of Reductionism

Practice Test 2

1. Dr. Kildoor takes a biological perspective on psychological research. He wants to understand why his poodle arrives in the kitchen to be fed exactly at 6 p.m., so he

a. compares his poodle to other dogs in the neighborhood.
b. records how quickly his dog is running at 6 p.m.
c. examines the environmental circumstances that gave rise to poodles as a species.
d. monitors his poodle's brain activity as the time approaches 6 p.m.

2. On your way to visit the department secretary, you overhear two psychologists having a loud discussion about what can properly be studied in the laboratory. One insists that psychologists should stick to observable behaviors. The other believes that psychologists can also study mental processes. These psychologists most likely represent the _____ perspectives.

a. behaviorist and cognitive
b. humanistic and psychodynamic
c. biological and cognitive
d. psychodynamic and biological

3. Which of the following is more than just a description of behavior?

a. Karla dropped the ball so she had to pick it up.
b. Karla was hungry so she ate a handful of cookies.
c. Karla chased another child around the playground.
d. Karla sat at her desk and sang along with the class.

4. For three years, Samantha has worked as a psychologist in a day care center for underprivileged children. She has developed a teaching program that enhances each child's self-esteem. This program most clearly satisfies psychology's goal of

a. description.
b. explanation.
c. prediction.
d. control.

5. Which of these is NOT a component of the definition of psychology?

a. mental processes
b. behavior
c. scientific study
d. level of analysis

6. The _____ perspective to the study of psychology is most likely to include researchers who focus on behaviors that are motivated by inner drives.

a. behaviorist
b. psychodynamic
c. cognitive
d. evolutionary

7. _____ focused on the way in which the mind understands organized wholes.

a. Edward Titchener
b. Max Wertheimer
c. John Dewey
d. William James

8. Structuralists and functionalists were all interested in the study of _____.

a. language
b. aggression
c. consciousness
d. scientific objectivity

9. To describe a piece of music, a friend first says "It's slow and sad" and then adds "It uses a lot of half notes and whole notes." These utterances illustrate

a. situational variables.
b. the difference between explanations and predictions.
c. the difference between the cognitive and biological perspectives.
d. levels of analysis.

10. _____ was the first woman to receive a PhD in psychology.

a. Anna Freud
b. Margaret Washburn
c. Karen Horney
d. Mary Calkins

Practice Test 3

1. Two housemates are arguing over the cause of a third housemate's poor social behavior. One attributes it to shyness, but the other believes it is due to a conceited personality. Researchers would probably judge which explanation is best by

a. measuring how strongly each housemate feels about his opinion.
b. attributing the social behavior to an intervening variable.
c. using informed imagination and inferences.
d. determining how well each explanation predicts behavior in new situations.

2. Surveys suggest that the number of practicing psychologists in the world is

a. between 100,000 and 200,000
b. between 50,000 and 100,000
c. over 500,000
d. two or three million

3. In her Research Methods course, Amy is giving a short classroom presentation on the "scientific method." She is most likely to mention the

a. steps used by researchers to analyze and solve problems.
b. general inability of scientists to draw conclusions from their research.
c. importance of authority and personal beliefs in the determination of truth.
d. reliance of researchers on biased methods.

4. While browsing in the bookstore, Roger flips through a book in the popular psychology section. Its emphasis is on the whole person, and it includes literary, historical, and artistic references. The book seems to be taking a _____ perspective.

a. humanistic
b. behavioristic
c. cognitive
d. evolutionary

5. Teachers' use of positive rewards, parents' intellectual stimulation of children, and the use of the principles of group dynamics in the workplace are all consistent with the idea that

a. psychology is little more than common sense.
b. explanation and prediction are the two most important psychological goals.
c. the use of animal participants has minimal relevance to modern psychological research.
d. psychological knowledge can be used to help improve the quality of life.

6. The best definition of behavior is

a. the means by which an organism adjusts to their environment
b. the workings of the human mind associating with others
c. internal events such as thinking, planning and reasoning
d. situational factors effecting the outcome of work

7. Many experts consider *The Principles of Psychology* to be the most important psychology text ever written. The author of this text was

a. Wilhelm Wundt
b. Max Wertheimer
c. William James
d. John Dewey

8. You see an advertisement that says "People don't read—brains read!" You suspect the person who wrote this advertisement is guided by the _____ perspective.

a. biological
b. cognitive
c. evolutionary
d. cultural

9. Which of these questions might be addressed by a developmental psychologist?

a. How can you teach a dog to fetch my slippers?
b. Why are some ideas easier to remember than other ideas?
c. What region of the brain predicts when people will be experiencing dreams?
d. Are babies color blind when they are first born?

10. Imagine being at an auction of rare manuscripts. Up for bid is a previously undiscovered early manuscript of Sigmund Freud. What would it most likely be entitled?

a. "You Are What You Eat"
b. "Evolution or Revolution?"
c. "Humans Are What Humans Do"
d. "Pushed and Pulled by Hidden Forces"

Comprehensive Test

1. Structuralism was based on the belief that

a. the mind understands many experiences as organized wholes, rather than the sum of simple parts.
b. all human mental experience could be understood as the combination of basic components.
c. introspective analyses of consciousness are too reductionistic.
d. consciousness is a property of mind in continual interaction with the environment.

2. Professor Constable has gathered data at her university in Iowa from which she has drawn the following conclusion: "All people who laugh frequently are valued by their peers." A psychologist with a _____ perspective would find this conclusion quite problematic.

a. biological
b. cognitive
c. sociocultural
d. humanistic

3. _____ psychologists attempted to answer questions relating to how people function in groups.

a. social
b. cognitive
c. human-factors
d. developmental

4. Imagine that you have decided to live your life based on the humanistic perspective. Your main task will be to

a. identify the antecedent environmental conditions that lead to your behavior.
b. try to understand the inner and outer forces that control you.
c. simply realize that life is a biochemical process.
d. strive for growth and the development of your potential.

5. All of the following are concerns of the sociocultural perspective EXCEPT the

a. role of cultural variables in the prediction of aggressive behavior.
b. effect of different languages on the way people experience the world
c. importance of advertisements in adolescents' decisions to begin smoking.
d. way cultural attitudes shape the experience of old age

6. An observer speculates that youth growing up in crime-infested environments become violent in order to survive, whereas those growing up in crime-free environments can divert their energies to less violent alternatives. This observer accepts that _____ factors are critical in explaining behavior.

a. biological
b. cultural
c. evolutionary
d. chemical

7. Dr. Soose has decided to do research on reading behavior. If he were to approach this topic from the broadest level of analysis, he would be most likely to study

a. whether there are cultural differences in attitudes toward reading.
b. the fixation points readers make while reading a page of text.
c. whether readers speak aloud while reading.
d. which parts of the brain are most active during the reading of a foreign language.

8. In his attempts to understand the violence in today's society, Desmond believes that we can learn from our early ancestors, who behaved aggressively because such adaptive behavior increased the chances of survival. It is likely that Desmond subscribes to the _____ perspective.

a. evolutionary
b. biological
c. psychodynamic
d. cognitive

9. Compared to Westerners, psychologists in Asian and African countries are more likely to have understanding as the ultimate goal in research. Which of the following perspectives promotes this view?

a. Evolutionary
b. Sociocultural
c. Psychodynamic
d. Humanistic

10. You see a list on a blackboard that contains words such as *antecedents* and *consequences*. You suspect that the list has been prepared for a lecture on the _____ perspective.

a. cognitive
b. behaviorist
c. evolutionary
d. humanistic

11. Which perspective believes that mankind is basically good and has the potential for positive growth?

a. cognitive
b. behavioral
c. psychodynamic
d. humanistic

12. Little Johnny was sent to the principle for misbehavior. He threw a spitball that hit the teacher. Lately he has been in trouble a lot. His mother recently ran off with a neighbor. Which goal of psychology does the preceding scenario answer?

a. describe
b. explain
c. predict
d. control

13. Which of the following is the best definition of psychology?

a. the study of behavior and the mind
b. the study of human and animal behavior
c. the study and practice of human psychopathology
d. the scientific study of behavior and mental processes

14. Who is considered the father of psychology?

a. Sigmund Freud
b. Wilhelm Wundt
c. John Watson
d. Ivan Pavlov

15. Dr. Clementine works with executives in a unique training program to develop leadership skills. Which specialty of psychology does he practice?
a. neuropsychology
b. human factors
c. educational
d. industrial/organizational

True/False Questions

1. The best definition of psychology is the study of behavior and mental processes.   T   F

2. Sigmund Freud was a well-known psychologist.   T   F

3. Believers of the psychodynamic perspective view the unconscious as a major determinant of behavior.   T   F

4. The goals of psychology are to describe, explain, predict and control.   T   F

5. Early psychology traces its roots to Edward Titchener, an early functionalist.   T   F

6. Functionalists used the technique of introspection.   T   F

7. The evolutionary perspective seeks to connect contemporary psychology with the life sciences.　　　　T　F

8. A cognitive psychologist would be most interested in the unconscious.　　　　T　F

Essay Questions

1. Compare and contrast the early schools of structuralism and functionalism. Which school was considered more "scientific"; which school used the technique of introspection?

2. Analyze the seven contemporary perspectives of psychology. Which theoretical concepts are important to each?

When you have finished . . . Weblinks

American Psychological Association

http://www.apa.org/

Check out the American Psychological Association's (APA) website. APA Online has many links to organizations and practical information. It is the nation's premier professional association for the field of psychology.

History of Psychology

http://elvers.stjoe.udayton.edu/history/welcome.htm

The History of Psychology website provides links to people relevant to psychology listed categorically, alphabetically and chronologically. Since the University of Dayton maintains it, it also has library links if you are in the OhioLINK system

The Psi Café

http://www.psy.pdx.edu/PsiCafe/

The Psi Café provides a gateway to the vast amount of information and resources that can be found on the internet about the general field of psychology; subfields; theories; programs; institutes; organizations; as well as application of psychological issues in everyday life.

Social Psychology Network

http://www.socialpsychology.org/career.htm

The Social Psychology website provides links to career tips for psychology students, academic careers, job listings, research in psychology, Stanford Prison experiment and interactive forums.

The Society for General Psychology – APA Division 1

http://www.apa.org/divisions/div1/pioneers.html

Portraits of Pioneers in Psychology is a history series published under the sponsorship of the Society for General Psychology, Division 1 of the American Psychological Association.

Psychology and Life

Across

3. model that emphasizes maximizing potential
7. perspective concerned with observable behavior and the environment
8. perspective that stresses human thought
9. observational reports about the behavior of organisms
10. perspective that stresses behavioral and mental adaptiveness

Down

1. model that focuses on cross-cultural differences as the cause of behavior
2. study of the structure of mind and behavior as a combination of simple elements
4. scientific approach that relies on measurable or observable behavior
5. scientific study of behavior and mental processes
6. procedures that minimize error and yield dependable generalizations

Puzzle created with Puzzlemaker at DiscoverySchool.com

Chapter 1 - Answers

Practice Test 1

1. a (p. 6)
2. b (p. 4)
3. c (p. 10)
4. b (p. 13)
5. d (p. 12)
6. c (p. 15)
7. a (p. 9)
8. a (p. 8)
9. c (p. 14)
10. a (p. 10)

Practice Test 2

1. d (p. 13)
2. a (p. 12)
3. b (p. 12)
4. d (p. 7)
5. d (p. 4)
6. b (p. 11)
7. b (p. 10)
8. c (p. 10)
9. d (p. 6)
10. b (p 19)

Practice Test 3

1. d (p. 7)
2. c (p. 18)
3. a (p. 4)
4. a (p. 12)
5. d (p. 8)
6. a (p. 4)
7. c (p. 9)
8. a (p. 13)
9. d (p. 17)
10. d (p. 11)

Comprehensive Test

Multiple Choice

1. b (p. 10)
2. c (p. 15)
3. a (p. 17)
4. d (p. 12)
5. c (p. 15)
6. b (p. 15)
7. a (p. 6)
8. a. (p. 14)
9. b (p. 15)
10. b (p. 12)
11. d (p. 12)
12. b (p. 6)
13. d (p. 4)
14. b (p. 9)
15. d (p. 17)

True/False

1. T (p. 4)
2. F (p. 11)
3. T (p. 11)
4. T (p. 5)
5. F (p. 9)
6. F (p. 10)
7. T (p. 13)
8. F (p. 13)

Crossword Key

Across

3. Humanistic
7. Behavioral
8. Cognitive
9. Behavioral Data
10. Evolutionary

Down

1. Sociocultural
2. Structuralism
4. Behaviorism
5. Psychology
6. Scientific Method

 **Chapter 2**

Research Methods in Psychology

Before you read . . .

This chapter introduces you to the process of research and explains how psychologists develop the ideas they test. It all begins with experimental methods. How are experiments designed to yield causal explanations? The chapter goes on to explore correlational methods. You'll learn why correlation does not imply causation. The issues of reliability and validity are important concepts covered in the psychological measurement portion of this chapter. These issues are just as important in self-report and behavioral measures. No coverage of scientific methods would be complete without exposure to ethical issues in human and animal research. The chapter ends with an exploration of the critical thinking skills needed to be an informed consumer. Attached to this chapter is a statistical appendix that is designed to briefly familiarize you with descriptive and inferential statistics.

Chapter Objectives

After reading this chapter you should be able to:

- Explain how a researcher formulates a theory and generates hypotheses.

- Describe the steps of the scientific method.

- Discuss how researchers combat observer biases by standardized procedures and observational definitions.

- Explain experimental research methods and the relationship between variables.

- Discuss how researchers rule out alternative explanations by using controls.

- Discuss correlation and understand why correlations do not prove causation.

- Understand how research affects your attitudes.

- Differentiate between reliability and validity.

- Describe psychological measurements including self-reports and behavioral measures.

- Appreciate the issues involved in the ethical treatment of animals and humans in research.

- Understand how to think critically and how to evaluate web information.

As you read . . . Term Identification

Behavioral Measures	Representative Sample
Between-subjects Design	Sample
Case Study	Self-report Measures
Confounding Variable	Standardization
Control Procedures	Theory
Correlation Coefficient	Validity
Correlational Methods	Variable
Debriefing	Within-subjects design
Dependent Variable	Descriptive Statistics
Determinism	Frequency Distribution
Double Blind Control	Inferential Statistics
Expectancy Effects	Mean
Experimental Methods	Measures of Central Tendency
Hypothesis	Measures of Variability
Independent Variable	Median
Observer Bias	Mode
Operational Definition	Normal Curve
Placebo Control	Range
Placebo Effects	Significant Difference
Population	Standard Deviation
Reliability	

As you read . . . Questions and Answers

The Process of Research

1. What is meant by critical thinking skills?

2. What is meant by determinism?

3. What are hypotheses and their sources?

4. What kind of attitude is needed for scientific research?

5. Why is public verifiability important?

6. What conclusions does the scientific method allow researchers to make?

Observer Biases and Operational Definitions

1. Summarize the effects of observer biases.

2. Describe a situation from your own life that might have been affected by observer bias.

3. Why is standardization important? What is an operational definition?

Consider an experiment in which a researcher examines the effects of mood on memory. She is going to use hypnotic induction to place participants in a happy, sad, or neutral mood, and then ask them to share childhood memories. The researcher wants to determine whether the emotional tone of the memories matches the mood in which the participants have been placed.

4. What is/are the independent variable(s)?

5. What is/are the dependent variable(s)?

6. How might you operationalize the "emotional tone" of the memories? That is, how would you measure their "emotional tone?"

Experimental Methods: Alternative Explanations and the Need for Controls

1. You see a man running out of a building. What are some explanations for this behavior? Suppose you wanted to test one explanation. What might some confounding variables be?

2. Why do researchers worry about expectancy and placebo effects?

3. A researcher wishes to show that people who are given chocolate to eat have an easier time memorizing lists of words. Consider these procedures:

    A. The experimenter who gives each participant chocolate (or not) is different from the experimenter who administers the memory test.

    B. One group of participants is not given any food, but each participant in this group spends as much time in the experimental room before taking the memory test as do the "chocolate" participants.

        a) Which of these is a double-blind control? Which is a placebo control? Why?

        b) What problems in interpretation of the results do these two controls prevent?

        c) Is this a between-subjects or within-subjects design? How could you change the experiment to transform it from one to the other?

Correlational Methods

1. Make sure you understand the difference between positive and negative correlations. Can you think of a real-world example in which high values on one dimension are generally matched by high values on a second dimension (a positive correlation)? Can you think of a real-world negative correlation?

2. Summarize an example from the textbook of why correlation does not imply causation.

Subliminal Influence

What was the result when researchers examined subliminal influence in the laboratory?

Psychology In Your Life

What do you need to consider when answering 'research' questions?

Psychological Measurement

What are reliability and validity?

Self-Report Measures

1. What types of information are gathered through self-report?

2. What are common self-report methods?

Behavioral Measures and Observations

1. What is meant by behavioral measures?

2. What do observations focus on?

3. What sets naturalistic observation apart from other behavioral measures?

4. Why is Jane Goodall's research an example of naturalistic observation?

5. What would be a self-report measure for sleepiness? What would be a behavioral measure? (Challenge yourself to provide more than one measure for other phenomena that interest you.)

6. How is a case study different/the same as self-report measures? Behavioral observations?

Ethical Issues in Human and Animal Research

1. For these four brief sections, focus on the types of ethical issues researchers must consider before they set out to conduct a study.

   A. Informed Consent
   B. Risk/Gain Assessment
   C. Intentional Deception
   D. Debriefing

2. Why are informed consent and debriefing such crucial parts of ethical research?

Issues in Animal Research:

Summarize the debate over the uses of nonhuman animals in psychological research by describing how each of the following might respond.

Professor Yes (supports the use of nonhuman animals in restricted circumstances):

Professor No (believes all nonhuman research should be banned):

Becoming a Wiser Research Consumer

1. Make sure you understand what the authors mean by "becoming a wiser research consumer".

2. How can studying psychology help you in becoming a wiser research consumer?

Critical Thinking In Your Life

1. What standards should you use to evaluate the authenticity of information on the web?

Statistical Supplement

What were the hypotheses of the *sudden murderers* study?

Analyzing the Data: Descriptive Statistics

1. What is the purpose of frequency distributions?

2. What do you learn from bar graphs?

3. What are three different measures of central tendency? How are they defined or calculated?

4. What is variability? What are two measures of variability? How are they defined?

5. What is measured by correlation coefficients?

Inferential Statistics

1. What is the role of the normal curve for inferential statistics?

2. What is meant by statistical significance? How are significant differences defined?

1. What steps can you take to be a wise consumer of statistics?

2. Overall, do the statistical analyses provide evidence in favor of the hypotheses of the sudden murderers study?

For Group Study

The Process of Research

Choose some real-life issues for which psychological data might be relevant (you may already have done this for Chapter 1). Discuss in what ways the current societal context might influence the hypotheses people would develop to explain important phenomena. You might consider, for example, the roots of criminal behavior or concerns about violence on television.

Observer Biases and Operational Definitions

Challenge each other to operationalize abstract concepts. How would you measure equality? Freedom? Honesty? Courage?

Experimental Methods: Alternative Explanations and the Need for Controls

Watch a television program with the sound off and try to come up with alternative explanations for the behavior you see. Discuss what evidence you would need to decide among the alternative explanations. (If you don't have a television handy, try watching people who are far enough away so that you can't hear them.)

Self-Report Measures

Find a recent newspaper or magazine that presents poll or survey data. Discuss the wording of the questions that were asked. Do you think the wording or type of question (for example, open-ended vs. fixed alternatives) influenced the answers that were given or the conclusions that were drawn?

Behavioral Measures and Observations

Look out the window at people walking by and try to describe as precisely as possible what they are doing. Discuss how you can reach agreement on judgments that are potentially subjective. Are the people happy? Are they angry? Are they in love? Are they having a fight?

Practice Test 1

1. Ms. Gap does a study to determine the relationship between age and amount of money spent on new clothing. She discovers that the older an adult gets, the less money he or she generally spends on clothing. This is a

a. base rate estimate.
b. negative correlation.
c. dependent variable.
d. positive correlation.

2. Your history professor catches you yawning during his lecture and asks you how much sleep you got last night. When you say, "five hours," he concludes that you wouldn't be yawning if you got more sleep. One possible confounding variable that your professor may be overlooking is that

a. you get only five hours of sleep every night.
b. the professor was giving a boring lecture.
c. you got up early to come to history class.
d. the professor got eight hours of sleep.

3. You heard a report on the news this morning that 72% of car owners drive over the speed limit because they don't believe they will get caught. The most likely source of this information is

a. case histories.
b. behavioral observations.
c. self-report questionnaires.
d. placebo biases.

4. You are given a list of test scores to analyze: 100, 94, 97, 94, 94, 62, 75, 88, 94, 92. Without doing any calculations, it would be pretty easy for you to identify the _____ of the distribution.

a. mean
b. mode
c. range
d. standard deviation

5. Which of the following is likely to be the conclusion from a study using a correlational method?

a. Children sleep better when they are read stories at bedtime.
b. Rats learn mazes best when they receive food as a reward.
c. People find horror movies less scary after they have viewed a television program that explains special effects.
d. Women are more likely than men to talk with friends about personal problems.

6. A critic of Professor Clark's research has suggested that all of his results can be explained in terms of expectancy effects. The strongest counterargument that Professor Clark could offer would be to say that

a. he operationalized all his variables.
b. he used a case history.
c. he used a double-blind control.
d. he used a between-subjects design.

7. While walking past an auditorium, you overhear, "There are no morally relevant differences between human and nonhuman animals." The debate is likely to be about the

a. ethics of using nonhuman animals as participants in psychological research.
b. ethics of using deception without informed consent.
c. importance of studying basic psychological processes in a wide range of species.
d. importance of debriefing all experimental participants.

8. You are looking at a friend's notes from a lecture on the scientific method. You discover that the only statement he got down correctly is that

a. independent variables must be operationalized.
b. some variables cannot be operationalized.
c. experiments must have more dependent variables than independent variables.
d. dependent variables are more valid than independent variables.

9. One day when you have nothing better to do, you decide to try out two new recipes for chocolate chip cookies. You want to determine which of them yields tastier cookies. You ask ten friends to try one cookie from each recipe and then tell you which one he or she prefers. This is a(n)

a. naturalistic design.
b. between-subjects design.
c. within-subjects design.
d. placebo control.

10. Prior to an experiment, participants must give their informed consent. This means that they

a. have been made aware of the risks and benefits of the experiment.
b. have agreed that the risks of the experiment outweigh the benefits.
c. will try to recall all the information given to them during the experimental session.
d. will try to provide data in line with the experimenter's predictions.

Practice Test 2

1. Tommy claims that he doesn't believe in the assumption of determinism. Which of the following is a statement he's likely to make?

a. "Sometimes people fail no matter how determined they are to succeed."
b. "The scientific method is only appropriate for research with humans."
c. "You can test some hypotheses without using an independent variable."
d. "Some behaviors are not brought about by specific causal factors."

2. Imagine that you are a new teacher and that you want to study the effect of rewards on children's performance in school. You might choose as a dependent variable

a. the number of As each child gets.
b. each child's age at the beginning of the study.
c. the number of brothers and sisters each child has.
d. each teacher's attitude toward rewards.

3. Mrs. Kim thought that her son was the best actor in his high school play. A psychologist might say that Mrs. Kim's judgment was influenced by

a. an ordeal of proof.
b. an observer bias.
c. standardization.
d. placebo effects.

4. Hiroko is planning research on advertisements. She wishes to show that teenagers are more likely to buy soft drinks that contain extra amounts of caffeine. If she wants her conclusions to be valid, it's important that Hiroko start with a

a. double-blind control.
b. placebo control.
c. context of justification.
d. representative sample.

5. Which correlation coefficient must be a mistake?

a. -0.7
b. 0.0
c. +1.0
d. +2.4

6. Which of these is NOT an example of a descriptive statistic?

a. range
b. significance test
c. standard deviation
d. correlation coefficient

7. Fillmore announces that he has collected convincing data that support the existence of extrasensory perception. As the next step in the research process, Fillmore should

a. carefully operationalize and standardize each of the variables in the study.
b. keep his methods secret to protect the anonymity of his participants.
c. publicly verify that he is a trained experimentalist.
d. reveal his methods so that other researchers can attempt to replicate his findings.

8. Research on subliminal audiotapes demonstrated that participants believed their memory improved when they "listened" to tapes that were marked "memory" but were actually about "self-esteem." This is a good example of a

a. confounding variable.
b. correlation.
c. placebo effect.
d. expectancy effect.

9. A key feature of naturalistic observation is that the experimenter

a. uses only open-ended questions.
b. does not interfere with the behavior being studied.
c. observes the same participants for several years.
d. attempts to re-create a natural behavior in a laboratory setting.

10. Mia complains that her weight scale gives her vastly different measurements of her weight from hour to hour. You assume that the scale is

a. valid.
b. consistent.
c. reliable.
d. not reliable.

Practice Test 3

1. In a _____ research design, each participant serves as his or her own control.

a. between-subjects
b. double-blind
c. placebo effect
d. within-subjects

2. In a national survey, a researcher determines that states that have instituted a death penalty have shown a decrease in violent crimes. Assuming that the data are accurate, what can the researcher conclude?

a. The death penalty is a deterrent to violent crime.
b. Violent criminals have probably moved to states that do not have a death penalty.
c. There are fewer violent crimes in states that have a death penalty.
d. A third variable is causing the relationship.

3. Johan is conducting an experiment. When he is in the right mood, he gives participants the instructions orally and answers their questions. At other times, he has the participants read the instructions on a computer screen. It sounds like Johan has forgotten to be careful about

a. standardization.
b. placebo effects.
c. double-blind controls.
d. representative samples.

4. You have been hired to do research for a perfume company. You are testing two new perfumes to see which customers prefer. However, the samples you are using are numbered so that you do not know which is which, nor do the customers know which sample they are getting. You are using a

a. double-blind control procedure.
b. correlational method.
c. placebo control procedure.
d. naturalistic observation procedure.

5. You are applying for a job at a clothing store. To get the job, you are asked to complete a test that asks you questions about the most popular movies of 1929. You would probably argue that the test is NOT a _____ measure of your potential job performance.

a. reliable or valid
b. reliable
c. correlational
d. valid

6. A researcher is interested in how best to prevent panic behavior. As part of his procedure, he plans on locking participants in a room, pumping fake smoke under the door, and sounding the fire alarm. How should he handle the issue of deception?

a. He must tell the participants everything he plans to do.
b. Once the participants consent to participate, he can do whatever he wants.
c. It would be best if he said nothing to the participants about the deception.
d. He should consider alternatives to deception and reduce potential risks.

7. In a study described in the text, an investigator designed an experiment to test the hypothesis that "morning people" feel best performing tasks in the morning. He administered coffee to participants to enhance performance. What happened to the people in the treatment condition?

a. Participants were asked to fill out a questionnaire about their evening/morning preference.
b. Their performance on a memory task improved regardless of the time of day.
c. Their performance on a memory task declined regardless of the time of day.
d. Their performance on a memory task improved in the morning.

8. You read in the newspaper that there is a positive correlation between hat size and intelligence. From this statistic, you know that people who have _____ hat sizes also have _____ intelligence.

a. larger; higher
b. larger; lower
c. smaller; higher
d. smaller; lower

9. A researcher is investigating the effects of breathing techniques on the reduction of stress. Some participants use one breathing technique and others use a different technique. Each participant's level of stress is then measured with a paper-and-pencil questionnaire. What are the independent (IV) and dependent variables (DV)?

a. The IV is the type of breathing technique, and the DV is the number of participants in the study.
b. The IV is the level of stress, and the DV is the number of participants in the study.
c. The IV is one breathing technique, and the DV is the other breathing technique.
d. The IV is the type of breathing technique, and the DV is the level of stress.

10. Carol wishes to determine the central tendency for age in her family. The five ages are 12, 15, 23, 50, and 55. For Carol's family the _____ is bigger than the _____.

a. mean; range
b. median; mean
c. median; range
d. mean; median

Comprehensive Test

1. An investigator is interested in whether ignoring a child's misbehavior will reduce its occurrence. In the first and third week of a study, a child's acts of misbehavior are recorded. In the second week, teachers are instructed to ignore such misbehavior, and the number of incidents is also recorded. What type of research design is being used?

a. between-subjects
b. within-subjects
c. placebo control
d. experimental and control group

2. A teacher is interested in measuring the amount of time that a student in her class is on-task versus off-task. Your recommendation to this teacher is that she use

a. a questionnaire.
b. a self-report measure.
c. a behavioral measure.
d. a face-to-face interview.

3. If a driver is given a ticket for speeding, he or she will be less likely to exceed the speed limit in the future. This statement is an example of a(n)

a. hypothesis.
b. control attempt.
c. operational definition.
d. expectancy effect.

4. In a classic experiment, students were given rats that were all from the same group. However, half the students were told their rats were "maze-bright," and half were told their rats were "maze-dull." When their performance on the mazes were measured,

a. the labels had no impact on the rats' ability to learn.
b. the "bright" rats did not meet the students' expectations.
c. the "dull" rats were unable to learn the mazes at all.
d. the "bright" rats learned better than the "dull" rats.

5. Your friend Charlie is very excited about the new subliminal tape he has just purchased to help him quit smoking. Knowing something about the research on subliminal influences, you feel the need to inform him that

a. you are glad he finally has chosen a strategy that will work for him.
b. he is probably wasting his money.
c. all you have read about subliminal influences supports its validity.
d. subliminal tapes will not help him quit smoking, but may help him lose weight.

6. A researcher is interested in testing the effects of alcohol on driving ability. She believes alcohol will slow reaction time enough to interfere with driving. She varies the amount of alcohol ingested in the experimental and control groups and measures reaction time. In this experiment the independent variable is

a. the amount of alcohol ingested.
b. the reaction time.
c. the driving ability.
d. the control group.

7. In a drug trial there are four groups. One group gets the experimental drug x, another group gets an older drug, a third group gets a placebo and the last group receives no treatment. Researchers measure life expectancy by recording the number of days until death. What is the dependent variable?

a. drug X
b. the older drug
c. the placebo
d. life expectancy

8. Psychology is considered a science because it

a. follows rules of the scientific method
b. allows for experimentation
c. supports critical thinking
d. proposes theories

9. _____ is the degree to which a test produces similar scores, while _____ is the extent to which a test measures what it was intended to measure.

a. Validity, reliability
b. Reliability, validity
c. Self-report, honesty
d. Honesty, self-report

10. Which of the following is NOT an issue in the ethical treatment of participants in research?

a. deception
b. debriefing
c. deviance
d. informed consent

11. Jack is a fan of the Red Flops. Jill is a fan of the White Flops. They both wish to describe to you what happened in a controversial game between the two teams. You suspect that their accounts will show the influence of

a. confounding variables.
b. observer biases.
c. expectancy effects.
d. placebo effects.

12. As a class exercise, Nancy is required to carry out a naturalistic observation. Which of these would be appropriate? She:

a. visits a mall to see how many people shop by themselves or with others.
b. plays with children at a park to see how they respond to a stranger.
c. interviews her fellow students about their most and least favorite courses.
d. administers a survey about the food in her college's main cafeteria.

13. An experimenter completes a study on movie-going. In his sample, right-handed people had seen an average of 11 movies in the past year and left-handed people had seen 15. To determine whether that difference can be generalized beyond his sample, the experimenter will use _____.

a. inferential statistics
b. descriptive statistics
c. correlational methods
d. control procedures

14. Bettina claims that every time she goes jogging, bees come out to attack her. She takes this very personally. You've even heard her say, "The bees are out to get me." You might explain to her that

a. she needs a placebo control group to test her hypothesis.
b. correlation does not imply causation.
c. bees are not appropriate research subjects.
d. she needs to operationalize her claim.

15. Imagine that a researcher has just completed a study. During the study, participants were partly deceived, and some were made to feel embarrassment. After collecting the data, the researcher met briefly with the participants, thanking them for their participation, and paying them for their time. Should the researcher have done anything else after the study?

a. Since the participants were paid, the researcher was under no obligation to do more than was done.
b. The participants should have gone through a formal debriefing process.
c. The researcher should have addressed their embarrassment, but not mention the deception.
d. The participants should have been asked to give informed consent after the study was over.

True/False Questions

1. The dependent variable is the thing that is measured in an experiment.		T	F
2. Correlation helps prove causation.		T	F
3. Psychologists often disregard ethical principles when it comes to research with animals.		T	F
4. A single representative score that can be used as an index of the most typical score in a group is known as a measure of central tendency.		T	F
5. Debriefing occurs at the start of a research project when participants are given a description of the procedures.		T	F
6. In a double-blind control, only the experimenter knows who gets the treatment.		T	F
7. Questionnaires or surveys are also known as self-report measures.		T	F
8. Correlation coefficients vary between −1.0 and +1.0.		T	F

Essay Questions

1 Discuss the steps to becoming a wise consumer of research.

2. Is psychology a science? Why or why not? Explain the steps of the scientific method.

When you have finished . . . Weblinks

Online Experiments

http://psychexps.olemiss.edu/

Participate in online experiments. This site maintained by the University of Mississippi contains experiments and demonstrations that can be done totally online.

Psych Crawler

http://www.psychcrawler.com

With Psych Crawler, the official APA sponsored search engine, you can find quality sites on the Internet related to research or whatever topic you choose.

APA Ethical Principles

http://www.apa.org/ethics/code2002.html

View the ethical principles of psychologists and conduct code at the official American Psychological Association (APA) web site. Revised in June 2003, these are the standards to which academic, research and professional psychologists adhere.

Research Methods in Psychology

http://du.edu/psychology/methods/

This site developed by the University of Denver provides resources for hands-on learning in research methods and statistics.

Psychology in America

http://serendip.brynmawr.edu/Mind/before.html

Psychological research by pre-contemporary researchers is explained in detail, as well as how it relates to the development of psychology as we know it today.

Research Methods in Psychology

Across

5. belief that treatment will be effective
6. conducted at the end of an experiment to minimize participant confusion
8. in depth observation of an individual
9. organized set of concepts that explains a phenomenon
10. entire set of individuals to which generalizations will be made from the experiment
11. subset of a population selected as participants in an experiment
12. variable that a researcher manipulates

Down

1. idea that all events are determined by causal factors
2. the degree to which a test produces the similar scores when repeated
3. variable that a researcher measures
4. extent to which a test measures what it intends to measure
6. when both participants and experimenters are unaware of who has received which treatment
7. testable explanation of the relationship between two variables
8. research method that determines the extent to which variables are related

Puzzle created with Puzzlemaker at DiscoverySchool.com

Chapter 2 - Answers

Practice Test 1

1. b (p. 33)
2. b (p. 30)
3. c (p. 37)
4. b (p. 49)
5. d (p. 33)
6. c (p. 31)
7. a (p. 41)
8. a (p. 28)
9. c (p. 32)
10. a (p. 40)

Practice Test 2

1. d (p. 26)
2. a (p. 29)
3. b (p. 27)
4. d (p. 32)
5. d. (p. 33)
6. b (p. 48)
7. d. (p. 26)
8. c (p. 31)
9. b (p. 38)
10. d (p. 37)

Practice Test 3

1. d (p. 32)
2. c (p. 33)
3. a (p. 28)
4. a (p. 31)
5. d (p. 37)
6. d (p. 41)
7. b (p. 28)
8. a (p. 33)
9. d (p. 29)
10. d (p. 50)

Comprehensive Test

Multiple Choice	True/False
1. b (p. 32)	1. T (p. 29)
2. c (p. 38)	2. F (p. 33)
3. a (p. 26)	3. F (p. 41)
4. d (p. 30)	4. T (p. 49)
5. b (p. 34)	5. F (p. 41)
6. a (p. 29)	6. F (p. 31)
7. d (p. 29)	7. T (p. 37)
8. a (p. 26)	8. T (p. 33)
9. b (p. 37)	
10. c (p. 40)	
11. b (p. 27)	
12. a (p. 38)	
13. a (p. 48)	
14. b (p. 33)	
15. b (p. 41)	

Crossword Key

Across

5. Placebo
6. Debriefing
8. Case Study
9. Theory
10. Population
11. Sample
12. Independent variable

Down

1. Determinism
2. Reliability
3. Dependent variable
4. Validity
6. Double blind
7. Hypothesis
8. Correlation

📖 Chapter 3

The Biological and Evolutionary Bases of Behavior

Before you read . . .

This chapter is technical, yet worth mastering. It begins with coverage on heredity and behavior. It explains the history of evolution and natural selection, then presents variations in the human genotype. Biological concepts will appear throughout this chapter. Starting with the basic unit of the nervous system, the neuron is presented in detail including its structure, the action potential, the neurotransmitters and their functions. The brain, brain imaging, structure, and physiology are thoroughly reviewed. Brief exposure to the endocrine system is included. The chapter concludes with the nervous system in action. These biological concepts serve as the foundation for subsequent chapters. We are, after all, a society in which complex issues are understood in ever increasing biological terms.

Chapter Objectives

After reading this chapter you should be able to:

- Discuss the principles of natural selection.

- Trace the advances made in the evolution of humans.

- Define the basic unit of heredity.

- Describe the function of the neuron.

- Explain the parts of the neuron and what each does.

- Discuss the action potential in terms of thresholds and the "All-or-None" law.

- Explain the action and role of the neurotransmitters.

- List and define the various brain imaging techniques.

- Describe the parts of the central nervous system.

- Elaborate on the brain's three layers, the brain stem, limbic system, and cerebrum.

- Describe the functions of the right and left-brain.

- Explain how the endocrine system releases hormones that help regulate growth, sexual characteristics, metabolism, digestion and arousal.

As you read . . . Term Identification

Action Potential	Lesions
All-or-None Law	Limbic System
Amygdala	Magnetic Resonance Imaging (MRI)
Association Cortex	Medulla
Auditory Cortex	Motor Cortex
Autonomic Nervous System (ANS)	Motor Neurons
Axon	Natural Selection
Brain Stem	Neurogenesis
Broca's Area	Neuromodulator
Central Nervous System (CNS)	Neuron
Cerebellum	Neuroscience
Cerebral Cortex	Neurotransmitters
Cerebral Hemispheres	Occipital Lobe
Cerebrum	Parasympathetic Division
Corpus Callosum	Parietal Lobe
Dendrites	Peripheral Nervous System (PNS)
DNA (Deoxyribonucleic Acid)	PET Scans
Electroencephalogram (EEG)	Phenotype
Endocrine System	Pituitary Gland
Estrogen	Plasticity
Evolutionary Psychology	Pons
Excitatory Inputs	Refractory Period
Frontal Lobe	Repetitive Transcranial Magnetic Stimulation (rTMS)
Functional MRI (fMRI)	Resting Potential
Genes	Reticular Formation
Genetics	Sensory Neurons
Genome	Sex Chromosomes
Genotype	Sociobiology
Glia	Soma
Heredity	Somatic Nervous System
Heritability	Somatosensory Cortex
Hippocampus	Sympathetic Division
Homeostasis	Synapse
Hormones	Synaptic Transmission
Human Behavior Genetics	Temporal Lobe
Hypothalamus	Terminal Buttons
Inhibitory Inputs	Testosterone
Interneurons	Thalamus
Ion Channels	Visual Cortex

As you read . . . Questions and Answers

Heredity and Behavior

What is meant by the contrast between nature and nurture?

Evolution and Natural Selection

1. What observations led Darwin to propose the mechanism of natural selection? What has Peter and Rosemary Grant's research added to Darwin's observations?

2. What is meant by the phrase "survival of the fittest"?

3. Define genotype and phenotype.

4. Why are bipedalism and encephalization landmarks in human evolution?

5. How is language important for cultural evolution?

Variation in the Human Genotype

1. Describe is the study of genetics.

2. How many chromosomes did you inherit from each parent? Try to invent a strategy to remember that women have XX pairings and men XY.

3. What comparisons are necessary to draw conclusions about genetic influences on behavior?

4. What is the value of comparing monozygotic and dizygotic twins?

5. Why should conclusions about genetic aspects of happiness be drawn cautiously?

6. What are the goals of sociobiology and evolutionary psychology?

The Neuron

1. Draw your own picture of a neuron and label each of its parts.

2. What are three types of neurons?

3. What functions do glia serve?

Action Potentials

1. What is the contrast between excitatory and inhibitory inputs?

This is a section of the textbook with several figures that should help you understand the text. Try to work back and forth between the text and the figures. After you have studied, try to re-create rough versions of the figures on a blank piece of paper.

2. Define:

Action potential

Resting potential

Ion channels

Depolarization

3. How is the action potential passed down the axon?

4. Define:

    All-or-None law

    Myelinated neurons

    Nodes of Ranvier

    Refractory period (what is its function?)

Synaptic Transmission

Draw a diagram of a synapse and label the parts of the presynaptic and postsynaptic neurons.

Neurotransmitters and Their Functions

Summarize the properties of each neurotransmitter:

    Acetylcholine

    GABA

    Dopamine

    Norepinephrine

    Serotonin

    Endorphins (what is a neuromodulator?)

This section outlines a number of techniques to acquire information from the brain. For each technique, summarize how it is used. Identify Paul Broca and Walter Hess with the appropriate methodology.

1. Interventions within the brain

    Lesions

    Electrical stimulation

2. Recording and imaging brain activity

    EEG

    PET scans

    MRI and fMRI

What is meant by 'it's genetic'?

1. Make sure you can recall the major divisions of the nervous system. What functions does each division carry out?

    Central nervous system (CNS)

    Peripheral nervous system (PNS)

    Somatic nervous system

Autonomic nervous system

Sympathetic division

Parasympathetic division

2. How do the sympathetic and parasympathetic divisions work in opposition?

Brain Structures and Their Functions

For each of the following structures, study the figures in the text to see where it is located, then briefly summarize its function.

1. The Brain Stem

    Medulla

    Pons

    Reticular Formation

    Thalamus

    Cerebellum

2. The Limbic System

    Hippocampus

    Amygdala

    Hypothalamus

3. The Cerebrum

    Make sure you are able to locate the four lobes. List them here:

    _____   _____

    _____   _____

4. Cerebral Cortex

5. Cerebral Hemispheres

6. Corpus Callosum

7. Motor Cortex

8. Somatosensory Cortex

9. Auditory Cortex

10. Visual Cortex

11. Association Cortex

Hemispheric Lateralization

1. Make sure you understand the logic of the experiments with split-brain patients. Use the research of Roger Sperry and Michael Gazzaniga as an example.

2. What does it mean that "many language-related functions are *lateralized*"?

3. Make sure you understand the distinction between analytic and holistic processing. Why are both valuable?

4. What evidence suggests that there are characteristic differences between the brains of males and females?

The Endocrine System

1. What are hormones and what do they do?

2. Study the figure and table in your book to see the locations of endocrine glands and their functions.

3. What role does the hypothalamus serve in the endocrine system? What functions does the pituitary gland serve?

4. What are the functions of testosterone and estrogen?

Plasticity and Neurogenesis

How does plasticity relate to life experiences?

1. How do pleasant or unpleasant stimuli produce different patterns of activity in your brain? Does music produce the same pattern?

2. Explain how music can send "chills" down your spine.

For Group Study

Heredity and Behavior

You can use a group of friends to make sure you understand the distinctions made in this section. Can you identify different genotypes and phenotypes in the room? Also, you can start to think about the effects of nature and nurture. How would each of you explain differences between you and your brothers and sisters?

Biology and Behavior

This chapter introduces a large number of specialized terms. The best way to learn them is by creating a set of flash cards with your study group. Help each other by going through the cards and making sure each person can reproduce the correct information. You can also devise strategies together for remembering the different terms. (Perhaps, for example, you can remember the function of the "reticular formation" because it reminds you of "tickle," which is something someone could do to keep you alert. We suspect your group can do better than that!) This same advice applies to later sections of the chapter. It will help you to join forces to develop strategies for mastering the material.

Hemispheric Lateralization

Try to think about "analytic" and "holistic" approaches to everyday tasks. Can you detect different approaches that seem characteristic of each member of the group? Do some people seem more analytic or more holistic?

After you read . . . Practice Tests

Practice Test 1

1. A movie director needs to cast someone who looks like a villain. He is most interested in the actor's

a. cultural evolution.
b. chromosomes.
c. phenotype.
d. genotype.

2. Carson has recently been diagnosed as suffering from clinical depression. If you had to guess which neurotransmitter is playing a role in his mood illness, you would be correct in saying

a. acetylcholine.
b. GABA.
c. norepinephrine.
d. endorphin.

3. Lara was in an accident that left her with some brain damage. She now has difficulty speaking. If Lara is right-handed, the area of damage is likely to be in the

a. corpus callosum.
b. brain stem.
c. left hemisphere.
d. right hemisphere.

4. A speaker is discussing how a special adaptation in humans allowed humans to engage in complex thinking, remembering, and reasoning. You know that the adaptation the speaker is referring to is

a. bipedalism.
b. encephalization.
c. social cooperation.
d. language.

5. If you suffered damage to your _____, you might experience difficulty learning the names of new acquaintances.

a. hypothalamus
b. hippocampus
c. reticular formation
d. pons

6. Which of the following might be the title of a book about endocrine activity?

a. <u>Be Happy about Hormones</u>
b. <u>My Favorite Synapse</u>
c. <u>Are You Sympathetic to Your Nervous System?</u>
d. <u>Those Nutty Neurons!</u>

7. Which of the following is NOT true of the resting potential?

a. There is a greater percentage of sodium in the fluid outside the neuron.
b. There is a greater percentage of potassium in the fluid inside the neuron.
c. The fluid inside the neuron is polarized with respect to the fluid outside the neuron.
d. Sodium channels are open to permit the flow of ions into the neuron.

8. How do Darwin's finches illustrate the principle of natural selection?

a. They are more likely than other species to live in family clusters.
b. They seek out environments where is is easy for them to obtain food.
c. Their phenotypes are unrelated to their genotypes.
d. The shapes of their beaks suggests adaptation to different environments.

9. Suppose you were having a conversation with a neuron. Which statement would it be likely to make?

a. "There are a whole lot of us, but I've never touched another neuron."
b. "I wish I had more terminal buttons on my dendrites."
c. "My myelin sheath slows down the rate at which I can transmit an action potential."
d. "Sometimes I generate a large action potential; sometimes I generate a small one."

10. You have decided to attend a costume party dressed as a neuron. Which of the following should NOT be a feature of your costume?

a. A wig on your head could represent myelin sheaths.
b. A "soma" tee shirt with a cell nucleus drawn on it.
c. You could use your arms as dendrites.
d. Receptor molecules painted on each of your fingers.

Practice Test 2

1. Research on patients who have undergone split-brain surgery has shown that

a. extensive therapy is usually required to teach the patient to speak correctly..
b. there will be a significant difference in how they process the written word.
c. their behavior after the surgery will be, for the most part, normal.
d. their spoken and written language centers will be reversed.

2. Repetitive transcranial magnetic stimulation (rTMS) allow researchers to

a. image several brain areas simultaneously.
b. monitor the flow of blood in the brain.
c. create temporary brain lesions.
d. study the effects of brain damage on cognitive processes.

3. Which statement is most accurate about the role of your two cerebral hemispheres in carrying out day-to-day life functions?

a. Most functions are performed in one hemisphere or the other.
b. Their different processing styles contribute to most of the functions you carry out.
c. The left hemisphere is responsible for the "duality of consciousness."
d. The two hemispheres play identical roles except that they control opposite sides of the body.

4. When a cell is polarized, the fluid inside the cell is more _____ charged with respect to the _____ charged exterior fluid.

a. positively; negatively
b. negatively; positively
c. equally; negatively
d. positively; negatively

5. If you do NOT inherit a Y chromosome from your father, you are born with

a. female characteristics.
b. only 45 chromosomes.
c. 200 genes.
d. male characteristics.

6. As you walk into the classroom, the teacher is erasing the blackboard. You catch a fleeting glimpse of the words "damage," "lesions," "stimulating," "recording," and "image" before they are erased. It is immediately clear to you that the teacher was discussing

a. research on evolution.
b. brain research.
c. language development.
d. behavioral genetics.

7. You are looking at a large painting with a wildly flowing river at the center of the canvas. On the left side of the river, there is a city with an impressive skyline. On the right side, there are acres of open wilderness. Connecting the two banks of the river is a wide bridge. The feature of this painting that should most remind you of your corpus callosum is the

a. wide bridge.
b. city with the impressive skyline.
c. acres of open wilderness.
d. wildly flowing river.

8. While you are under anesthesia, the _____ nervous system still takes care of basic life processes like breathing.

a. somatic
b. autonomic
c. synaptic
d. central

9. What happens when a region of a neuron enters an absolute refractory period?

a. The ion channels permit the flow of sodium into the neuron.
b. No amount of stimulation will allow another action potential to be generated.
c. That region of the neuron becomes particularly sensitive to inhibitory inputs.
d. The resting potential can only travel in one direction down the axon.

10. Joe is participating in an experiment that requires him to lift his left hand when he is touched on the right side of his body, and vice versa. Joe feels a gentle tap on his left shoulder, so he lifts his right hand. The "gentle tap" was sensed in the _____ side of Joe's brain, and the motor command to lift his hand was issued by the _____ side of his brain.

a. left; left
b. right; right
c. left; right
d. right; left

Practice Test 3

1. When excitatory inputs to a nerve cell are sufficiently strong with respect to inhibitory inputs, the neuron becomes _____ and a(n) _____ occurs.

a. polarized; action potential
b. polarized; refractory period
c. depolarized; refractory period
d. depolarized; action potential

2. There was one house to which Robbie didn't like delivering the morning paper. Today, when he saw the big dog coming at him, Robbie's _____ mobilized his body into action and his _____ told the muscles in his legs to run.

a. sympathetic nervous system; spinal cord
b. parasympathetic nervous system; brain
c. sympathetic nervous system; somatic nervous system
d. parasympathetic nervous system; somatic nervous system

3. Marie is walking through an exhibit at the science museum entitled, "The Living Brain." She enters through a waiting room called "the spinal cord," and then enters the brain. The exhibit takes her from the deepest recesses of the brain to the surface layer. What is the route she will follow?

a. cerebrum, limbic system, brain stem
b. limbic system, cerebrum, brain stem
c. brain stem, limbic system, cerebrum
d. cerebrum, brain stem, limbic system

4. Little Billy is learning how to flush the toilet. One day he notices that the toilet will not flush properly unless he waits for a while. Billy doesn't know it, but the fact that the toilet will not flush until the water level returns to normal is also an example of

a. nodes of Ranvier.
b. ion channels.
c. the synapse.
d. refractory periods.

5. A friend is playing a new game called "Be a Science Detective!" She has just received a clue card which tells her that the suspect has a Y chromosome. From this, it can be deduced that the suspect is

a. male.
b. female.
c. asexual.
d. an albino.

6. The all-or-none law states that

a. resting potentials are the same for motor neurons and sensory neurons.
b. all similar cognitive processes will be lateralized in the brain in the same way.
c. the size of the resting potential is affected only by the relative concentrations of sodium and potassium in the fluid outside the neuron.
d. the size of the action potential is unaffected by increases in the intensity of the stimulation beyond the threshold level.

7. Organisms with a selective advantage are

a. more likely to have a genotype.
b. more likely to have a phenotype.
c. more likely to pass on their genotypes.
d. less likely to pass on their phenotypes.

8. Cassie has no difficulty understanding what you say to her, but finds it impossible to produce words to convey her understanding. You suspect that she has damage to

a. the visual cortex.
b. the angular gyrus.
c. Wernicke's area.
d. the motor cortex.

9. Jack is making flash cards to help him learn the major brain structures and functions. Jill walks by and notices that Jack has incorrectly listed a certain structure as part of the brain stem. She points out to him that the brain stem does NOT include the

a. cerebrum.
b. medulla.
c. thalamus.
d. pons.

10. Studies of cerebral dominance have determined that many language-related behaviors are lateralized. For example, for most individuals spoken language is lateralized to the _____ hemisphere; for individuals who use American Sign Language, language is lateralized to the _____ hemisphere.

a. right; left
b. right; right
c. left; left
d. left; right

Comprehensive Test

1. Your friend Duke claims that the brain, encased in its protective environment, is not changed by life experiences such as stress. You decide to inform him of research that shows that

a. he is right.
b. changes in communication across existing synapses can form new synapses.
c. scientists will never be able to answer this question accurately.
d. stress can increase the number of connections in the brain.

2. Night Owl is drawing a representation of the relationship between the amount of area in the motor cortex devoted to different parts of the body. In his drawing, Night Owl should

a. devote more area to the shoulders and wrist.
b. have the largest area be the one that controls the thumb and the muscles involved in speech.
c. enlarge only the area that controls the eyes and ears.
d. enlarge the area that controls the back muscles and the bottom parts of the legs and feet.

3. Which of the following is NOT a function attributed to glia?

a. They provide insulation for axons.
b. They eliminate foreign substances inside neurons.
c. They prevent toxic substances from reaching the brain.
d. They guide newborn neurons to appropriate locations in the brain.

4. Chris and Chrissy are trying to match the lobes of the brain with their various functions. Which pairing do they have wrong?

a. frontal lobe—involved with motor control and cognitive activities
b. parietal lobe—makes plans, decisions, and sets goals
c. occipital lobe—the final destination for visual information
d. temporal lobe—processes auditory information

5. Suppose you were a neurotransmitter. Imagine that you have left one neuron and have been successful in binding yourself to a receptor molecule on another neuron. What effect will you have?

a. You will have increased the probability that the second neuron will fire.
b. You will have decreased the probability that the second neuron will fire.
c. You will have either increased or decreased the probability that the second neuron will fire.
d. You will have absolutely no effect on the second neuron.

6. "Studies show that males manifest higher levels of aggression than females across all cultures." If you assume that this statement is true, it would seem to implicate _____ as the primary basis for the observed higher level of aggression in males.

a. the environment
b. heredity
c. conditioning
d. nurture

7. Chester has written a science fiction novel. In his pretend world, as a character becomes more skilled in a certain behavior, the part of the brain that is related to that area becomes larger. Francesca is one of the best ballerinas in the world. Using Chester's logic, we can expect that her _____ will be especially large.

a. hippocampus
b. pons
c. thalamus
d. cerebellum

8. Imagine reading in a magazine that scientists have suggested genetics are at least partly responsible for the amount of time that adolescents spend talking on the telephone. Which of the following would be most consistent with the explanation a behavioral geneticist would give to such a finding?

a. The article has likely misinterpreted the actual research findings.
b. Although genetics can explain primitive behavior, genetics cannot explain modern behavior.
c. The behavior of talking on the telephone likely has been encoded into a person's genotype.
d. Some unknown factor must mediate the genetic influence on the behavior of talking on the telephone.

9. Mary is building a computer simulation of a human being, but she is having problems. Her 'human' behaves as though it does not have an endocrine system. When she was designing the brain, Mary probably left out the

a. hippocampus.
b. hypothalamus.
c. thalamus.
d. reticular formation.

10. Donna is an artist who is working on illustrations for an anatomy text. Her current efforts are directed toward cells that are specialized to receive, process, and/or transmit information to other cells within the body. Although these cells vary in size and shape, they all have the same basic structure.
Donna is drawing

a. glial cells.
b. neurons.
c. terminal buttons.
d. axons.

11. Which brain structure is most closely associated with aggression?

a. hippocampus
b. amygdala
c. thalamus
d. hypothalamus

12. Which of the following is the most basic genetic material?

a. DNA
b. genes
c. heredity
d. chromosomes

13. All of the following are ways to record and image the brain EXCEPT the

a. fMRI
b. CAT
c. RAS
d. EEG

14. Sally sees a bear in the woods. She runs away as fast as she can. After she is safe, she catches her breath and calms down. Which nervous system activated her flight?

a. central nervous system
b. sympathetic nervous system
c. parasympathetic nervous system
d. somatic nervous system

15. GABA is the most common inhibitory neurotransmitter in the brain. It also plays a role in which of the following?

a. memory
b. movement
c. paranoia
d. anxiety

True/False Questions

1. Dopamine is related to the memory loss associated with Alzheimer's disease.   T   F

2. The part of the brain that is responsible for our higher reasoning processes   T   F
   is the cerebral cortex.

3. Computerized Axial Tomography shows brain function rather than structure.   T   F

4. Genes are the biological units of heredity containing discrete sections of   T   F
   chromosomes responsible for transmission of traits.

5. The parasympathetic nervous system monitors routine operation of the body's   T   F
   internal functions.

6. The parietal lobe is involved in motor control and cognitive abilities such   T   F
   as planning, decision making, and goal setting.

7. Patients who undergo "split-brain" operations have their thalamus surgically   T   F
   removed.

8. The "All-or-None" law states that the size of the action potential is unaffected   T   F
   by the intensity of the stimulation beyond threshold.

Essay Questions

1. What are the three major types of neurons? Draw a diagram of a motor neuron and label the parts. Describe how the neuron generates an action potential.

2. Which brain structures make up the limbic system? Explain the function of the limbic system in the human brain.

When you have finished . . . Weblinks

Probe the Brain

http://www.pbs.org/wgbh/aso/tryit/brain/

This is a cool site from A Science Odyssey. It allows you to interact with the motor cortex of the brain. It requires a shock wave plug-in that you can download free from the site.

Neuron Tutorial

http://psych.hanover.edu/Krantz/neurotut.html

Basic Neural Processes, by John Kranz of Hanover College, is a good tutorial for basic anatomy and neural transmission. The animation makes it come alive.

Whole Brain Atlas

http://www.med.harvard.edu/AANLIB/home.html

The Whole Brain Atlas is an oldie but goody. The site is a classic from Harvard University Medical Center. You can see actual "slices" of the brain by selecting from various levels of CAT scans..

Human Anatomy Online

http://www.innerbody.com/image/nervov.html

Innerbody.com presents a series of interactive educational diagrams relating to nerves, nerve pain, and the peripheral and central nervous systems.

Virtual Body

http://www.medtropolis.com/VBody.asp

The Virtual Body website presents animated demonstrations, definitions and explanations of the human brain and nervous system – parts, neurons, facts, and functions.

The Biological and Evolutionary Bases of Behavior

Across

2. region of the brain that regulates higher cognitive functions
3. biological transmission of traits from a parents to offspring
5. branched fibers of neurons that receive incoming signals
8. part of the limbic system that controls aggression
9. specialized cell that processes and transmits information to other cells
11. extended fiber of a neuron through which nerve impulses travel
12. brain structure that relays sensory impulses to the body
13. region of the brain that contains the somatosensory cortex
14. cell body of a neuron containing the nucleus and cytoplasm

Down

1. chemical messengers released from neurons
2. part of the brain that controls coordination, posture and balance
4. region of the brain stem that regulates breathing
6. gap between one neuron and another
7. study of the inheritance of physical and psychological traits from ancestors
10. brain structure that regulates eating and drinking

Puzzle created with Puzzlemaker at DiscoverySchool.com

Chapter 3 - Answers

Practice Test 1

1. c (p. 58)
2. c (p. 69)
3. c (p. 82)
4. b (p. 58)
5. b (p. 77)
6. a (p. 84)
7. d (p. 66)
8. d (p. 57)
9. a (p. 64)
10. a (p. 64)

Practice Test 2

1. c (p. 81)
2. c (p. 72)
3. b (p. 83)
4. b (p. 66)
5. a (p. 60)
6. b (p. 72)
7. a (p. 79)
8. b (p. 74)
9. b (p. 67)
10. d (p. 82)

Practice Test 3

1. d (p. 66)
2. c (p. 74)
3. c (p. 75)
4. d (p. 67)
5. a (p. 60)
6. d (p. 67)
7. c (p. 58)
8. d (p. 79)
9. a (p. 79)
10. c (p. 83)

Comprehensive Test

Multiple Choice	True/False
1. b (p. 85)	1. F (p. 69)
2. b (p. 79)	2. T (p. 79)
3. b (p. 64)	3. F (p. 73)
4. b (p. 79)	4. T (p. 60)
5. c (p. 65)	5. T (p. 74)
6. b (p. 60)	6. F (p. 79)
7. d (p. 77)	7. F (p. 79)
8. d (p. 60)	8. T (p. 67)
9. b (p. 85)	
10. b (p. 63)	
11. b (p. 79)	
12. a (p. 60)	
13. c (p. 73)	
14. b (p. 74)	
15. d (p. 69)	

Crossword Key

Across

2. Cerebrum
3. Heredity
5. Dendrites
8. Amygdala
9. Neuron
11. Axon
12. Thalamus
13. Parietal Lobe
14. Soma

Down

1. Neurotransmitters
2. Cerebellum
4. Medulla
6. Synapse
7. Genetics
10. Hypothalamus

**Chapter 4**

Sensation and Perception

Before you read . . .

Sensation and perception is one of the oldest fields in psychology. In this chapter you will learn how we sense, organize, identify, and recognize stimuli. You will come to understand how illusions and ambiguities help define the challenges of perceptual theories. The chapter builds on psychophysics, which is the relation between physical stimulation and sensory experience. It moves from physical events to explore the mental events involved in sensory processing. The biological components of our sensory systems are covered in detail. They include the sensory systems of sight, hearing, smell, taste and touch. The organizational processes of attention, perceptual grouping, motion and depth, and perceptual constancies are clearly spelled out. The chapter finishes with identification and recognition processes. Understanding how sensation and perception differ and interact provides a building block to the cognitive and mental processes explained in later chapters.

Chapter Objectives

After reading this chapter you should be able to:

- Differentiate between sensation and perception.

- Explain the task of perception and what happens when ambiguity or illusions arise.

- Define psychophysics and describe its mathematical functions.

- Explain signal detection theory, difference threshold, and just noticeable difference.

- Describe transduction.

- Describe the parts of the visual system and explain how each works – including processes within the brain.

- Explain the properties of light, including wavelength, hue, saturation, and brightness.

- Contrast the trichromatic color vision theory with the opponent processes theory.

- Discuss how sound waves produce hearing.

- Differentiate between pitch, loudness, and timbre.

- Describe the parts of the ear and explain how each works.

- Differentiate between place theory and frequency theory.

- Discuss how the brain determines the direction of a sound.

- Explain how smell and taste work.

- Explain how the cutaneous senses, vestibular senses, and kinesthetic senses work.

- Define pain and explain its physiological response.

- Describe attentional processes.

- List and describe the 5 Gestalt laws of perception.

- Describe binocular, motion, and pictorial cues and how they contribute to the perception of depth.

- Explain perceptual constancies in term of size, shape, and lightness.

- Discuss bottom-up and top-down processes in perceptual identification.

- Explain how context, expectations, and perceptual sets guide recognition of ambiguous data.

As you read . . . Term Identification

Absolute Threshold	Opponent-Process Theory
Accommodation	Optic Nerve
Amacrine Cells	Pain
Ambiguity	Perception
Attention	Perceptual Constancy
Auditory Cortex	Perceptual Organization
Auditory Nerve	Pheromones
Basilar Membrane	Phi Phenomenon
Bipolar Cells	Photoreceptors
Bottom-up Processing	Pitch
Brightness	Place Theory
Cochlea	Proximal Stimulus
Complementary Colors	Psychometric Function
Cones	Psychophysics
Convergence	Receptive Field
Cutaneous Senses	Relative Motion Parallax
Dark Adaptation	Response Bias

Dichotic Listening	Retina
Difference Threshold	Retinal Disparity
Distal Stimuli	Rods
Figure	Saturation
Fovea	Sensation
Frequency Theory	Sensory Adaptation
Ganglion Cells	Sensory Receptors
Gate-Control Theory	Set
Gestalt Psychology	Shape Constancy
Goal Directed Selection	Signal Detection Theory (SDT)
Ground	Size Constancy
Horizontal Cells	Sound Location
Hue	Stimulus-Driven Capture
Identification and Recognition	Timbre
Illusion	Top-Down Processing
Just Noticeable Difference (JND)	Transduction
Kinesthetic Sense	Trichromatic Theory
Lightness Constancy	Vestibular Sense
Loudness	Visual Cortex
Olfactory Bulb	Volley Principle
	Weber's Law

As you read . . . Questions and Answers

Sensing, Organizing, Identifying, and Recognizing

1. Make sure you understand each of the stages in the perceptual process. How does each stage differ from the next?

2. Define sensation and the functions of identification and recognition.

The Proximal and Distal Stimuli

What are proximal and distal stimuli? Look at objects around the room and try to think about the two-dimensional image they cast on your retina. How can you tell what you're looking at based on that 2D image?

Reality, Ambiguity, and Illusions

1. Ambiguity is mentioned at the beginning of the chapter to help you understand why perception is a challenge. It is often the case that information arriving from the environment allows for several interpretations. Your perceptual system must determine which one is correct (or, at least, must settle on a best guess). Make sure you understand each of the examples.

2. How do illusions differ from ambiguities? From hallucinations? How can the study of illusions be helpful to researchers?

3. What kinds of illusions do you experience on a day-to-day basis? When are illusions helpful?

Psychophysics

1. What is psychophysics, and what role did Gustav Fechner play in its history?

2. How are absolute thresholds defined? What is a psychometric function?

3. Define and give an example of sensory adaptation.

4. What are response biases? How do they originate?

5. How does signal detection theory differentiate between sensory processes and decision processes? (Use yes sayers and no sayers as an example.)

6. Define and give an example of difference thresholds. What is a JND?

7. What law did Ernst Weber originate? (Make sure you follow the math shown on page 102)

From Physical Events to Mental Events

1. Define and give an example of transduction.

2. What is meant by sensory receptors?

The Visual System

This section has several figures to aid your understanding. As you read through the text, use the figures to help solidify your knowledge.

The Human Eye

Make sure you understand the analogy between a camera and an eye. What are the components of the analogy?

The Pupil and the Lens

Explain the physiology of accommodation.

The Retina

1. For each of these concepts, make sure you understand where you would find them and give a brief sketch of their function.

Retina

Photoreceptors

Rods

Cones

Fovea

Bipolar cells

Ganglion cells

Horizontal cells

Amacrine cells

2. What is dark adaptation?

3. Where are your blind spots? Why are you not aware of them?

Processes in the Brain

1. Trace the path of visual information toward your brain.

   Optic nerve

   Optic chiasma

   Visual cortex

2. What is blindsight? What does it suggest about visual processing?

Critical Thinking In Your Life

1. What is the cause of most types of blindness?

How does the MARC system attempt to remedy this problem?

Seeing Color

1. What are the physical properties of light waves?

2. What are the three psychological dimensions of color?

3. What is the difference between additive and subtractive color mixture?

4. How do negative afterimages demonstrate the existence of complementary colors?

5. What is color blindness? What are its most and least common forms?

6. Fill in this chart for two theories of color vision.

Name	Who supported it?	What does it explain?

7. What reconciliation did Leo Hurvich and Dorothea Jameson suggest between the two theories?

The Physics of Sound

Review the physical properties of sine waves. Distinguish between frequency and amplitude.

Psychological Dimensions of Sound

What aspects of the physical signal give rise to each of these dimensions?

1. Pitch

2. Loudness (decibels)

3. Timbre

The Physiology of Hearing

Use the figures in this section to help you master the material.

1. What role do each of these structures play in the transduction of the sound wave?

Pinna (external ear)

Tympanic membrane (eardrum)

Hammer, anvil, and stirrup

Cochlea

Basilar membrane

Auditory nerve

Auditory cortex

2. Fill in this chart for two theories of pitch perception.

Name	Who supported it?	What does it explain?

3. What is the volley principle? How does it help explain pitch perception?

4. For what range of stimuli do the two mechanisms overlap?

5. What two mechanisms account for sound localization?

Smell

Define:

1. Olfactory cilia

2. Olfactory bulb (note the growth of new neurons)

3. Pheromones

Taste

1. What is the relationship between odor and taste?

Where do you find papillae? Where do you find taste buds?

2. What are the basic taste qualities?

3. How easy is it to damage the taste system?

Touch and Skin Senses

1. Note that these senses are also called cutaneous senses. What are each of the cutaneous senses?

2. What are some of the properties of touch?

The Vestibular and Kinesthetic Senses

1. Define each of these senses and note the source of sensory information.

2. What may cause motion sickness?

Pain

1. Would you want to live without pain?

2. What are some of the costs of acute and chronic pain?

3. Contrast nociceptive and neuropathic pain. What types of receptors are there for pain?

4. How is the experience of pain affected by psychological factors? Give two examples.

5. What is gate-control theory?

1. What aspects of physiology can make the same foods both flavorful and painful?

2. What are supertasters? How does someone become a supertaster?

Organizational Processes in Perception

As a preview for this whole section, spend a few more minutes looking around your environment. Find things in your environment that should challenge your perceptual system. You might also want to work backwards from the text to look for the types of situations that are described. How do you know, for example, that you're looking at a poster that's hanging in front of a wall? How can you tell that the poster is in front of the wall? What depth cues are you using? Why do you take the wall to be the ground and the poster to be the figure?

Attentional Processes

1. Distinguish between goal-directed selection and stimulus-driven capture.

2. Make sure you understand how stimulus-driven capture operates to influence your senses.

3. What is the dichotic listening technique and the shadowing procedure? How was filter theory tested?

4. What research results suggest that attention does not function as an absolute filter?

How are supertasters similar and different from nontasters?

Principles of Perceptual Grouping

List the four laws this section presents. From your real-world experience, try to give a different application from the one given in the book.

Law	Application

Spatial and Temporal Integration

1. Why doesn't your visual memory preserve precise details of scenes?

2. How does this finding apply to "impossible" objects?

Motion Perception

1. How do you detect motion from the size of images on your retina?

2. What is the role of reference frames in induced motion?

3. Explain apparent motion and the phi phenomenon.

Depth Perception

1. Why does depth perception require interpretation of the sensory input?

2. List the cues for depth perception, and explain why each works.

   a. Binocular and motion cues

Cue	Why it works

b. Pictorial cues

Cue	Why it works

Perceptual Constancies

1. Define perceptual constancy.

2. Explain how each type of constancy is possible and give an example.

   Size constancy

   Shape constancy

   Orientation constancy

   Lightness constancy

Bottom-Up and Top-Down Processes

1. Define and give examples of bottom-up and top-down processes. Which type is also called data-driven processing? Which is called conceptually driven? Why?

2. How does phonemic restoration illustrate the impact of top-down processes?

1. How do expectations affect perception?

2. Define and give an example of each type of set.

For Group Study

Psychophysics

Do you want to try some psychophysics at home? Here's what we suggest. One member of your group should prepare a series of about eight glasses of sugar water, with different amounts of sugar mixed in to each glass (e.g., 1/4 tsp, 1/2 tsp, 1 tsp, and so on). Keep the physical change steady (that's why we suggested multiples of two). The glasses should be labeled so that only the preparer knows which is which.

The other group members should take a small taste of each mixture and perform magnitude estimation. What's the relationship between physical intensity and sensory experience?

You could also use the same approach to try absolute and difference thresholds. How much sugar do you need to put in a glass of water before you can differentiate it from a glass of plain water? (Have a friend prepare the two glasses and not tell you which is which.) How much more sugar do you have to add to make two glasses taste different to you? Measure JNDs starting with different concentrations. Can you re-create Weber's law?

The Visual System

There are many new terms in this chapter. You should take the same approach to studying as you did in Chapter 2. Make sets of flash cards with your group. Help each other develop strategies for remembering the material.

Your Other Senses

There are a number of exercises you can try to give you some firsthand experience with the properties of your sensory systems. Here are two suggestions:

For odor and taste, have a meal together. What are the prominent sensory qualities of the food you are eating? Do you all agree about how strong the flavors are? (If you tried the psychophysics experiment described earlier, you may have already discovered some individual differences in taste.) If you have spicy food, do some of you find it unpleasant? Do all flavors taste stronger to those people? What happens to taste when you hold your nose?

To discover properties of your skin senses, you should find two pointed objects (but not too sharp!). The idea is to see how far apart you can touch a partner's skin with the two points simultaneously without the partner being able to tell whether it's one or two. Sometimes you should touch with just one and sometimes with both. Your partner must respond, "one" or "two." You may be surprised how far apart you can touch with two stimuli on some parts of the body before your partner will say "two."

Organizational Process in Perception

Spend some time looking around the environment trying to apply the material in this chapter directly to the world around you. Ask yourselves questions such as

1. How am I determining what is figure and what is ground?
2. Where do I perceive depth? What cues am I using? (Does anything change when I shut an eye? Why or why not?)
3. What constancies are at work?

Work through these topics with the group.

Attentional Processes

Spend some time talking about how your focus of attention is directed both by what's in the world (stimulus-driven capture) and what's in your head (goal-directed selection). Watch a scene out a window. Does everyone notice the same things? Why or why not? Can you detect elements of the scene that you all *had* to look at? Can you detect the goals that made some aspects of the scene more interesting to some people than to others?

Practice Test 1

1. To discuss the difference between objects in the world and images on your retina, you have brought to class a large red ball and a cardboard circle painted the same color. In the demonstration, the ball will serve best as the _____ stimulus and the circle will serve best as the _____ stimulus.

a. distal; proximal
b. proximal; invariant
c. invariant; distal
d. proximal; distal

2. Thor has been given a new box of crayons. He draws a thick plus sign (+) with red for the horizontal line and blue for the vertical line. Thor notices that the overlap looks purple. He has just discovered the effects of

a. additive color mixing.
b. negative afterimages.
c. subtractive color mixing.
d. complementary colors.

3. How could you make a green circle look greener?

a. Stare at it for a long time.
b. Look at a red circle before looking at the green circle.
c. Close one eye.
d. Focus on the perimeter of the circle rather than the center.

4. You hear someone call out "Help!" The shout arrives at your right ear shortly after your left ear. The source is likely to be

a. off to your left.
b. directly in front of you.
c. off to your right.
d. directly behind you.

5. The volley principle suggests that

a. several neurons firing in sequence could signal high-frequency sounds.
b. complex sound waves stimulate successive locations on the basilar membrane.
c. combinations of pure tones combine to produce complex waves.
d. low-frequency sounds are detected more easily than high-frequency sounds.

6. You wash your new pair of blue jeans in bleach so that they have a faded look. The dimension of their color you have changed the most is _____.

a. intensity
b. hue
c. brightness
d. saturation

7. If all the cones in your eyes stopped functioning, then you would

a. no longer have color vision.
b. be totally blind.
c. only have sight at the center of the visual field.
d. have poorest vision when illumination was near darkness.

8. You've been watching television for a while. It seems, over time, that the volume on the TV has been getting softer and softer. This impression may be a consequence of

a. absolute thresholds.
b. response bias.
c. just noticeable differences.
d. sensory adaptation.

9. With your eyes closed, touch your finger to your nose. Your _____ sense allows you to succeed at this task.

a. olfactory
b. kinesthetic
c. auditory
d. vestibular

10. The _____ provides part of the link between the eardrum and the cochlea.

a. basilar membrane
b. anvil
c. pinna
d. tympanic membrane

Practice Test 2

1. In one experiment, participants did not notice relatively large changes between two arrays of familiar objects. What is one explanation for this result?

a. People tend to group together environmental objects that are similar to each other.
b. Attention is required for people to perceive objects that consist of more than one feature.
c. Perceptual identification must precede object recognition.
d. The world itself is generally a stable source of information.

2. You walk by a classroom and see a professor drawing a large rectangle on the blackboard. Next, he asks his class to tilt their heads about 45 degrees. It's likely that he is making a point about _____ constancy.

a. size
b. dimensional
c. shape
d. orientation

3. Lightness constancy works because the _____ of light reflected off an object remains about the same even as the _____ changes.

a. percentage; absolute amount
b. percentage; gestalt
c. absolute amount; illumination
d. absolute amount; percentage

4. Erika is viewing a display that has a row of three red circles on top of a row of three green circles (all the circles are evenly spaced). Erika reports that she sees three columns, each with a red circle and a green circle. Call the perception police! Erika's percept violates the Gestalt law of

a. common fate.
b. proximity.
c. similarity.
d. closure.

5. A friend asks you to close your eyes and then places an object in your hand. You can tell that it is in the shape of a cube, but not much else. The process of perception has been halted when you reached the stage of

a. perceptual organization.
b. object recognition.
c. sensation.
d. closure.

6. Try this demonstration. Hold your pen or pencil as far away from your head as you can. Now keep your eyes focused on it as you bring it toward you. Can you feel the strain on your eye muscles? You have just experienced the way that _____ can be used as a cue to depth.

a. relative motion
b. occlusion
c. retinal disparity
d. convergence

7. You are looking at a painting that consists of a circular canvas with a black circle painted in the middle. The name of the painting is "White Doughnut on Black Table." Suppose the title were changed to "Black Disk on White Iceberg." The black circle should now look _____ you.

a. closer to
b. farther from
c. larger to
d. smaller to

8. Your friend Hiram believes that illusions are only things that psychologists make up to trick people in the classroom. To convince him otherwise, you ask him to think about why

a. some of the planets aren't always visible.
b. it looks like the moon is always chasing you.
c. the sun appears to be overhead at midday.
d. the moon is easier to see at night than at day.

9. Dichotic listening tasks have often been used to study the extent to which

a. capacity limitations affect preattentive processing.
b. internal representations become suppressed in memory.
c. unattended information is processed for meaning.
d. the filter applies to attended information.

10. Even though she reread her research paper three times, Selena still missed several typographical errors. This is best explained by

a. bottom-up processing.
b. spatial integration.
c. percept.
d. component recognition.

Practice Test 3

1. The children are at a walk-through science museum exhibit entitled "The Ear." They are to act as vibrating air molecules entering the ear. What is the order in which they will encounter the structures listed below as they move through the ear?

a. tympanic membrane, middle ear, pinna, cochlea
b. cochlea, middle ear, pinna, tympanic membrane
c. tympanic membrane, pinna, cochlea, middle ear
d. pinna, tympanic membrane, middle ear, cochlea

2. By using light of various wavelengths, vision researchers have discovered that different cone cells are maximally responsive to

a. dark, light, and shades of gray.
b. blue, green, and red.
c. seven wavelengths of light, representing the seven primary colors.
d. hundreds of different wavelengths, representing all colors.

3. While at the art museum, Juán learns a neat trick. If he stares at a painting for a few minutes, then looks away at a blank wall, he "sees" colors that are opposite to those in the original painting. Juán has discovered the

a. opponent-process theory.
b. subtractive color mixture.
c. color blindness.
d. negative afterimage.

4. The value of the difference threshold is known as a

a. just noticeable difference.
b. barely perceptible minimum.
c. sensory difference threshold.
d. psychological separation unit.

5. Your uncle, recently arrived from South America, finds it difficult to distinguish the difference in sound between the word *man* and the word *men*. As far as he is concerned, the words sound the same, although you can detect a difference. The judgments that you and your uncle are making about these sounds are similar to that of a participant in a study of

a. difference thresholds.
b. absolute thresholds.
c. magnitude estimation.
d. the response bias.

6. Jeremy's father is celebrating his 50th birthday. When he tries to read the card his son has given him, he jokes that his arms have gotten too short to be able to read without his glasses. In reality, his vision problem is most likely due to

a. accommodation.
b. flattening of the cornea.
c. the loss of elasticity of the lens.
d. contraction of the ciliary muscles.

7. The sense that tells us whether the elevator we are riding is going up or down is called the _____ sense.

a. proprioceptive
b. vestibular
c. cutaneous
d. kinesthetic

8. In signal detection theory, a "payoff matrix" is

a. an indication of the strength with which a stimulus is presented.
b. a reflection of anticipated gains and losses associated with a decision.
c. the actual likelihood that a stimulus will be presented.
d. the actual likelihood that a stimulus will not be presented.

9. Kim is confused about how external sensations, such as light, are changed to neural sensations by the brain to produce the experience of seeing. Once Kim learns about _____, she will have the answer to her question.

a. difference thresholds
b. signal detection theory
c. psychophysical scales
d. transduction

10. Herbie is a "yea sayer." On a signal detection task, he is likely to be _____ on hits and _____ on false alarms.

a. low; high
b. high; low
c. high; high
d. low; low

Comprehensive Test

1. Joyce stared at the lovely trees. Several different species were growing together, their branches intertwined and overlapped. However, the leaves of each variety could easily be seen as separate, somehow grouping themselves together. What Joyce is witnessing is the Gestalt law of

a. proximity.
b. common fate.
c. similarity.
d. effect.

2. When two stationary spots of light in different positions in the visual field are turned on and off alternately, it may seem like a single light is moving back and forth between the two spots. This effect is known as

a. relative motion parallax.
b. depth perception.
c. the phi phenomenon.
d. interposition.

3. You are still a novice when it comes to skiing, so when you find yourself heading for a tree, you fall to the side in order to avoid a potential collision. What mechanism allowed you to sense that the tree was getting closer and closer?

a. The feedback from muscular tension and pressure from the eyes.
b. The rate at which your retinal image of the tree expanded.
c. The feeling of air rushing into your face.
d. The buildup of pressure as the air between you and the tree became compressed.

4. Your psychology teacher asks students to break into small groups to discuss the relative merits of different theories of attention. As the groups begin their separate discussions, the room becomes quite noisy and you have a difficult time hearing the members of your own group. Suddenly, you hear your name being mentioned by someone in another group. The fact that you attended to your name has been called

a. dichotic listening.
b. the cocktail party phenomenon.
c. shadowing.
d. unselected channel attending.

5. As you read this question, the words stand out against a backdrop. This illustrates the concept of

a. figure and ground.
b. subjective contour.
c. closure.
d. reference frames

6. Despite your reckless journey down the sidewalk on Roller blades, you see the world as stable even though there are dramatic changes in stimulation of your sensory systems. This is referred to as

a. the size/distance relation.
b. relative motion parallax.
c. the Ponzo illusion.
d. perceptual constancy.

7. A friend's 4-year-old daughter shows you a drawing she made in preschool. You have no idea what the picture shows until she says, "It's a doggie!" At that point, you are able to see that the picture portrays a dog. This is an example of _____ processing.

a. bottom-up
b. preattentive
c. top-down
d. parallel

8. You are watching children at play. One group is playing on the swings, a few feet away is another group on the slide, and removed from these two is a third group playing catch. Your tendency to see separate groups of children playing is explained by

a. your knowledge of what children like to play.
b. the law of common fate.
c. the law of proximity.
d. the law of figure and ground.

9. You are taking a walk through a forest with your friend Ricardo. After 10 minutes, you emerge from the forest into bright sunlight. Despite the change in illumination, your white t-shirt looks equally as light to you inside and outside the forest. This is an example of

a. illumination equivalence.
b. the importance of the proximal stimulus.
c. top-down processing.
d. lightness constancy.

10. Courtney, a new mother, is typically a sound sleeper. Yet, when her newborn cries in the middle of the night, Courtney is the first to hear her. Courtney's response is due to the presence of

a. a percept.
b. the phi phenomenon.
c. figure and ground.
d. ambiguity.

11 Norman has a strange picture of a woman on his wall. First, it looks as though it is a picture of a young woman, but as one stares at it, it suddenly looks as though it is a picture of an older woman. This important characteristic of ambiguous figures is known as

a. instability.
b. an illusion.
c. lateral inhibition.
d. a hallucination.

12. The fifth-grade teacher has his students engaged in a "treasure hunt." He asks his students to look around in the room and find as quickly as possible the following objects: a red circle, an object that is soft that one can sit on it, anything colored yellow, and an object that can be used for holding a book but will also roll on the floor. Based on your reading of the information in the textbook, which of the objects is most likely to be found first?

a. The red circle.
b. The soft object that one can sit on.
c. Any object colored yellow.
d. The object to be used for holding and rolling.

13. Sensory evidence is the starting point for _____ processing.

a. top-down
b. bottom-up
c. conceptually driven
d. contextual

14. Knowing that illusions exist, you can accurately conclude that

a. perceptual systems are sometimes imperfect in recovering the distal stimulus from the proximal stimulus.
b. people are unable to overcome the influence of illusions.
c. sensory receptors do not operate in a predictable manner.
d. either the proximal stimulus does not exist or the distal stimulus does not exist.

15. Synthesis occurs in the _____ stage of perceptual processing.

a. perceptual organization
b. identification and recognition
c. sensation
d. invariant

True/False Questions

1. Psychophysics is the correspondence between physical stimulation and psychological experience.   T   F

2. Weber's law sates that as the size of the pupil increases the image on the retina decreases.   T   F

3. We see color thanks to the photoreceptors located in the vitreous humor.   T   F

4. Pain is the body's response to noxious stimuli.   T   F

5. Artists such as Salvador Dali have used perceptual ambiguities in their artwork.   T   F

6. The Gestalt law of proximity states that objects moving in the same direction at the same rate are grouped together.   T   F

7. The phi phenomenon occurs when the size of an image expands on your retina as the object approaches.   T   F

Essay Questions

1. Trace how the nerve impulses for your sense of smell and taste go through your sensory systems.

2. List 5 of the Gestalt laws of perceptual organization. Define and give an example of each from your daily life.

When you have finished . . . Weblinks

Sensation and Perception Tutorials

http://psych.hanover.edu/Krantz/sen_tut.html

The sensation and perception tutorials were developed by John Krantz of Hanover College. Illustrations and clear explanations of perceptual illusions are presented on this classic web site. Although first developed in1994, they are still pertinent today.

Sensation and Perception Jeopardy

http://www.uni.edu/walsh/jeopardy.html

This game of jeopardy was developed by Linda Walsh of the University of Northern Iowa. It's a fun and good review of the visual system and perceptual processes. See if you can beat your opponents.

Optical Illusions

http://dragon.uml.edu/psych/illusion.html

More optical illusions. This site was developed not just for fun but also to explain some of the common optical illusions and how they relate to sensation and perception.

Impossible Figures

http://www.fink.com/papers/impossible.html

This site takes optical illusions one step further – explaining why our perception of impossible figures is distorted. Pictorial cues are examined from two and three dimensional perspectives.

Sensation and Perception Tutorials

http://www.indiana.edu/~iuepsyc/topics/s_p.htm

This site, developed by Indiana University East, provides numerous links to tutorials in sensation, perception, psychophysics, vision and more.

Sensation and Perception

Across

2. idea that the size of a difference threshold is proportional to intensity of the stimulus
4. photoreceptors that are responsible for the perception of color
7. organization and interpretation of sensory images
10. when the cillary muscles change the thickness of a lens for focusing
11. the layer at the back of the eye that contains photoreceptors
12. fluid filled inner tube found in the inner ear

Down

1. study of correspondence between physical stimulation and psychological experience
3. sensory experience that is incorrect but shared by other in the same perceptual environment
5. stimulation of sensory receptors which cause neural impulses
6. sound quality of highness or lowness
8. transformation of one form of energy into another
9. area of the retina that forms the point of sharpest vision

Puzzle created with Puzzlemaker at DiscoverySchool.com

Chapter 4 - Answers

Practice Test 1

1. a (p. 96)
2. c (p. 110)
3. b (p. 109)
4. a (p. 116)
5. a (p. 115)
6. d (p. 109)
7. a (p. 104)
8. d (p. 100)
9. b (p. 119)
10. b (p. 114)

Practice Test 2

1. d (p. 129)
2. c (p. 130)
3. a (p. 130)
4. c (p. 124)
5. b (p. 94)
6. d (p. 127)
7. a (p. 98)
8. b (p. 98)
9. c (p. 123)
10. c (p. 94)

Practice Test 3

1. d (p. 114)
2. b (p. 109)
3. d (p. 109)
4. a (p. 101)
5. a (p. 101)
6. c (p. 104)
7. b (p. 119)
8. b (p. 101)
9. d (p. 102)
10. c (p. 101)

Comprehensive Test

Multiple Choice

1. c (p. 124)
2. c (p. 126)
3. b (p. 129)
4. b (p. 123)
5. a (p. 124)
6. d (p. 129)
7. c (p. 131)
8. c (p. 124)
9. d (p. 130)
10. a (p. 94)
11. b (p. 98)
12. c (p. 131)
13. b (p. 131)
14. a (p. 96)
15. a (p. 94)

True/False

1. T (p. 99)
2. F (p. 102)
3. F (p. 104)
4. T (p. 120)
5. T (p. 97)
6. F (p. 124)
7. F (p. 124)

Crossword Key

Across

2. Weber's Law
4. Cones
7. Perception
10. Accommodation
11. Retina
12. Cochlea

Down

1. Psychophysics
3. Illusions
5. Sensation
6. Pitch
8. Transduction
9. Fovea

📖Chapter 5

Mind, Consciousness, and Alternate States

📰 Before You Read

This chapter covers the contents of consciousness. If consciousness is awareness, then there are different levels of conscious experience. The chapter describes the various functions and uses of consciousness. Many students are very interested in this chapter, which goes into detail about sleep, why we sleep, disorders of sleep and dreams. Next, altered states of consciousness are explained. Lucid dreaming, hypnosis, meditation, and religious ecstasy are part of the fascinating journey. The chapter ends with a discussion of mind-altering drugs including what causes dependence and addiction as well as the varieties of psychoactive drugs.

Chapter Objectives

After reading this chapter you should be able to:

- Define consciousness.

- Differentiate between consciousness, nonconscious, unattended, and unconscious processes.

- Describe some of the research techniques used to study the contents of consciousness.

- Explain the functions and constructions of consciousness.

- Define circadian rhythms and explain why they are important.

- Explain the change of brain activity over the course of a night's sleep (the sleep cycle).

- Discuss the different functions served by REM and NREM sleep.

- List and describe the various sleep disorders.

- Identify the potential impact of getting too little sleep.

- Contrast the dream theories of Freud and those in other cultures.

- Discuss possible biological explanations for the origin of dreams, including activation-synthesis.

- Describe and explain lucid dreaming.

- Describe and explain hypnosis, including induction, hypnotizability, and effects.

- Describe and explain mediation.

- Identify how religious ecstasy relates to levels of consciousness.

- Define tolerance, dependence, addiction, and hallucinations.

- Identify how psychoactive drugs alter consciousness.

- List and describe the psychoactive drug classifications.

- Identify the potential effects of ecstasy on the brain.

As you read . . . Term Identification

Addiction	Meditation
Circadian Rhythm	Narcolepsy
Consciousness	Nonconscious
Daytime Sleepiness	Non-REM (NREM)
Dream Work	Physiological Dependence
Experience-Sampling Method	Preconscious Memories
Hallucinations	Psychoactive Drugs
Hypnosis	Psychological Dependence
Hypnotizability	Rapid Eye Movement (REM)
Insomnia	Sleep Apnea
Latent Content	Somnambulism
Lucid Dreaming	Think-Aloud Protocol
Manifest Content	Toler

As you read . . . Questions and Answers

Awareness and Consciousness

1. Use the various levels of consciousness to summarize the material in this section.

2. For each concept, give a brief description and an example from the text.

Nonconscious processes

Preconscious memories

Unattended information

The unconscious

3. How has the idea of the unconscious changed from Freud to contemporary theories? How can information stored in your unconscious have an effect on your behavior?

Studying the Contents of Consciousness

Describe two techniques researchers use to study consciousness:

1.

2.

The Uses of Consciousness

1. What functions do each of the following aspects of consciousness accomplish to aid survival?

Restrictive

Selective storage

Planning or Executive control

2. How do the following constructions of consciousness contribute to your interpretation of reality?

Personal

Cultural (consensual validation)

Studying the Functions of Consciousness

Summarize the research techniques described in this section.

Circadian Rhythms

1. What are circadian rhythms? What variables influence jet lag?

2. Draw yourself a diagram to help remember how traveling east and west affects your circadian rhythms.

The Sleep Cycle

How does the EEG help sleep researchers? Make sure you understand the distinction between REM and NREM sleep. Study Figures 5.3 and 5.4 to master the sleep cycle.

Why Sleep?

Suppose someone told you that sleep was unnecessary. How would you respond?

Summarize the major types of sleep disorders.

1. Insomnia (what is subjective insomnia?)

2. Narcolepsy

3. Sleep apnea

4. Somnambulism

1. Why do experts worry that adolescents and college students don't get enough sleep?

2. Summarize the consequences of receiving too little sleep.

1. Why did Freud distinguish between manifest and latent content? How is the latent content determined?

2. What traditions of dream interpretation exist in non-Western cultures?

3. What is the physiological explanation of dream interpretation? What evidence contradicts physiological theories?

4. What are some properties of nightmares?

Lucid Dreaming

How are individuals trained to become lucid dreamers?

Hypnosis

1. What is hypnosis?

2. How is hypnosis induced? What has been found with respect to individual differences in hypnotizability?

3. How have researchers demonstrated that hypnosis is more than simulation?

4. How does research on pain control suggest that the effects of hypnosis are not just placebo effects?

Meditation

1. What is the purpose of meditation?

2. What is controversial about meditation?

Religious Ecstasy

1. How do meditation, prayer, fasting, and spiritual communication contribute to intense religious experiences?

2. What experiences are associated with religious ecstasy?

Dependence and Addiction

1. How do psychoactive drugs relate to tolerance, physiological dependence, addiction, and psychological addiction?

2. What are the physiological and psychological aspects of tolerance, dependence, and addiction?

3. What are the medical uses of psychoactive drugs?

Varieties of Psychoactive Drugs

1. Summarize the effects of each type of psychoactive drug.

   Hallucinogens

   Opiates

   Depressants

   Stimulants

2. What two stimulants are common in day-to-day experience? What effects do they have?

Critical Thinking In Your Life

How does ecstasy affect your thought process?

For Group Study

Awareness and Consciousness

Work through the different categories (nonconscious processes, preconscious memories, and so on). Choose everyday experiences and make sure you all agree how to analyze the contributions of consciousness. What types of things do you regularly do outside of conscious awareness?

Studying the Functions of Consciousness

Try to remember some slips of the tongue you have heard others use. Can you analyze how they emerge? Recently, for example, we heard someone say, "He's just like Homer Fudd" (which was a combination of Elmer Fudd and Homer Simpson). There doesn't seem to be much influence from unconsciousness in this example (the textbook returns to these ordinary slips of the tongue in Chapter 9). Can you do better? You should see if you and your friends can find instances in which the slip may indicate some meaning lurking in the unconscious.

Sleep and Dreams

If you have never seen REM sleep (that is, if you have never seen a sleeper's eyes moving), then you should consider asking a friend or lover for permission to watch him or her sleeping. When during the night would it be best to watch?

Try to have each group member write down whatever dreams he or she can remember for a few mornings. (Trying to remember your dreams is a good way to start remembering more of them.) Do all of the group members' dreams share similar characteristics? Are some of the same concerns expressed in many of your dreams? Can you find sources for individual details? How vivid are your dreams? Do some of you dream in color and others in black and white? Try to understand the theories of dreaming given in this section in terms of your individual experiences.

Mind-Altering Drugs

During college, many people experiment with mind-altering drugs. With your group, discuss why this might be so. What are the dangers of this practice? Why do people use drugs even given these risks? Work through the list of psychoactive drugs and try to understand the effects that each of them has on the brain and body.

After you read . . . Practice Tests

Practice Test 1

1. A person who practices meditation may minimize external stimulation with the goal of

a. preventing hallucinations.
b. eliminating unconscious processes.
c. improving automatic thinking.
d. enhancing self-knowledge.

2. According to Freud, which of the following would be an example of an unconscious process?

a. You tell the punch line to a joke.
b. You are afraid of rabbits, but do not know why.
c. You put a key in a lock to open a door.
d. You wave at a friend across the street.

3. Each day that Paul shoots up with heroin, he needs a slightly bigger dose to get the same effect. This is a phenomenon called _____.

a. psychological dependence
b. craving
c. neurotransmitter depletion
d. tolerance

4. Self-hypnosis is particularly valuable for controlling pain because patients can

a. determine whether they are high or low in hypnotizability.
b. avoid the use of placebo medications.
c. use the procedure whenever they need it.
d. avoid the side effects of other-induced hypnotic trances.

5. Which statement is true about patterns of hypnotizability in adulthood?

a. Women are considerably more hypnotizable than men.
b. People's hypnotizability mostly depends on the skill of the hypnotist.
c. Men are somewhat more hypnotizable than women.
d. People's hypnotizability is relatively stable over time.

6. You find it very difficult to tune out information that is not relevant to the immediate goals you are pursuing. You might be concerned that your consciousness is not serving its proper _____ function.

a. restrictive
b. selective storage
c. executive control
d. consensual validation

7. Danielle believes that she may suffer from sleep apnea. How could you determine if she is correct?

a. Ask her to report how much sleepiness she experiences during the day.
b. Monitor her eye movement patterns during the night.
c. Monitor her breathing patterns during the night.
d. Follow her for a day and determine how often she spontaneously falls asleep.

8. A man is telling his friends about his hallucinations. How are his friends most likely to react?

a. His friends will probably assume that the man is mentally ill.
b. They are most likely to react as though he has taken a drug.
c. They will probably assume that the hallucinations are religious revelations.
d. Their reaction will depend on the culture in which the man lives.

9. Which of the following is NOT a function of consciousness? .

a. planning
b. restricting stimuli
c. selecting stimuli
d. categorizing stimuli

10. Memories that are accessible to consciousness only after something calls your attention to them are known as _____ memories.

a. nonconscious
b. preconscious
c. unattended
d. unconscious

Practice Test 2

1. Participants sometimes will incorrectly report that an individual is famous because they fail to remember that they had read the name on an earlier list. What lesson does this result provide about the functions of consciousness?

a. Conscious judgments can affect the construction of unconscious memories.
b. The executive control function of consciousness sometimes fails.
c. Conscious processes contribute to judgment errors.
d. Unconscious memories can influence conscious judgments.

2. Carmen is mesmerized by the television documentary depicting the Holy Ghost people of Appalachia handling poisonous snakes and fire. She learns that these intensely religious people prepare for their participation in the "signs of the spirits" by

a. drinking strychnine poison.
b. listening to long sermons, singing, and dancing wildly.
c. quietly meditating in groups of seven.
d. taking psychoactive drugs.

3. Flying east generally creates greater jet lag than flying west because your

a. biological clock can be more readily extended than shortened.
b. circadian rhythms follow the ticking of an internal clock.
c. sleep cycle depends on the relationship between body time and clock time.
d. circadian rhythms are more influential early in the morning than late in the evening.

4. One feature of many non-Western approaches to dream interpretation is that dreams are believed

a. to provide a vision of the future.
b. to be the side effects of other brain activities.
c. to arise from unconscious wishes.
d. to signal the onset of religious ecstasy.

5. For a research project, you are asked to wear an electronic pager. At random times during the day, the pager signals you to write down the most recent thoughts you were having. The research project is probably studying the _____ of consciousness.

a. functions
b. levels
c. contents
d. processes

6. You tell your therapist that you had a dream in which "a bear growled at you in the woods and then chased you." Your therapist tells you that you are concerned about being yelled at by your boss. This interpretation suggests that your therapist believes in the importance of the _____ content of dreams.

a. manifest
b. analytic
c. latent
d. holistic

7. Different drugs can affect the messages neurotransmitters send to the body: _____ decrease arousal; _____ increase arousal.

a. opiates; barbiturates
b. cannabinoids; opiates
c. barbiturates; amphetamines
d. cannabinoids; amphetamines

8. During a typical night you go through the sleep cycle about _____ times; you have the most REM sleep in the _____ cycles.

a. four to six; early
b. four to six; late
c. one to three; early
d. one to three; late

9. Olga claims to be a lucid dreamer, which means that she can

a. have vivid dreams during non-REM sleep.
b. have daydreams that are as lucid as night dreams.
c. control the content of her dreams.
d. keep her eyes still during her dreams.

10. Right before you started to read this question, its answer was _____.

a. a preconscious memory
b. a nonconscious process
c. unattended information
d. an unconscious process

Practice Test 3

1. The chemicals in nicotine stimulate patterns in the brain which are similar to those activated when one is addicted to

a. alcohol.
b. cocaine.
c. heroin.
d. opium.

2. Substances such as _____ and _____ tend to depress the body's mental and physical activity.

a. alcohol; cannabinoids
b. cannabinoids; barbiturates
c. alcohol; barbiturates
d. barbiturates; hallucinogens

3. If you are a modern sleep researcher, your work has probably been most influenced by the

a. invention of the EEG and the discovery of rapid eye movements.
b. theories of Sigmund Freud and Carl Jung.
c. discovery of circadian rhythms and the principle of hibernation.
d. phenomenon of jet lag and the invention of the electrocardiogram.

4. One day a friend confides in you that she has narcolepsy. You understand this to mean that she

a. is addicted to narcotics.
b. has a chronic, mildly contagious disease.
c. has a periodic compulsion to sleep during the daytime.
d. experiences total loss of muscle control brought on by emotional excitement.

5. Timothy "sees" nonexistent mice running up and down the building walls and "hears" voices speaking to him from his unplugged radio. Timothy is apparently experiencing

a. illusions.
b. hallucinations.
c. delusions.
d. a reality check.

6. Just for the fun of it, you have decided to keep a dream diary. Today, when you wake up, you remember a very long and interesting dream. It is most likely that this dream occurred

a. about 90 minutes after you fell asleep.
b. shortly before you awakened.
c. during NREM sleep.
d. during Stage 3 or Stage 4.

7. Which of the following procedures would be most likely to be a part of the SLIP technique?

a. Asking participants to say a series of words.
b. Distracting participants while they are memorizing a list of names.
c. Asking blindfolded participants to run across a wet floor.
d. Rewarding accuracy and punishing errors.

8. Professor Templin's students are participating in a study in which they have to report what they are thinking about when a bell goes off at different times during the class. The research that Professor Templin's students are participating in is using the _____ method.

a. experience-sampling
b. think-aloud
c. "beeper"
d. randomized participation

9. The use of mind-altering drugs

a. began shortly after World War I.
b. can be treated by the ingestion of sophora seeds.
c. can be traced to ancient times.
d. was first inspired by Aldous Huxley's book, *The Doors of Perception*.

10. Curtis is an anthropologist who is visiting a Mayan village in Guatemala in order to learn more about the Mayan Indians' views on dreams. He will find out that

a. in Mayan culture only the shamans are allowed to recount and discuss dreams.
b. formal instruction about religious rituals is not provided to shamans because it is expected they will receive such information by way of dreams.
c. dreamers take care not to wake up at night in order to preserve memory for their dreams.
d. Mayan mothers are curious about the dreams of their children and will ask them to recount their dreams.

Comprehensive Test

1. Hillary is participating in an experiment on pain reduction. Assuming Hillary is highly hypnotizable she will experience the most pain relief

a. following the induction of hypnotic analgesia.
b. with highly motivating instructions to ignore the pain.
c. after ingesting a placebo capsule.
d. after engaging in directed self-awareness.

2. The regulation of blood pressure, the beating of your heart, and the automatic process of breathing are all examples of

a. preconscious memories.
b. nonconscious processes.
c. self-conscious processes.
d. autobiographical knowledge.

3. How do we know when children have developed a sense of self? When they have

a. acquired the ability to dream.
b. the knowledge that they have siblings.
c. realized that they are separate from others.
d. consciousness of what they are doing and that they are doing it, and that others will react to those actions.

4. Zoltan the Magnificent is sharing information with his pupil Voltan about using hypnosis as part of his stage act. Which of the following statements would be accurate information?

a. Women are more susceptible to hypnosis than are men.
b. Most people fall asleep on their way to being deeply hypnotized.
c. More people have more low responses to hypnotic inductions than high responses.
d. Most people are more hypnotizable as older adults than they are as teenagers.

5. To explain the importance of the _____ function of consciousness, Stanley says, "Suppose you never threw out any junk mail? How cluttered would your home become?"

a. restrictive
b. executive control
c. consensual validation
d. selective storage

6. One of the most important functions of REM sleep is maintenance of

a. learning and memory
b. sleep cycles
c. relaxation
d. breathing

111

7. Dee Dee is studying botany. She comes across a plant with psychoactive effects, whose active ingredient is THC. It can impair motor coordination and affects receptors common in the hippocampus. This psychoactive plant is probably a

a. cannabis.
b. cocoa.
c. cactus.
d. mushroom.

8. Hal believes that the scientists of the future will be able to "create" androids that will have a sense of self. It can be inferred that the androids probably will

a. have a well-developed personality.
b. experience consciousness.
c. have normal intelligence.
d. be able to speak as humans do.

9. A man claims that he has terrible insomnia and hardly sleeps at all. The fact that his wife complains that his constant snoring disturbs her sleep suggests that the man's condition is

a. cataplexy.
b. subjective insomnia.
c. narcolepsy.
d. sleep apnea.

10. Max is playing the part of a hypnotized person in a school play. In order for the audience to believe that Max is hypnotized, he needs to communicate to them that he

a. is deeply asleep.
b. has lost all sense of self-control.
c. is in a state of heightened responsiveness.
d. is tense and nervous.

11. Which of the following is the sleep disorder in which the person stops breathing while asleep?

a. narcolepsy
b. insomnia
c. sleep apnea
d. somnambulism

12. Freud believed that memories that are too painful to remember are repressed, or put out of our awareness. According to Freud these memories go into the _____.

a. preconscious
b. unconscious
c. latent content
d. manifest content

13. Due to our circadian rhythms, our 24-25 hour biological clock, it is much easier to fly on a _____ flight because we can expect to experience less jet lag.

a. eastbound
b. westbound
c. northerly
d. southerly

14. The _____ content of a dream conveys the deeper, hidden meaning according to Freud.

a. latent
b. manifest
c. biological
d. cognitive

15. All of the following are major psychoactive drug classifications EXCEPT:

a. opiates
b. depressants
c. stimulants
d. steroids

True/False Questions

1. Psychological dependence is a situation in which an individual needs greater dosages to get the same effect.　　　　T　　F

2. Few people suffer from the chronic inability to sleep normally.　　　　T　　F

3. Narcolepsy is a sleep disorder that is sometimes accompanied by cataplexy.　　　　T　　F

4. Our circadian rhythms operate according to a 12 hour clock.　　　　T　　F

5. There are several theories, but no one knows why people sleep.　　　　T　　F

6. If you were to be deprived of REM sleep for a night you would have more REM sleep the next night.　　　　T　　F

7. Cocaine is a stimulant.　　　　T　　F

8. Delusions are vivid perceptions that occur in the absence of objective stimulation.　　　　T　　F

Essay Questions

1. Outline the stages and progression of a normal night's sleep. Differentiate between REM and NREM sleep by explaining what occurs during each.

2. List the drug classifications. Give an example of each and tell how each affects the central nervous system.

When you have finished . . . Weblinks

Sleepnet

http://www.sleepnet.com/

Sleepnet is a great clearinghouse for links and any other information on sleep. You can take a sleep test, learn about sleep disorders, get tips for healthy sleep, or join one of the many discussion forums.

Straight Talk on Alcohol and Other Drugs

http://www.alcoholandotherdrugs.com/

This site was designed with input from students taking general psychology. It's called Straight Talk on Alcohol and Other Drugs: A Website for College Students. Look through the five chapters to find why students use alcohol and other drugs.

American Society for Clinical Hypnosis

http://www.asch.net/genpubinfo.htm

This is the general public information page on the American Society for Clinical Hypnosis' (ASCH) website. Pay particular attention to the definitions and myths about hypnosis. Hypnosis is not acting like a chicken.

The Dreams Foundation

http://www.dreams.ca/

This site provides resources for the understanding of nightmares, lucid dreaming, sleep research, disorder treatment, precognitive dreams and dreamwork. Suggestions for improving dream recall as well as dream consciousness are provided.

Meditation

http://1stholistic.com/Mediation/hol_meditation.htm

HolisticOnline takes pride in providing in-depth treatment of meditation via this internet website.

Mind, Consciousness and Altered States

Across
3. altered state of consciousness designed to enhance self-knowledge and well being
4. chronic inability to sleep normally
8. hidden meaning of a dream
9. needing more and more of a drug to get the same effect
10. when the body requires a drug in order to function
11. sleep disorder causing the person to stop breathing while asleep
12. sleepwalking
13. awareness of internal events and the external environment

Down
1. conscious awareness of dreams
2. false perceptions
5. irresistible sleepiness during the daytime
6. surface content of a dream
7. altered state characterized by deep relaxation and susceptibility to suggestion

Puzzle created with Puzzlemaker at DiscoverySchool.com

Chapter 5 – Answers

Practice Test 1

1. d (p. 155)
2. b (p. 141)
3. d (p. 158)
4. c (p. 155)
5. d (p. 154)
6. a (p. 143)
7. c (p. 149)
8. d (p. 157)
9. d (p. 143)
10. b (p. 141)

Practice Test 2

1. d (p. 141)
2. b (p. 156)
3. a (p. 146)
4. a (p. 151)
5. c (p. 140)
6. c (p. 151)
7. c (p. 159-160)
8. b (p. 146)
9. c (p. 153)
10. a (p. 141)

Practice Test 3

1. b (p. 161)
2. c (p. 159)
3. a (p. 146)
4. c (p. 149)
5. b (p. 158)
6. b (p. 150)
7. a (p. 144)
8. a (p. 142)
9. c (p. 157)
10. d (p.151)

Comprehensive Test

Multiple Choice	True/False

Multiple Choice

1. a (p. 154)
2. b (p. 141)
3. d (p. 141)
4. c (p. 154)
5. d (p. 144)
6. a (p. 146)
7. a (p. 158)
8. b (p. 140)
9. b (p. 148)
10. c (p. 153)
11. c (p. 149)
12. b (p. 142)
13. b (p. 145)
14. a (p. 151)
15. d (p. 157)

True/False

1. F (p. 158)
2. F (p. 148)
3. T (p. 149)
4. F (p. 145)
5. T (p. 148)
6. T (p. 148)
7. T (p. 160)
8. F (p. 158)

Crossword Key

Across

3. Meditation
4. Insomnia
8. Latent Content
9. Tolerance
10. Addiction
11. Sleep Apnea
12. Somnambulism
13. Consciousness

Down

1. Lucid Dreaming
2. Hallucinations
5. Narcolepsy
6. Manifest Content
7. Hypnosis

Chapter 6

Learning and Behavior Analysis

Before You Read

The study of learning is the focus of this chapter. The chapter begins with a definition of terms. Learning is a relatively consistent change of behavior based on experience. The chapter goes on to cover the different types of learning. First, classical conditioning is defined and Pavlov's experiments are highlighted. The process and applications of classical conditioning are explained. Next, operant conditioning is explained with Thorndike's law of effect leading to Skinner's principle of reinforcement. The properties and schedules of reinforcement are described. Coverage continues with the biology of learning, which asks, "How do species-specific tendencies affect learning?" The chapter closes with the final type of learning, cognitive learning. You will come to appreciate how you can learn by watching others.

Chapter Objectives

After reading this chapter you should be able to:

- Define learning.

- Explain classical conditioning using the terms UCS, UCR, CS and CR.

- Describe extinction and explain how it occurs.

- Define and contrast stimulus generalization and discrimination.

- Explain classical conditioning of emotional responses and drug tolerance.

- State Thorndike's Law of Effect.

- Describe Skinner's behavior analytic approach.

- Differentiate between positive reinforcement, negative reinforcement, and punishment.

- Differentiate between primary and secondary reinforcers.

- Identify the 4 schedules of reinforcement and give an example of each.

- Explain how complex behaviors are shaped.

- Describe instinctual drift.

- Explain how taste-aversion is based on genetically prepared associations.

- Describe cognitive maps and conceptual behavior.

- Explain how humans and other animals can learn through observation.

As you read . . . Term Identification

Acquisition	Operant Conditioning
Animal Cognition	Operant Extinction
Behavior Analysis	Partial Reinforcement Effect
Biological Constraints on Learning	Positive Punishment
Classical Conditioning	Positive Reinforcement
Cognitive Map	Primary Reinforces
Conditioned Reinforcers	Punisher
Conditioned Response (CR)	Reflex
Conditioned Stimulus (CS)	Reinforcer
Discriminative Stimuli	Reinforcement Contingency
Extinction	Schedules of Reinforcement
Fixed-Interval Schedule	Shaping by Successive Approximations
Fixed-Ratio Schedule	Spontaneous Recovery
Habituation	Stimulus Discrimination
Instinctual Drift	Stimulus Generalization
Law of Effect	Taste-Aversion Learning
Learning	Three-Term Contingency
Learning-Performance Distinction	Unconditioned Response (UCR)
Negative Punishment	Unconditioned Stimulus (UCS)
Negative Reinforcement	Variable-Interval Schedule
Observational Learning	Variable-Ratio Schedule
Operant	

As you read . . . Questions and Answers

What Is Learning?

Give an example for each of these components of the definition of learning. What changes in behavior don't fit the definition?

1. A change in behavior or behavior potential (learning-performance distinction)

2. A relatively consistent change

3. A process based on experience

Behaviorism and Behavior Analysis

1. What is radical behaviorism?

2. Summarize the influential ideas of John Watson and B. F. Skinner. What did they have to say about mental states?

3. What is behavior analysis? Why does it assume that learning is conserved across species?

Pavlov's Surprising Observation

1. What observation prompted Pavlov to study classical conditioning?

2. Describe the main features of Pavlov's procedure. What did his dogs do?

3. Define:

   Reflex

   Unconditioned stimulus

   Unconditioned response

   Conditioned stimulus

Conditioned response

Processes of Conditioning

1. What is acquisition? Why does timing matter?

2. What is extinction?

3. What is spontaneous recovery?

4. What is stimulus generalization and how is a generalization gradient produced?

5. How is training in stimulus discrimination done?

6. Explain why generalization and discrimination must occur in a balanced fashion.

Focus on Acquisition

1. Contrast contiguity and contingency.

Applications of Classical Conditioning

1. How does classical conditioning explain feelings of disgust?

2. How does classical conditioning explain the acquisition of fears? Describe Watson and Rayner's experiment.

3. Summarize Shepard Siegel's research on tolerance with rats (identify the UCS, UCR, and so on).

4. How have Siegel's findings been applied to human situations?

The Law of Effect

What was the purpose of Thorndike's puzzle boxes? What did he conclude about stimulus-response connections, trial and error, and the law of effect?

Psychology In Your Life

Explain why some aftereffects of chemotherapy remain after treatment has ended?

Experimental Analysis of Behavior

1. What are important assumptions of the experimental analysis of behavior?

2. What are operants? What is an operant chamber?

Reinforcement Contingencies

1. Make sure you understand how each of these types of reinforcers and punishments are different. Give examples of each:

Positive reinforcement

Negative reinforcement

Operant extinction

Positive punishment

Negative punishment

2. What is a good way to differentiate punishment and reinforcement?

3. What are discriminative stimuli?

4. Give an example of a three-term contingency.

You should work your way through the questions and answers in the text by calling to mind real-life situations. We repeat each question here. Try to give an answer without looking back at the text.

5. How can you define a behavior that you would like to reinforce or eliminate?

6. How can you define the contexts in which a behavior is appropriate or inappropriate?

7. Have you unknowingly been reinforcing some behaviors?

1. What is a primary reinforcer? What is a conditioned reinforcer? Give examples.

2. How do token economies work?

3. What is the Response Deprivation Theory? Give examples of the Premack principle at work.

1. How common is it for parents to spank their children?

2. What has research revealed about the relationship between physical punishment and children's classroom behavior?

1. Describe the effect of partial reinforcement.

Make sure you understand the notation (F vs. V; R vs. I). For each of the schedules of reinforcement, bolster your memory by trying to think of a real-life example.

2. Fixed-ratio (FR) schedules

3. Variable-ratio (VR) schedules

4.Fixed-interval (FI) schedules

5. Variable-interval (VI) schedules

Shaping

How does shaping work? (Give an example.)

Biology and Learning

What is meant by biological constraints on learning?

Instinctual Drift

Give examples of instinctual drift.

Taste-Aversion Learning

1. Summarize John Garcia's research on taste-aversion learning.

2. Describe two applications of taste-aversion learning.

Cognitive Influences on Learning

What is meant by cognition?

Animal Cognition

1. What did Edward Tolman's research demonstrate?

2. What are three functions of cognitive maps?

3. What are the capabilities of Clark's nutcrackers?

4. Summarize the results of Edward Wasserman's research with pigeons.

Observational Learning

1. What is meant by vicarious reinforcement and vicarious punishment?

2. What is meant by observational learning?

3. What general conclusions have been drawn from studies of observational learning?

4. How does research on observational learning apply to television and movie viewing?

For Group Study

Applications of Classical Conditioning

The text challenges you to examine your life for instances of classical conditioning. Take up that challenge with your group. Start with the situations given in the book. Do the examples alarm or disgust you? Why? Are there fears or preferences that any of you can't attribute to conscious processes? For each example, remember that classical conditioning must start with a UCS → UCR pairing. If you can't figure out what that pairing would be, you're not dealing with classical conditioning.

Reinforcement Contingencies

You should have lots of ideas about how this material applies to day-to-day life. As a group, choose some behaviors you'd like to make more or less frequent (your own behaviors, or others'). Discuss how you might use each of the different types of reinforcement contingencies to bring the change about.

Shaping

Do any of you have pets? Think of something you'd like to train the pet to do and discuss how you might accomplish the goal using shaping or chaining.

You can also practice shaping as a group. Choose one member to leave the room. While he or she is gone, select some behavior that is complex and interesting. You might, for example, want your friend to do a jumping jack, spin, and then touch the ground. You will use applause for reinforcement. After you have chosen the behavior, talk about how you will differentially reinforce each step on the way to performing the full behavior. Bring your friend back in and go to it.

After you read . . . Practice Tests

Practice Test 1

1. Katie's parents want her to stop screaming. She is warned that if she doesn't stop screaming, she will not be allowed to have a slice of the chocolate cake she loves so much. What type of reinforcement contingency have Katie's parents established?

a. negative punishment
b. positive punishment
c. negative reinforcement
d. operant extinction

2. Which statement might a person who espouses behavior analysis be most likely to make?

a. People eat when they are hungry because they receive internal messages from the hypothalamus.
b. Forms of learning are not conserved across species.
c. I seek to identify the mechanisms that explain people's actions in response to experience.
d. We focus on the subjective experiences that people find important.

3. In positive punishment, the probability of a response decreases over time when a stimulus is _____; in negative punishment; the probability of a response decreases over time when a stimulus is _____.

a. presented; presented
b. presented; removed
c. removed; removed
d. removed; presented

4. Gloria has just come from her doctor. The doctor has prescribed a drug that must be taken on a full stomach, but will inevitably make Gloria feel sick. Gloria, who is an expert on principles of learning, decides to have meatloaf for dinner. You would guess that meatloaf is

a. not one of Gloria's primary reinforcers.
b. one of Gloria's favorite foods.
c. not one of Gloria's favorite foods.
d. one of Gloria's discriminative stimuli.

5. You go to the Rialto and watch a horror film that terrifies you. The next time a friend invites you to the movies, you are unwilling to set foot in the Rialto. In this situation, the Rialto is the _____, and your fear response is the _____.

a. CS; UCR
b. CS; CR
c. UCS; UCR
d. UCS; CR

6. You would like to train your new puppy using the Response Deprivation Theory (Premack principle). To get started, you should determine

a. which behaviors are low- and high-probability.
b. what stimulus you can use as a positive punisher.
c. how often the puppy requires negative reinforcement.
d. what stimuli function as primary reinforcers.

7. You are watching an experiment in which a rabbit's eye blink is being classically conditioned. In the procedure, a tone sounds followed shortly by a puff of air to the eye. However, you notice that the air puff follows a 100-Hz tone but not a 120-Hz tone. It's likely that the rabbit is undergoing _____ training.

a. extinction
b. recovery
c. generalization
d. discrimination

8. You hear on the news that a famous rock star has died of a heroin overdose. Apparently, he shot up twice every day. What other piece of information may have been an important part of the story?

a. He had been using heroin since he was 22.
b. He was shooting up for the first time in his new home.
c. Every time he shot up, he did it in the company of his wife.
d. Other members of his band were heroin users as well.

9. Using classical conditioning, you have trained a rat that a bell predicts an electric shock. You now would like the rat to learn that a light also predicts the shock. In a long series of trials, you provide it with the sequence bell—light—shock. The outcome of this training is likely to be that the rat responds

a. only to the light.
b. only to the bell.
c. to both the light and the bell.
d. to neither the light nor the bell.

10. Shirlee works as an animal trainer for a circus. She is about to try training a ferret for the first time. She has spent the last few days at the library reading up on ferrets' innate behavior patterns. Shirlee is trying to avoid problems with

a. instinctual drift.
b. behavior chaining.
c. discriminative stimuli.
d. operant extinction.

Practice Test 2

1. You are conducting an experiment in which dogs receive electric shocks and produce fear responses. The whole time the experiment is going on, a loud fan is keeping the room cool. The next time the dogs are brought into the room, will the sound of the fan elicit a fear response?

a. No, because the electric shock is not contiguous with the fan.
b. No, because the electric shock is not contingent on the fan.
c. Yes, because the electric shock is contiguous with the fan.
d. Yes, because the electric shock is contingent on the fan.

2. Which of the following scenarios sounds like an instance in which maladaptive behavior may be reinforced by secondary gains?

a. Each time a young girl throws a tantrum she loses TV privileges.
b. Patients in a psychiatric hospital earn tokens for taking their medication.
c. The grandparents of a shy child bring him extra gifts.
d. A playground bully is rewarded when he helps prevent a fight.

3. Taylor thinks she may have discovered a violation of the law of effect. She has been trying to teach her cat Jeffrey to jump on her lap by scratching him behind the ears each time he does so. Strangely, Jeffrey is spending less and less time in Taylor's lap. You suggest to Taylor that her scratching may not be _____ for Jeffrey.

a. an operant
b. a stimulus
c. contingent
d. rewarding

4. Emily wants her son to learn a new behavior through vicarious reinforcement. She should try to find a situation in which her son can watch someone

a. having a reward taken away for failing to carry out the relevant behavior.
b. having a reward taken away for carrying out the relevant behavior.
c. being given punishment for failing to carry out the relevant behavior.
d. being given a reward for carrying out the relevant behavior.

5. It is not always possible to judge the extent of learning by observing a person's behavior because some learning

a. lasts for only a brief time.
b. is not immediately expressed in performance.
c. is the result of physical maturation.
d. does not rely on experience.

6. You are a dog named Mr. Peabody. At first, your owner gave you a dog biscuit every time you sniffed around his slippers. Now you only get the biscuit when you actually pick up one of the slippers. Your owner is probably using _____ to teach you a complex behavior.

a. chaining
b. partial reinforcement
c. conditioned reinforcers
d. shaping

7. For your classical conditioning experiment, you have selected a buzzer as your CS. Which of the following would be the LEAST likely UCR?

a. whistling
b. an eye blink
c. salivation
d. nausea

8. In the first phase of an experiment, pigeons learned to peck an orange key after viewing photographs of people and cars and a red key after viewing a flower or a chair. The second phase included only pictures of cars and chairs. The pigeons learned to peck a green key after seeing cars and a white key after seeing chairs. In the third phase, the pigeons see flowers again. The researcher can conclude that a pigeon has learned a category if it pecks a

a. white key when it sees a chair.
b. white key when it sees a flower.
c. green key when it sees a car.
d. green key when it sees a flower.

9. Edward Tolman's research on cognitive maps demonstrated that rats could

a. press a bar in the right pattern to gain access to a maze.
b. find their way to hidden food after long delays.
c. solve mazes by observing other rats being reinforced.
d. find paths through mazes that had never previously been reinforced.

10. You are watching a rat in an operant chamber. It presses the bar vigorously for a short period of time and then hardly presses at all for about 5 seconds. That pattern is repeated for as long as you watch. You suspect that the rat is on a _____ schedule.

a. FR-5
b. VR-5
c. FI-5
d. VI-5

Practice Test 3

1. You are playing the part of John Watson in a classroom debate on different approaches to the study of learning. Someone raises a question about the use of introspection in psychological research. You should take the position that introspection _____ an acceptable means of studying behavior because it is _____.

a. is; objective
b. is; subjective
c. is not; objective
d. is not; subjective

2. Ms. Crabtree likes to use conditioned reinforcers to help motivate her second graders. If asked why she prefers conditioned reinforcers to primary reinforcers, she is LEAST likely to respond that they

a. satisfy biological needs.
b. are readily available.
c. are portable.
d. can be dispensed rapidly.

3. Using a puff of air as the UCS, Enid classically conditions her dog to blink whenever she says "blink." Her parrot overhears the procedure and says "blink" all day long when Enid is out. When she returns, Enid says "blink" to her dog, but he does not blink. It appears as though

a. the dog's behavior has generalized.
b. spontaneous recovery has occurred.
c. the dog is now under the parrot's control.
d. extinction has taken place.

4. The research of Robert Rescorla challenged Pavlov's belief that conditioning will occur if the CS and UCS

a. stimulate different sensory modalities.
b. stimulate the same sensory modality.
c. are only spatially contiguous.
d. are only temporally contiguous.

5. Pat and Judy both work in clothing assembly, but in two different companies. Pat is paid every two weeks for her work, while Judy is paid after assembling 100 pieces of clothing. Pat is under a _____ schedule of reinforcement, and Judy is under a _____ schedule of reinforcement.

a. variable-ratio; fixed-interval
b. fixed-interval; variable-ratio
c. fixed-ratio; fixed-interval
d. fixed-interval; fixed-ratio

6. Shirley notices that a classmate is praised by the teacher for helping another child with her homework. Shirley then decides that she would like to help her classmates with their homework also. Shirley is exhibiting learning through

a. vicarious punishment.
b. vicarious reinforcement.
c. the application of cognitive maps.
d. the Premack principle.

7. When the young B. F. Skinner economized on his supply of rat pellets, he found that compared to rats who were reinforced after every response, the animals who were put on a partial reinforcement schedule

a. learned less quickly.
b. responded less frequently during extinction.
c. stopped responding immediately.
d. responded more vigorously during extinction.

8. Reinforcers always are defined in terms of

a. the probability of a behavior.
b. cultural values.
c. indications of pleasure.
d. the temporary state of the organism.

9. Your friend Teresa doesn't believe that whether she was physically punished as a teenager has anything to do with her emotional or psychological state now, many years later. Is she correct?

a. Yes, most effects of physical punishment are not long lasting.
b. Yes, as teenagers develop into adults, formal thinking allows them to understand their parents' use of physical punishment intellectually, reducing or eliminating the effects of physical punishment.
c. No, those individuals who were physically punished as adolescents experience problems later in life, although they disappear in a very short time.
d. No, those individuals who were physically punished as adolescents are put at higher risk for negative outcomes such as depression and suicide.

10. Nellie's mom thinks that Nellie could be neater. She is constantly nagging Nellie to keep her room tidy. When Nellie increases her room cleaning, her mom stops nagging her. The nagging provides

a. positive punishment.
b. negative punishment.
c. positive reinforcement.
d. negative reinforcement.

Comprehensive Test

1. The students in the psychology class have decided to get the teacher to lecture from a corner of the classroom. They smile and make eye contact with him only when he moves closer and closer to the corner. If he moves in the wrong direction, they avert their eyes and look bored. The students are using

a. observational learning techniques.
b. primary reinforcement.
c. shaping.
d. the Premack principle.

2. Professor Boone has a pet raccoon named Danny that he is trying to teach a trick. He wants Danny to put some coins into a toy bank, and is using food as a reinforcer. Danny, however, simply rubs the coins together in his paws, and won't let go. This sounds like what Keller and Marion Breland referred to as

a. taste-aversion learning.
b. a token economy.
c. instinctual drift.
d. an internal cognitive map.

3. Karma has rehearsed her speech so many times that she recites it in her sleep. When she gets up in class to give her speech, however, she forgets most of it. Karma's inability to give her speech reflects problems in

a. learning.
b. performance.
c. learning and performance.
d. personality traits such as shyness.

4. Whenever Manfred injects himself with heroin, he is in his bedroom. One day he is asked to go over to his friend's house for a party. During the party he sneaks away to inject himself with his usual dose of heroin in his friend's bedroom. What do you predict is likely to happen, if Shepard Siegel's findings with rats are valid for humans?

a. Manfred is more likely to overdose.
b. Manfred is less likely to overdose.
c. Manfred will experience effects no different than before.
d. Manfred's addiction will lessen.

5. When a softball player is late for practice, she loses a day's pay. When Jamie watches television instead of doing his household chores, he has to turn over the keys to the family car. These examples illustrate the process of

a. positive reinforcement.
b. negative reinforcement.
c. positive punishment.
d. negative punishment.

135

6. Taste-aversion learning demonstrates that animals

a. respond to operant conditioning procedures best when their survival is at stake.
b. can overcome the effects of blocking when their survival is at stake.
c. are more likely to produce UCRs in the presence of CSs than UCSs.
d. have inborn biases to associate particular stimuli with particular consequences.

7. The sudden reappearance of the CR to the CS after a period of time following extinction is referred to as

a. extinction.
b. stimulus generalization.
c. spontaneous recovery.
d. stimulus generalization.

8. Dr. Thunder is a colleague of Pavlov's who believes he can classically condition anything. You tell him that classical conditioning is not very effective for

a. voluntary responses.
b. involuntary responses.
c. emotional responses.
d. habit responses.

9. As part of a lab exercise on classical conditioning, the students are experimenting with different temporal patterns. In one study, they present the CS, but then turn it off before the UCS is presented. This is known as _____ conditioning.

a. simultaneous
b. delayed
c. backward
d. trace

10. Fred is designing an experiment using B. F. Skinner's approach as a model. When choosing a variable to measure, Fred should focus on

a. the number of trials it takes to escape from a puzzle box.
b. the amount of saliva his participants secrete.
c. the probability that a given response will occur.
d. changes in a participant's conceptualizations.

11. All of the following are critical for learning to occur EXCEPT :

a. it must be relatively consistent.
b. it is based on experience.
c. there must be a behavior change.
d. the environment must be conducive.

12. Pavlov won a Nobel Prize in 1904 for his research on _____.

a. digestion in dogs
b. classical conditioning
c. operant conditioning
d. cognitive learning

13. In conditioning, the weakening of a conditioned association in the absence of a reinforcer is called:

a. shaping
b. extinction
c. spontaneous recovery
d. stimulus generalization

14. Little Albert was trained to fear a white rat, a stimulus he had initially not feared, by pairing it with an aversive _____.

a. CS
b. CR
c. UCS
d. UCR

15. You go to Las Vegas to play the slot machines. Now that you have taken psychology you know that the machines are set to pay off on which schedule of reinforcement?

a. FR
b. FI
c. VR
d. VI

True/False Questions

1. Operant conditioning relies on reflex responses.   T   F

2. Ivan Pavlov won a Nobel Prize for his work with dogs.   T   F

3. Rescorla found that the role of contingency in classical   T   F
   conditioning is very important.

4. The law of effect states that there is a consistent relationship   T   F
   between a response and environmental changes.

5. In negative reinforcement, a behavior is followed by the presentation   T   F
   of an aversive stimuli decreasing the probability of that behavior.

6. Conditioned reinforcers, such as food and water, are biologically determined. T   F

7. Fixed-ratio schedules of reinforcement depend on time.   T   F

8. In observational learning, humans or animals learn by watching others.   T   F

Essay Questions

1. Describe the 4 schedules of reinforcement. Give an example of each. Which one creates high rates of response with no pauses?

2. Explain how extinction, spontaneous recovery, generalization and discrimination work in the classical conditioning paradigm.

When you have finished . . . Weblinks

Classical Conditioning

http://sun.science.wayne.edu/~wpoff/cor/mem/conditnl.html

This is an enlightening tutorial from Wayne State University on conditioning. Types of conditioning, generalization, and extinction are explored in detail.

The Behaviorism Tutorial

http://psych.athabascau.ca/html/Behaviorism/

The Behaviorism Tutorial is produced by Jay Moore of Athabasca University. It consists of three parts, narrative, definitions, and quotations, each with built in quizzing features.

Psych Lab Operant Conditioning

http://www.uwm.edu/~johnchay/oc.htm

Try your hand at operantly conditioning your own bird. This simulation from PsychLab allows you to do just that. Click on the food tray and watch the bird peck. See how the schedule of reinforcement is tracked on the cumulative recorder.

Observational (Social) Learning

http://chiron.valdosta.edu/whuitt/col/soccog/soclrn.html

The four step pattern developed by Bandura as well related experiments are explained and demonstrated at this website.

Token Economy System

http://www.minddisorders.com/Py-Z/Token-economy-system.html

You can learn the basics of behavior modification as well as the components needed for an effective token economy system. The definition, purpose, description, and risks of token economy systems are explored. A link to the token economy system forum is provided.

Learning and Behavioral Analysis

Across

7. stimulus that decreases the probability of a response
8. weakening of a conditioned association
9. reinforcer delivered after a fixed number of responses
11. removal of an aversive stimuli to increase the likelihood of a response
12. reinforcer delivered after a variable number of responses

Down

1. reinforcer delivered after a variable period of time
2. conditioned response is first elicited by the conditioned stimuli
3. relatively permanent change in behavior that results from experience
4. reinforce responses that successfully approximate the desired response
5. reinforcer is delivered after a fixed period of time
6. any stimulus that increases the probability of a response
10. unlearned response that has biological relevance for an organism

Puzzle created with Puzzlemaker at DiscoverySchool.com

Chapter 6 - Answers

Practice Test 1

1. a (p. 180)
2. c (p. 167)
3. b (p. 180)
4. c (p. 179)
5. b (p. 176)
6. a (p. 183)
7. d (p. 180)
8. b (p. 176)
9. b. (p. 171)
10. a (p. 187)

Practice Test 2

1. b (p. 173)
2. c (p. 182)
3. d (p. 178)
4. d (p. 192)
5. b (p. 166)
6. d (p. 186)
7. a. (p. 170)
8. b (p. 180)
9. d (p. 190)
10. c (p. 185)

Practice Test 3

1. d (p. 167)
2. a (p. 179)
3. d (p. 171)
4. d (p. 172)
5. d (p. 185)
6. b (p. 192)
7. d (p. 183)
8. a (p. 179)
9. d (p. 184)
10. d (p. 179)

Comprehensive Test

Multiple Choice

1. c (p. 186)
2. c (p. 187)
3. b (p. 166)
4. a (p. 176)
5. d (p. 180)
6. d (p. 188)
7. c (p. 171)
8. a (p. 170)
9. d (p. 170)
10. c (p. 178)
11. d (p. 166)
12. a (p. 168)
13. b (p. 171)
14. a (p. 175)
15. c (p. 185)

True/False

1. F (p. 178)
2. T (p. 168)
3. T (p. 172)
4. F (p. 177)
5. F (p. 179)
6. F (p. 182)
7. F (p. 185)
8. T (p. 192)

Crossword Key

Across

7. Punisher
8. Extinction
9. Fixed Ratio
11. Negative Reinforcement
12. Variable Ratio

Down

1. Variable Interval
2. Acquisition
3. Learning
4. Shaping
5. Fixed Interval
6. Reinforcer
10. Reflex

Chapter 7

Memory

Before you read . . .

What is memory? Are you aware of all the memories you possess? How do you remember how to do things? All of these questions and more are answered in the memory chapter. It begins with an overview of the origins of contemporary memory research and moves on to the types of memory and memory processes. The chapter follows the stage model of memory by introducing sensory memory, short- term memory and long-term memory. You will learn about context and encoding, retrieval, and memory improvement. Some of the mnemonic devices and tips could be very helpful in your coursework. The chapter continues with discussion on memory structures. How is memory organized? How do memory structures guide your moment-by-moment experience? The chapter ends with the biological aspects of memory. Scientists are currently searching for the biological correlates of memory, for example, how much the new brain imaging techniques reveal about the structures and biological processes of memory.

Chapter Objectives

After reading this chapter you should be able to:

- Define memory.

- Differentiate between implicit, explicit, declarative, and procedural memory.

- Elaborate on the three stages of memory; encoding, storage, and retrieval.

- Describe iconic memory.

- Discuss short-term memory in terms of its limited capacity and duration.

- Discuss maintenance rehearsal and chunking in terms of how each can extend the limits of STM.

- Define working memory, discuss its capacity, and identify its three components.

- Discuss the connection between retrieval, recall and recognition.

- Differentiate between episodic and semantic memory.

- Explain encoding specificity.

- Describe the serial position effect.

- Elaborate on the levels of processing theory.

- Discuss how implicit memory is assessed.

- Explain the effects of interference on memory.

- Explain how memory can be improved through elaborative rehearsal and mnemonics.

- Explain how memory research can be used to your advantage.

- Differentiate between prototypes, concepts, and schemas.

- Explain the unreliability of eyewitness testimony.

- Identify some of the brain structures associated with memory.

- Explain how Alzheimer's affects memory.

- Discuss how individuals with amnesia have helped in the study of memory.

As you read . . . Term Identification

Amnesia	Primacy Effect
Basic Level	Priming
Chunking	Proactive Interference
Concepts	Procedural Memory
Contextual Distinctiveness	Prototype
Declarative Memory	Recall
Elaborative Rehearsal	Recency Effect
Encoding	Recognition
Encoding Specificity	Reconstructive Memory
Engram	Retrieval
Episodic Memories	Retrieval Cues
Exemplars	Retroactive Interference
Explicit Uses of Memory	Schemas
Iconic Memory	Semantic Memories
Implicit Uses of Memory	Serial Position Effect
Levels-of-Processing Theory	Short Term Memory
Long-Term Memory	Storage
Memory	Transfer-Appropriate Processing
Metamemory	Working Memory
Mnemonics	

As you read . . . Questions and Answers

What Is Memory?

What does it mean to describe memory as a type of information processing?

Types of Memory

1. Distinguish between implicit and explicit memory. (Which kind of memory task are you performing?)

2. Define and give examples of declarative and procedural memory. (Which type of memory allows you to write without thinking much about the process?)

3. What is knowledge compilation? When will it lead to errors?

An Overview of Memory Processes

1. Define:

   Encoding (and mental representations)

   Storage

   Retrieval

2. What is the flow of information through these processes?

Iconic Memory

1. How did Sperling's experiments demonstrate the existence of iconic memory?

2. What properties did he discover?

The Capacity Limitations of STM

1. What is memory span? Why does it differ from the capacity of STM?

2. What is the capacity of STM?

Accommodating to STM Capacity

1. What is maintenance rehearsal? How does a distracter task prevent people from rehearsing?

2. What is chunking? How can it be used to expand the capacity of STM?

3. What did Saul Sternberg demonstrate about retrieval from STM?

Working Memory

1. Describe the three components of working memory.

   Phonological loop:

   Visuospatial sketchpad:

Central executive:

2. What are some consequences of working memory span?

Long-Term Memory: Encoding and Retrieval

1. What is long-term memory?

2. What general conclusion about memory performance will this chapter support?

3. What is the difference between recall and recognition? How can each be tested?

4. How are episodic and semantic memories alike and different?

Context and Encoding

1. What is encoding specificity? Describe research studies of encoding specificity.

2. What is the serial position effect? Which is the primacy effect and which the recency effect?

3. What is contextual distinctiveness? How does it explain the serial position effect? Summarize the logic of the experimental test.

1. What is meant by levels of processing? What happens when you process information at a deeper level?

2. What claim is made by researchers who adopt the transfer-appropriate processing perspective?

3. List and illustrate five techniques that are used to evaluate implicit memory. (Don't forget category association, which comes later in this section.)

4. What is priming? How is it shown on implicit memory tests?

5. Describe the logic of the experiment that demonstrated the importance of a match between processes at the encoding and retrieval stages.

6. Why did Ebbinghaus use nonsense syllables for his pioneering research?

7. What did he learn from using the savings method?

8. Describe interference. Differentiate between proactive and retroactive interference. Give an example of each from your own life.

Improving Memory for Unstructured Information

1. Describe and give an example of elaborative rehearsal.

2. List and describe two types of mnemonics.

1. What is meant by metamemory? What are feelings-of-knowing?

2. Are feelings-of-knowing generally accurate?

3. What two theories explain the accuracy of feelings-of-knowing?

Critical Thinking in Your Life

Summarize the text's advice based on each type of research.

1. Encoding specificity:

2. Serial position:

3. Elaborative rehearsal and mnemonics:

4. Metamemory:

Memory Structures

1. What are concepts? Give your own examples. What is the relationship between concepts and categories?

2. What are schemas? How are they formed?

3. What are prototypes? What evidence suggests that you form them?

4. How do prototypes change over time?

5. Describe exemplars and how they are different from prototypes.

Remembering as a Reconstructive Process

1. What three processes did Sir Frederic Bartlett find that led to distortions in reconstructive memory?

2. How can schemas lead to distortions in reconstructive memory?

3. In what circumstances is it appropriate not to remember exactly what happened? Explain how quotation is relevant.

4. Describe two experiments that demonstrate some of the difficulties of eyewitness memory.

Searching for the Engram

1. What did Karl Lashley mean by the "engram"? List the conclusions from his research.

2. What brain structures have been implicated in memory processes?

What are the brain changes, first described by Alois Alzheimer, found in individuals with that disease?

Amnesia

1. From what memory problems did Nick A. suffer after his injury?

2. Summarize an experiment that suggests that implicit memory may be spared when brain damage impairs explicit memory.

Brain Imaging

What have PET scans and MRI shown about the distribution of memory operations to parts of the brain?

For Group Study

Types of Memory

This section of the chapter makes distinctions among different types of memory. A later section (IV. B. Retrieval Cues) also introduces semantic versus episodic memory. Make sure you understand each of these distinctions by talking about examples provided by the group. You should also share problems you've had with different types of memory. If you've learned to drive, for example, talk about what that experience was like. Was it easy or hard for your teacher to try to turn procedural knowledge back into declarative instructions?

You are also probably more likely to benefit from the memory exercises suggested in the text if you try each of them in the group. Don't focus on who does better and who does worse. Instead, talk about what is important about each exercise.

Context and Encoding & Metamemory

This chapter should give your group another excuse to have some fun together. One of the best ways to reflect on your memory processes is to play a board game such as Trivial Pursuit (or make up your own trivia questions). As you play, sometimes you'll know the answer right away. Sometimes you'll know right away that you *don't* know the answer (which is a type of metamemory). Often, however, you'll be caught in the middle—you'll have a feeling-of-knowing but not be able to remember. So how can you get the memory out? Try to reconstruct the context in which you first learned the information, right? Even if you only play over the course of a brief study break, playing a trivia game can help make you more comfortable with many of the ideas in the chapter.

Improving Memory for Unstructured Information

Try some mnemonic devices as a group. You could, for example, try to make up a mnemonic for the names of each of the types of memory (implicit, explicit, and so on). Choose information in the text you all wish to memorize, and practice with these mnemonics. This is a good habit to get into!

Remembering as a Reconstructive Process

If the members of your group know each other pretty well, it's likely that some of you will have experienced events together. Choose two people who have some story in common (as a last resort, they could both talk about one of the lectures from class). Have one of them leave the room while the first one tells the story. Make sure he or she tells the story in reasonable detail (that is, more than just a plot outline). Take informal notes. Have the second one return and tell his or her version of the story. How different are the versions? Can you trace the differences to the work of schemas? Have they reconstructed parts of the story differently? Do they have any fundamental disagreements about what happened?

After you read . . . Practice Tests

Practice Test 1

1. The textbook describes a famous participant, S.F., who was able to memorize 84 digits even though his memory for letters was still only about seven items. This study made the point that

a. chunking is a valuable memory strategy.
b. memory can be improved through maintenance rehearsal.
c. the capacity of short-term memory has been underestimated.
d. there are large individual differences in short-term memory capacity among adults.

2. Renaldo is part of a family of acrobats that performs at the circus. When he performs his maneuvers, Renaldo is likely to find _____ memory to be most useful to him.

a. declarative
b. procedural
c. semantic
d. episodic

3. You are at a crowded party. A woman waves to you from across the room. You know she looks familiar, but you can't quite figure out who she is. Finally, it dawns on you: it's your dentist's assistant. Your memory difficulty can probably be explained by

a. encoding specificity.
b. proactive interference.
c. retroactive interference.
d. levels of processing.

4. Research with PET scans suggests that the encoding and retrieval of episodic information takes place in _____ of the brain.

a. the right hemisphere
b. the left hemisphere
c. the hypothalamus
d. different hemispheres

5. Carol is a researcher working with a patient who has suffered damage to his hippocampus. She would like to see if her patient can remember Carol's name. Carol wants to use a technique with the best possibility of showing positive evidence of memory. She should ask her patient

a. which name is right out of the group "Carolyn, Carmen, Carol, Catherine."
b. to try as hard as possible to recall her name.
c. to say what name first comes to mind to complete "Ca_____."
d. to list all the names she can think of beginning with "C" and then choose the one that sounds correct.

6. In research on eyewitness memory, did warning people that post-event information was misleading eliminate its effect?

a. Yes—when they have been warned, people try harder to remember the real events.
b. Yes—the warning allows people to ignore post-event information.
c. No—in eyewitness situations, people can't use reconstructive memory.
d. No—even with the warning, post-event information has an effect.

7. Charlie was attending his tenth high school reunion. He was disappointed when he entered the room because no one seemed to _____ his face. Of course, he had grown a mustache and beard since high school. Perhaps the _____ weren't good enough. Charlie decided to go back to his hotel room and shave.

a. recognize; retrieval cues
b. recall; retrieval cues
c. recognize; encoding cues
d. recall; encoding cues

8. Josef and Kirsten are in a class in which eight students must make a presentation each day. Kirsten hopes the professor will remember her presentation well. Josef prefers that the professor forgets his presentation. Kirsten is thinking, "Please let me go _____." Josef is thinking, "Please let me go _____."

a. in the middle; last
b. in the middle; first
c. last; first
d. last; in the middle

9. You walk into a classroom at the end of a lecture. On the blackboard you see:

　　　　_el_p__ne　　　pleetheon　　　tel_____

You suspect that the lecture was on tests for _____ priming in _____ memory.

a. physical; implicit
b. meaning; implicit
c. physical; explicit
d. meaning; explicit

10. Your friend Doug doesn't believe that the mental processes used to encode information have much of an effect on retrieval. You should give him a brief summary of research on

a. encoding specificity.
b. feelings-of-knowing.
c. reconstructive memory.
d. levels of processing.

Practice Test 2

1. Andre wants to learn how to play tennis, so he goes to his friend Jimmy for some instruction. Jimmy has been playing tennis for a long time, but he finds it difficult to put into words what Andre needs to do. The problem is most likely that

a. Jimmy doesn't have conscious access to the content of his procedural memory.
b. Jimmy no longer has a procedural memory for playing tennis.
c. the knowledge compilation process has not yet taken place with respect to Jimmy's tennis skills.
d. knowledge of tennis is a declarative memory.

2. You are trying to find out from a friend whether a particular piece of information he can recall is an episodic memory or a semantic memory. A good question to ask would be,

a. "How easy is it for you to remember the information?"
b. "Do you remember the context in which you acquired the information?"
c. "Do you need short-term memory to recall the information?"
d. "Can you remember the information without retrieval cues?"

3. Timmy is getting ready to leave for school. Of these four questions his mother asks him, which is a metamemory question?

a. Did you remember to bring your lunch?
b. Are you going to learn about dinosaurs today?
c. Will you remember to bring your report card home tonight?
d. Did Helene pay you the 50 cents she owes you?

4. You go to an international cat show that includes a large number of breeds you've never seen before. It's likely that by the end of the day, there would be subtle changes in your _____ for the category of cats.

a. basic level
b. stereotype
c. feelings-of-knowing
d. prototype

5. On Friday afternoon you memorized a poem. On Monday morning, you discover that you've completely forgotten it. You wonder if it will be easier to learn a second time around. The research of _____ is most directly relevant to this question.

a. Elizabeth Loftus
b. Saul Sternberg
c. Hermann Ebbinghaus
d. Endel Tulving

6. George Sperling's comparison between a whole-report and partial-report procedure allowed him to conclude that iconic memory

a. is associated with vision.
b. has a large capacity.
c. lasts for at least 20 seconds.
d. preserves letters but not numbers.

7. Which of the following was a conclusion from Karl Lashley's studies in search of the engram?

a. Memories for maze running are not found in the cortex.
b. Memory was not affected by the location of the tissue that was removed.
c. The amount of tissue removed had no effect on rats' ability to relearn the mazes.
d. The engram was localized in small portions of the brain.

8. For a memory experiment, participants are asked to read a story called, "A Visit to the Doctor." The story includes the sentence, "Velma had to wait for a while to see the doctor." An hour later, participants had to try to recall the story word for word. Which of the following sentences shows the LEAST evidence that a participant used his or her schema to reconstruct the sentence?

a. Velma read a magazine while she waited to see the doctor.
b. The nurse told Velma she would have to wait a while before she saw the doctor.
c. Before she could see the doctor, Velma had to wait a while.
d. Velma sat in a room full of patients waiting to see the doctor.

9. You ask your friend Kermit to name the three mental processes required for memory. He tells you that he used to know but now he can't remember. If Kermit's report is accurate, his difficulty is with

a. retrieval.
b. storage.
c. representation.
d. encoding.

10. It is best to think of short-term memory as a(n)

a. place to which information gets sent.
b. extension of iconic memory.
c. process that brings representations into focus.
d. repository for procedural knowledge.

Practice Test 3

1. Virginia is participating in an experiment that replicates Sperling's study of iconic memory. A visual display of three rows of letters is presented to her very briefly, then a tone is presented to her immediately after the letters. The purpose of the tone is to

a. keep her awake.
b. signal which row she should report.
c. interfere with her memory trace.
d. make her memory trace last longer.

2. Sure of your ability to remember a phone number without writing it down, you get the phone number of the shoe store from the operator. Just then, a loud siren that lasts approximately 18 seconds and prevents you from rehearsing the phone number. Which of the following statements is most accurate about your ability to remember the phone number?

a. You will probably remember the complete number.
b. You will probably remember about half of the number.
c. You will probably remember two digits from the middle part of the number.
d. You will probably forget the whole number.

3. Which of these is a feature that differentiates human memory search from most Web searches?

a. Human searches use concepts rather than words as retrieval cues.
b. Web searches use context to limit searches.
c. Human searches favor recall over recognition.
d. Web searches use schemas as retrieval cues to limit searches.

4. Which of the following terms does NOT belong with the others?

a. retrieval cue
b. central executive
c. phonological loop
d. visuospatial sketchpad

5. Participants are given a list of paired words to learn (e.g., *phone—yellow*), and told they only have to remember the second word of the pair. Later, they are asked to either recognize whether the second word appears on the list they generate, or recall the second word given the first word of the pair. If the performance of these participants is similar to the performance of the participants in Endel Tulving and Donald Thomson's study, performance will be

a. better on recognizing the words from the list they generate.
b. better on recalling the second words after being provided with the first word.
c. the same for both recognition and recall tasks.
d. best in the situation that is most different from the situation in which the words were first learned.

6. The finding that participants typically leave out the word "Liberty" when drawing a picture of a U.S. coin best illustrates the point that

a. schemas are quite resistant to change.
b. most schemas do not represent a person's average experience in the environment.
c. schemas tend to be inaccurate.
d. schemas are based on what people have noticed about the world.

7. A researcher is studying the serial position effect. She has participants read a list of unrelated words in order, then tests their memory for the words. If she were to draw a graph illustrating the probability of correct recall as a function of the position of the item on the list, the results would look most like

a. the letter U.
b. a straight horizontal line.
c. a diagonal line from lower left to upper right.
d. the letter S placed on its side.

8. Howard is a hypochondriac. He is always worried about having some terrible health problem. One day, he notices that he has trouble remembering facts, dates, names, and memories of emotional significance. You can expect that Howard will believe that he is experiencing problems with his

a. amygdala and hippocampus.
b. cerebral cortex.
c. cerebellum
d. striatum.

9. Josh waits until the last minute to study for tests. When you ask him why he does this, he says that Ebbinghaus's forgetting curve showed a rapid initial loss of memory, followed by a gradually declining rate of loss. Is Josh's description of the curve correct?

a. Yes, it is correct.
b. Yes, but it only applies to Ebbinghaus himself.
c. No, Josh is confusing it with findings on the memory span.
d. No, he has it backward.

10. Ollie thinks that an orange is a typical fruit and that a coconut is an atypical fruit. It is most likely that he has come to this conclusion because

a. oranges share more features with the prototypical member of the category than do coconuts.
b. he has eaten oranges, but has only seen coconuts.
c. he can identify oranges more quickly than he can identify coconuts.
d. he has been told that oranges are better examples of the category than coconuts.

Comprehensive Test

1. When Jacob moved, he found it difficult to remember his new telephone number. Two years later, he can't remember the old one when he tries to. The difficulties that Jacob has had remembering his telephone numbers can be attributed to

a. proactive interference.
b. retroactive interference.
c. first retroactive interference and now proactive interference.
d. first proactive interference and now retroactive interference.

2. At the grocery store you notice a woman looking at various parts of her body and then picking up certain grocery items. Curious about her behavior, you ask her what she is doing. She says that she prefers not to use shopping lists, but rather "stores" the items she needs by imagining they are located in different parts of her body. This woman is using the mnemonic device known as

a. the method of loci.
b. the acrostic-like.
c. acronyms.
d. place mnemonics.

3. Suppose you wanted to carry out a memory experiment on priming. You would be most likely to assess the effect that

a. a prior experience with a word has on a later experience.
b. a monetary reward has on a participant's future performance.
c. hints have on the ability to remember.
d. a new experience has on the recollection of an earlier experience.

4. Episodic memory

a. is the same as procedural memory.
b. is a type of procedural memory.
c. consists of semantic memories.
d. is a memory for personally experienced events.

5. Alfred is taking an intelligence test. One of the items requires him to listen to a list of numbers several times, then repeat as many as he can in the order that they were presented. It sounds like Alfred is being given a test of

a. implicit memory.
b. iconic memory.
c. rote learning.
d. knowledge compilation.

6. In one of the studies of Elizabeth Loftus and her colleagues, participants were shown a film of an automobile accident. A week later, it was found that the participants' memory of whether they had seen broken glass after the accident was influenced by

a. seeing pictures of the accident.
b. being asked which car had a broken window.
c. the words used to describe the impact of the two cars.
d. the testimony of other eyewitnesses.

7. Jan and Dean are discussing the test they just completed. They feel confident that they answered some of the questions correctly, but both feel uncertain about other questions. Research on these "feelings-of-knowing" has shown that

a. such feelings are generally accurate.
b. such feelings are generally inaccurate.
c. most individuals do not have strong feelings-of-knowing.
d. females are more likely to have feelings-of-knowing than are males.

8. Lim is a music major, and Tan is an engineering major. Both go to the same lecture about genres of music. Afterward, they find that they both remember about the same amount of information from the lecture. Which of the following is the most likely explanation for their equal recall performance?

a. Lim does not have a working memory span.
b. Tan is a high-span individual.
c. Lim liked the lecture.
d. Tan is a low-span individual.

9. The last time they were in the city, Sandy and Dennis had a great time at a restaurant, but now they can't remember its name. Sandy is looking at the restaurant listings in the telephone book in the hope that seeing the name will jog her memory. The procedure Sandy is using is similar to a _____ test of memory.

a. recall
b. recognition
c. word fragment completion
d. word identification

10. Margot's abilities were definitely affected by the accident. Although she could still manage to dress herself and make her own meals, at the end of the day she could not remember what she had done. She also had trouble remembering where things were kept, and sometimes even forgot the names of her children. Margot seems to be having the LEAST problem with her _____ memory.

a. declarative
b. procedural
c. explicit
d. episodic

11. Memory for information, facts and events is _____ while memory for how things get done is known as _____ .

a. declarative; procedural
b. procedural; declarative
c. implicit; explicit
d. explicit; implicit

12. Ebbinghaus was an early memory researcher. When studying the recall of nonsense syllables he found the learning curve's shape,

a. increased rapidly then tapered off
b. increased at the beginning and later again
c. decreased rapidly then reached a plateau
d. decreased slowly but showed later increases

13. Which of the following memory systems contain iconic memories?

a. sensory memory
b. short-term memory
c. working memory
d. long-term memory

14. George Miller suggested the "magic" number for memory capacity in STM was,

a. five to seven
b. five to nine
c. three to six
d. three to seven

15. Joan was a foreign exchange student in Germany. When she called home her first Christmas, she momentarily forgot her native English and lapsed into German. This type of forgetting is due to

a. proactive interference
b. retroactive interference
c. elaborative rehearsal
d. maintenance rehearsal

True/False Questions

1. Memory is defined as conscious efforts to recover information.   T   F

2. The 3 processes of memory are encoding, storage and retrieval.   T   F

3. Echoic memory is memory for images.   T   F

4. Chunking is the process of reconfiguring items by grouping them to increase the capacity of STM.   T   F

5. The serial position effect is made up of the primacy and recency effect.   T   F

6. You can expect items in short-term memory to last about 2 minutes.   T   F

7. A recall test is much easier than a recognition test.   T   F

8. Memories emerge most efficiently when the context of retrieval matches the context of encoding.   T   F

Essay Questions

1. Define mnemonic. List and describe two types of mnemonic devices. How might you put them to use in your studies?

2. Explain the levels of processing theory. How is it that deeply processed information will be recalled? Give examples.

When you have finished . . . Weblinks

Mind Tools: Memory and Mnemonics

http://www.mindtools.com/memory.html

Improve your memory with MindTools. This site gives you plenty of tips and tricks in how to improve your long and short-term memory. From remembering simple lists to using conncept maps, this site may help you in other areas of study.

Exploratorium: Memory Exhibits

http://www.exploratorium.edu/memory/index.html

San Francisco's renowned science museum, the Exploratory, maintains this site. Play interactive games to enhance memory. See what brain structures are important in memory.

Alzheimer's Association

http://www.alz.org

This is the official site of the Alzheimer's Association. It contains much information and many links to current memory research. There is even a section on how to maintain your brain.

Thinker: Serial Position Effect

http://cat.xula.edu/thinker/memory/working/serial

To demonstrate features of working memory, Thinker provides an interactive demonstration as well as explanations of memory terminology.

Learning and Teaching: Memory

http://www.learningandteaching.info/learning/memory.htm

A site designed especially for those planning to enter the teaching field, especially college or university, it provides an overview of learning and memory with accessible information for discussion, review and application.

After you finish . . . Puzzle it out

Memory

Across

2. strategies to enhance memory
4. retention of encoded material
6. identification of previously experienced stimuli
7. failure of memory
9. the memory trace
10. mental capacity to encode, store and retrieve information
11. grouping information into memory

Down

1. conceptual frameworks
3. visual sensory memory
5. method of retrieval in memory
8. mental representation is formed in memory

Puzzle created with Puzzlemaker at DiscoverySchool.com

Chapter 7 – Answers

Practice Test 1

1. a (p. 206)
2. b (p. 201)
3. a (p. 210)
4. d (p. 229)
5. c (p. 202)
6. d (p. 226)
7. a (p. 209)
8. d (p. 211)
9. a (p. 214)
10. d (p. 213)

Practice Test 2

1. a (p. 201)
2. b (p. 210)
3. c (p. 220)
4. d (p. 223)
5. c (p. 215)
6. b (p. 204)
7. b (p. 228)
8. c (p. 222)
9. a (p. 202)
10. c (p. 205)

Practice Test 3

1. b (p. 204)
2. d (p. 216)
3. a (p. 221)
4. a (p. 208)
5. b (p. 211)
6. d (p. 222)
7. a (p. 211)
8. a (p. 228)
9. a (p. 215)
10. a (p. 223)

Comprehensive Test

Multiple Choice

1. d (p. 216)
2. a. (p. 217)
3. a (p. 214)
4. d (p. 210)
5. c (p. 215)
6. c (p. 226)
7. a (p. 220)
8. b (p. 208)
9. b (p. 209)
10. b (p. 201)
11. a (p. 201)
12. c (p. 216)
13. a (p. 204)
14. b (p. 205)
15. b (p. 216)

True/False

1. T (p. 200)
2. T (p. 202)
3. F (p. 204)
4. T (p. 206)
5. T (p. 211)
6. F (p. 205)
7. F (p. 209)
8. T (p. 210)

Crossword Key

Across

2. mnemonics
4. storage
6. recognition
7. Amnesia
9. Engram
10. memory
11. Chunking

Down

1. schemas
3. iconicmemory
5. recall
8. encoding

 **Chapter 8**

Cognitive Processes

Before you read . . .

This chapter is about studying cognition, or thought processes. It begins with an introduction to the mind and mental processes. Language is a reflection of mental processes so the chapter continues with language production, language understanding, and culture. There are other ways besides language that we process information. For example, in visual representations, how do you put pictures to use? Can you combine verbal and visual representations? How does visual imagery connect with memory processes? The chapter goes on to discuss problem solving and reasoning. What general strategies can guide problem solving? The chapter explains the difference between deductive and inductive reasoning. It closes with a discussion on judgment, heuristics, and the psychology of decision-making. With luck, you will be able to apply these problem solving strategies in your life.

Chapter Objectives

After reading this chapter you should be able to:

- Explain what cognition is and what cognitive psychologists do.

- Describe the similarities and differences between serial and parallel processes.

- Describe the similarities and differences between controlled and automatic processing.

- Discuss how speakers design their utterances to suit particular audiences.

- Explain how the languages individuals speak play a role in how they think.

- Identify several means of resolving ambiguity.

- Discuss the products of understanding.

- Describe how language has evolved, including the impact of culture.

- Explain why people lie.

- Discuss the purpose of visual representations.

- Explain why people form visual representations.

- Describe the process of combining verbal and visual representations.

- Describe the various steps that problem solvers must go through to reach a goal.

- Differentiate between deductive and inductive reasoning.

- Define heuristics.

- Discuss availability, representativeness, and anchoring, and how they can lead to errors in decision making when misapplied.

- Explain the various factors involved in making difficult decisions.

As you read . . . Term Identification

Algorithm	Functional Fixedness
Anchoring Heuristic	Heuristics
Audience Design	Inductive Reasoning
Automatic Processes	Inferences
Availability Heuristic	Judgment
Belief-Bias Effect	Language Production
Cognition	Mental Set
Cognitive Processes	Parallel Processes
Cognitive Psychology	Problem Solving
Cognitive Science	Problem Space
Controlled Processes	Reasoning
Decision Aversion	Representativeness Heuristic
Decision Making	Serial Processing
Deductive Reasoning	Think-Aloud Protocols
Frame	

As you read . . . Questions and Answers

Discovering the Processes of Mind

1. What is cognition? Give some examples of cognitive processes.

2. What aspects of Donders's subtraction method logic do researchers still use and which have they abandoned?

Mental Processes and Mental Resources

1. Give examples of serial and parallel processes.

2. What claims do serial and parallel processes typically make on mental resources?

3. How is attention defined with respect to mental processes?

4. Define controlled and automatic processes.

Language Use

Define sentence meaning and speaker's meaning.

Language Production

What is audience design?

Use Table 8.3 to help you understand Grice's cooperative principle and each of the four maxims. Try to fill in this chart from memory:

Maxim	What it means

1. Describe the three types of evidence that allow you to judge whether information is a source of common ground.

2. Summarize the evidence on the use of community membership in language production.

3. What are spoonerisms? Give an example. Can you catch yourself making similar slips? Why is the study of speech errors useful?

4. What have researchers shown about the processes and representations that underlie fluent speech production?

Language Understanding

1. Give examples of lexical and structural ambiguities.

2. What have experiments demonstrated about the role of context in disambiguation?

a) For lexical ambiguities:

b) For message-level ambiguities:

3. What are propositions? How have researchers demonstrated that meanings are represented with propositions?

4. What are inferences? Do understanders draw all possible inferences? Why or why not?

Language and Evolution

1. Why are the results of early efforts to teach chimps language considered controversial?

2. What has research with bonobos revealed?

3. Can nonhuman animals engage in audience design?

Psychology in Your Life

What conclusions can be made regarding why and how people lie?

Language, Thought, and Culture

1. What ideas are captured by the Sapir-Whorf hypothesis?

2. What type of evidence has been offered in support of one form of this hypothesis?

Using Visual Representations

1. What anecdotes suggest that great thinkers have used visual images?

2. How have researchers studied mental rotation and what have they found?

3. In what ways are visual images like real perceptual images? What kinds of research show this?

Combining Verbal and Visual Representations

1. What are spatial mental models? What evidence suggests that you form them?

2. How do verbal representations affect visual representations?

Problem Solving

1. What three elements define a problem space?

2. Give examples of well-defined and ill-defined problems.

3. Explain the contrast between algorithms and heuristics.

4. What are think-aloud protocols and what can researchers learn from them?

5. Why can practice improve your problem solving?

6. What role do representations play in problem solving? Use the monk puzzle, Table 8.6, as an example.

7. What is functional fixedness? Give an example.

Deductive Reasoning

1. Give an example of deductive reasoning. Be able to give an example of a syllogism.

2. What is the belief-bias effect?

3. What is the Wason selection task and why do pragmatic reasoning schemas improve performance on it? At what age can children put permissions schemas to work?

Inductive Reasoning

1. Give an example of inductive reasoning.

2. What is the role of inductive reasoning in problem solving? How can research on analogical problem solving be applied in educational settings?

3. What are mental sets and how can they be overcome?

Judging and Decision Making

1. What is meant by "bounded rationality"?

2. Differentiate judgment from decision-making.

Heuristics and Judgment

1. What are heuristics? Why do researchers often focus on the errors that heuristics lead to?

2. For each heuristic, summarize how it operates and give examples.

a) Availability

b) Representativeness

c) Anchoring

1. Frames focus attention on the positive/negative or gain/loss features of a situation. What are the consequences?

2. What are "reference points" and why are they important?

3. What is "decision aversion"? What factors contribute to its existence?

4. Under what circumstances are people "decision seeking"?

For Group Study

Studying Cognition

You have probably noticed situations in which your attentional resources were suddenly strained. That's why, for example, you can't carry on much of a conversation if you're trying to drive in difficult traffic. Try to think about other situations in which you have to apportion your resources to different mental processes.

Speech Execution and Speech Errors

We're back to speech errors. In Chapter 5, we asked you to discuss whether speech errors revealed anything hidden in your unconscious. Here, you should look to speech errors to understand how planning takes place in language production. Have a casual conversation in your group about some lively topic such as politics or religion. Every time someone makes an error, try to detect its origins. This will make people somewhat self-conscious, but it's also a fun game to try to find the roots of your slip-ups.

Problem Solving

Encourage some of your group members to reveal real-life problems they have been trying to solve. It should help to think about the problems in the terms described in the chapter. What can you do as a group to assist problem solving?

Judgment and Decision Making

For this section of the chapter, see if you can find real-world examples of your own. Any time you are asked to make a judgment or a decision, you should think about what heuristics are at work and how the issues are being framed. Can you show how people make errors? Can you see how people on two sides of a debate frame problems differently?

After you read . . . Practice Tests

Practice Test 1

1. Research has suggested that you have cognitive processes that try to detect potential speech errors. That's why you are LEAST likely to produce a spoonerism based on the words

a. dart board.
b. darn bore.
c. dell bark.
d. duck bean.

2. You present participants in an experiment with this syllogism:

Premise 1: All mammals walk.
Premise 2: Whales are mammals.
Conclusion: Whales walk.

You find that your participants are reluctant to accept "Whales walk" as a valid conclusion. This is a case of _____ at work.

a. the belief-bias effect
b. the availability heuristic
c. decision aversion
d. functional fixedness

3. You are visiting New York City for the first time. You stop a man on the sidewalk and ask for directions to the Empire State Building. The man responds, "How well do you know Manhattan?" He is probably trying to figure out whether you share

a. linguistic copresence.
b. community membership.
c. maxims of cooperation.
d. physical copresence.

4. If you must solve problems regularly, it is a good strategy to practice the components of a complex solution because then

a. you won't suffer from functional fixedness.
b. all problems will be well-defined.
c. you can use a visual representation for problem solving.
d. those components will take up fewer resources.

5. If you have reached your attentional limits, it could be because you are trying to carry out too many _____ processes.

a. automatic
b. parallel
c. bottleneck
d. controlled

6. The monkeys that were part of Cheney and Seyfarth's research seemed to

a. have the same communication capabilities as the great apes.
b. be able to modify danger calls depending on their audience.
c. be able to modify danger calls depending on their audience and on what their audience knew.
d. not be able to modify danger calls depending on their audience.

7. Which of the following would be an appropriate representation for *The dog pushed the cat off the mat*?

a. OFF (dog, PUSH (cat, mat))
b. OFF (cat, PUSH (dog, mat))
c. PUSH (dog, OFF (cat, mat))
d. PUSH (cat, OFF (dog, mat))

8. Which of Bob's beliefs about language understanding is NOT correct?

a. Nonliteral language is always harder to understand than literal language.
b. People use context to make efficient choices among the meanings of ambiguous words.
c. People draw only a limited number of inferences when they understand a sentence.
d. Propositions are always the main ideas of sentences

9. Which of these statements was NOT true of language and evolution?

a. Vervet monkeys make distinct calls regarding dangers.
b. Chimps can produce spoken language.
c. Bonobos are more similar to humans than are chimpanzees.
d. Gibbons were able to locate toys based upon gaze direction within pictures.

10. Martha tells you that she is trying to study stimulus categorization using Donders's logic. You would expect her to try to create two experimental tasks

a. that both require stimulus generalization.
b. in which stimulus generalization precedes response selection.
c. that differ by only one mental process.
d. that involve only parallel processes.

Practice Test 2

1. You want to buy a new car. You think the car dealer may try to cheat you. Which of the following questions suggests that he is trying to use the anchoring bias against you?

a. "Doesn't this car have all the features of a luxury car?"
b. "Isn't this a better car than the last three cars you've looked at?"
c. "Don't you want to spend your money on the most popular car in the country?"
d. "What's the most you think someone would pay for a car this beautiful?"

2. Which of these is essential for successful inductive reasoning?

a. valid premises
b. past experience
c. valid conclusions
d. rules of logic

3. Andy wants Ellen to bet on the contents of a paper bag. Andy tells Ellen that he's just been at the grocery store and has picked up some supplies to make juice. Andy gives Ellen the four options listed below. Ellen can bet five dollars. If she guesses what's in the bag, Andy will give her ten. If Ellen is able to overcome the effects of representativeness, she will bet on

a. fruit.
b. oranges.
c. carrots.
d. eggs.

4. Which of the following is NOT an accurate conclusion from research on visual representations?

a. Mental rotation has very different properties than does physical rotation.
b. Similar brain structures are used to carry out visual perception and to generate visual images.
c. People scan visual images as if they were scanning real objects.
d. People often use mental rotation as part of the process of object recognition.

5. Studies in which participants are asked to scan visual images for information have suggested that

a. it is easier for participants to scan visual images than it is for them to scan real objects.
b. the use of an image has little in common with the properties of real visual perception.
c. people scan visual images as if they were scanning real objects.
d. visual images cannot be used to answer questions in the same way that real objects can be used.

6. Which of the following is NOT an explanation for decision aversion?

a. People don't like to be held accountable for decisions that lead to bad outcomes.
b. People like having other people make decisions for them.
c. People don't like to make decisions that will cause some people to have more and others less of some desired good.
d. People are able to anticipate the regret they will feel if the option they choose turns out worse than the option they didn't choose.

7. You are hearing a debate between an executive and an environmentalist about whether a new factory should be built. The executive emphasizes how many new jobs will be created. The environmentalist emphasizes how much plant and animal life will be lost from the pollution. The issue is going to be decided in an election. Each debater is trying to influence your vote by

a. allowing you to carry out deductive reasoning.
b. having you adopt a particular decision frame.
c. encouraging you to use the representativeness heuristic.
d. making sure you can't overcome a mental set.

8. While you are watching a movie on television, you see an advertisement for the soft drink Poopsie during every commercial break. The next day a friend asks you what you need at the store. You ask her to buy you some Poopsie. You might be able to explain this request, in part, by virtue of the _____ heuristic.

a. representativeness
b. anchoring
c. availability
d. rationality

9. When Sam said, "I wish we had a hammer," Diane took off her shoe and handed it to him. Diane was able to overcome

a. the belief-bias effect.
b. serial processing.
c. functional fixedness.
d. the availability heuristic.

10. Researchers on problem solving are most likely to use think-aloud protocols to learn about

a. initial states.
b. well-defined problems.
c. mental operations.
d. goal states.

Practice Test 3

1. Imagine that you are a teacher. You would like to help your students improve their problem solving skills, and you know that analogical problem solving is a useful technique. One difficulty you are likely to face is that your students

a. do not always see the relevance of past problems.
b. try to use analogical problem solving techniques for all problems.
c. do not do well with concrete analogies.
d. prefer to use deductive reasoning techniques.

2. If you were a research assistant to a cognitive psychologist, you would be LEAST likely to be helping to collect data on the

a. acquisition of language skills.
b. development of conditioned fear.
c. role of long-term memory in problem solving.
d. perception of visual patterns.

3. You are asked to read the sentence, "The cart that was in the driveway was colored bright red." Based on the research with propositional representation in memory, will the words *cart* and *red* be represented in memory together?

a. No, because they are very far apart in the actual structure of the sentence.
b. We don't know, research has not yet determined whether this happens.
c. Yes, because these words belong to the same proposition.
d. Yes, because these words are closely linked in meaning.

4. Which of the following statements would Edward Sapir most likely have uttered?

a. "Differences in language create differences in thought."
b. "Language and thought are not related."
c. "Language processes are primarily learned, while thought processes, which are indicative of intelligence, are primarily inborn."
d. "The linguistic communities that we are born into are within themselves fairly complex and will lead one speaker of that language to think very differently from another speaker of that same language."

5. The Monk Puzzle, which is presented in the textbook, becomes relatively easy to solve if one uses a _____ representation.

a. verbal
b. mathematical
c. visual
d. hierarchical

6. "Keep your head down, bend your knees, don't overswing, don't hold the club too tightly, spread your feet, keep your eyes on the ball!" Sometimes keeping track of all these instructions overwhelms young Jack, who is just learning to play golf. If you want to use research on problem solving to improve Jack's performance, you should suggest that he

a. practice each of his required behaviors separately so that over time they require fewer resources.
b. think less about what he has to do and respond more on the basis of instinct.
c. focus his attention on the least difficult demand during each of his practice sessions.
d. use think-aloud protocols just before he swings to give himself insight into the cause of his problems.

7. Today you are in a happy mood, and all the memories that come to mind are also happy memories. This pattern can be explained by the _____ heuristic.

a. representativeness
b. belief-bias
c. availability
d. anchoring

8. The SLIP technique is used in order to study

a. speech errors.
b. problem solving.
c. memory.
d. reasoning.

9. You are part of a study in which you are asked to memorize an image of a 12-story building with a flag on top. Later, you are asked to recall the image and focus on the front door of the building. Which of the following will be true with respect to your visual scanning abilities?

a. It will take you somewhat longer to determine that there was a shrub next to the front door of the building than to determine there was a flag on top of the building.
b. It will take you somewhat longer to determine that there was a flag on top of the building than to determine there was a shrub next to the front door of the building.
c. It will take you approximately the same amount of time to say there was a shrub next to the front door than to say there was a flag on top of the building.
d. The time dimension is not important in making judgments about the relative position of objects in the image as much as whether the objects stand out or not.

10. A friend says to you, "I wonder how many number one hits the Beatles had. Do you suppose it was more than 100?" The _____ provides one reason why your answer to your friend's question may not be accurate.

a. availability heuristic
b. subtraction method
c. belief-bias effect
d. anchoring heuristic

Comprehensive Test

1. Martha loves to drive as a way to relax. A psychologist interested in attentional processes would say that the situation that places the greatest demand on Martha's mental resources is

a. Situation A: Martha is driving by herself on a sunny day enjoying the beauties of nature.
b. Situation B: Martha is driving with her friend to work.
c. Situation C: Martha is driving while her friend is talking and there is construction on the road.
d. Situation D: Martha is driving while her friend is talking about her headache that won't seem to leave her.

2. Which of the following is a spoonerism?

a. Life is like a box of chocolates.
b. Come to us for unwanted pregnancies.
c. Let me sew you to your sheet.
d. A rolling stone gathers no moss.

3. Sondra became so involved with the vivid descriptions in the novel that she found herself thinking about the characters and setting throughout the day. She could picture their houses, where they worked, what they wore, and even what they looked like. Sondra's behavior best illustrates

a. the limitations of research comparing mental and physical representations.
b. the difference between literal and structural ambiguity.
c. that readers fill gaps with inferences.
d. that verbal descriptions can be used to form visual representations.

4. Collette has many interests. She is majoring in both psychology and computer science, but also loves philosophy and neuroscience. It sounds as though Collette would find that she is also interested in the interdisciplinary field of

a. linguistics.
b. developmental psychology.
c. cognitive science.
d. exercise physiology.

5. Can nonhuman animals learn and use language? Considering the information provided in the textbook, the correct answer to this question is

a. a definite yes.
b. yes, but only in bonobos and chimpanzees.
c. it is still an open question.
d. a definite no.

6. If a mental process requires attention, it is most likely to be a(n) _____ process.

a. serial
b. automatic
c. controlled
d. parallel

7. Sandy expects to get an A in the physics class, while her friend Shasha would be happy with a C. At the end of the semester, they both receive Bs for their course grade. Which of the following scenarios is more likely to happen?

a. Sandy will be happy with her grade.
b. Shasha will be happy with her grade.
c. Sandy and Shasha will be equally happy with their grades.
d. Shasha will be disappointed because she will feel as though she could have had an A.

8. Helen Keller's realization that the word *water* represents the liquid water underscores the relationship between

a. language and thought.
b. language and learning.
c. language and objects.
d. language and experience.

9. Only when you are working on a well-defined problem do you know

a. where you are and where you want to go.
b. that there is a single solution to the problem.
c. that you will eventually solve the problem.
d. the starting conditions, goal, and things you can do.

10. You have heard that some experimenters at your university are conducting research with apes in an attempt to teach them language. They are working with a species of apes that are nearer to us than the common chimpanzee, called

a. gorillas.
b. bonobos.
c. panpanzees.
d. vervets.

11. It is often difficult to carry on more than one _____ process because it requires more resources and more attention.

a. automatic
b. controlled
c. attentional
d. intentional

12. Language users have judgments of common ground based on all of the following EXCEPT:

a. community membership
b. copresence for actions
c. socioeconomic status
d. perceptual copresence

13. The statement, "We see and hear and otherwise experience very largely as we do because the language habits of our community predispose certain choices of interpretation", reflects the premise of which theory?

a. Sapir-Worf hypothesis
b. Cannon-Bard theory
c. Clark judgment theory
d. Muller-Lyer proposition

14. Problem solving often involves the use strategies or rules-of-thumb called

a. algorithms
b. problem spaces
c. protocols
d. heuristics

15. With the help of _____ reasoning, we can draw conclusions that are intended to follow logically from two or more statements or premises.

a. deductive
b. inductive
c. abstract
d. real world

True/False Questions

1. An algorithm is a step-by-step procedure that always provides the   T   F
   correct answer for a particular type of problem.

2. Deductive reasoning is a form of reasoning in which a conclusion is   T   F
   made based on available evidence and past experience.

3. Chimpanzees have greater cognitive potential than bonobos.   T   F

4. Visual imagination has no limits.   T   F

5. Inductive reasoning is based on the correct application of logic   T   F
   and rules.

6. People usually make judgments using a heuristic.   T   F

7. Our thought processes are represented through our language.   T   F

8. Cognition is a term for thought processes.   T   F

Essay Questions

1. Discuss the Sapir-Wolf hypothesis and how the languages people speak affect the way they think about the world. Give concrete examples.

2. The study of cognitive processes includes at least 4 mental processes. Compare and contrast serial processes with parallel processes and controlled processes with automatic processes.

When you have finished . . . Weblinks

The Gorilla Foundation

http://www.koko.org

Meet Koko the gorilla at the Gorilla Foundation website. Learn about human language and cognition from our primate cousins. This site is filled with videos and other interesting facts.

Figure This

http://www.figurethis.org/index.html

Figure This is designed as a family website for middle school age students to study Math challenges. But don't let that fool you! It is a bright, colorful, fun way to learn about puzzle solving and cognition.

Concept Mapping

http://trochim.human.cornell.edu/tutorial/katsumot/conmap.htm

This is a good tutorial on concept mapping written in question and answer style. If you like the idea of concept mapping, you could find one of the many software packages available that computerizes the process.

Judgemental Heuristics and Biases

http://www.nku.edu/~garns/165/pptj_h.html

A series of hypothetical cases are presented for you to try your hand at making judgments about. Explanations of possible responses and related consequences are reviewed, as well as operational definitions related to heuristics.

Cognitive Versus Behavioral Psychology

http://www.udel.edu/fth/pbs/webmodel.htm

There is a clear distinction between cognitive and behavioral psychology. This site explains, in great detail, the origin, similarities and differences between these two fields of psychology.

After you finish . . . Puzzle it out

Cognitive Processes

Across

2. reaching a goal by means of mental operations
3. thinking directed toward a goal
8. processes of knowing
9. step-by-step procedure for problem solving
10. filled in missing information

Down

1. selecting or rejecting options
4. process of forming opinions
5. rules of thumb to solve a task
6. to respond to a problem the same way as before
7. perspective or description of a choice

Puzzle created with Puzzlemaker at DiscoverySchool.com

Chapter 8 – Answers

Practice Test 1

1. a (p. 242)
2. a (p. 259)
3. b (p. 241)
4. d (p. 239)
5. d (p. 239)
6. b (p. 247)
7. c (p. 246)
8. a (p. 240)
9. b (p. 247)
10. c (p. 237)

Practice Test 2

1. d (p. 265)
2. b (p. 260)
3. a (p. 264)
4. a (p. 250)
5. c (p. 252)
6. b (p. 268)
7. b (p. 266)
8. c (p. 263)
9. c (p. 257)
10. c (p. 256)

Practice Test 3

1. a (p. 257)
2. b (p. 236)
3. c (p. 246)
4. a (p. 248)
5. c (p. 250)
6. a (p. 239)
7. c (p. 263)
8. a (p. 243)
9. b. (p. 251)
10. d (p. 265)

Comprehensive Test

Multiple Choice

1. c (p. 239)
2. c (p. 242)
3. d (p. 250)
4. c (p. 236)
5. c (p. 247)
6. c (p. 239)
7. b (p. 268)
8. a (p. 248)
9. d (p. 255)
10. b (p. 247)
11. b (p. 239)
12. c (p. 241)
13. a (p. 248)
14. d (p. 256)
15. a (p. 257)

True/False

1. T (p. 256)
2. F (p. 258)
3. F (p. 247)
4. T (p. 251)
5. F (p. 260)
6. T (p. 256)
7. T (p. 240)
8. T (p. 236)

Crossword Key

Across

2. Problem Solving
3. Reasoning
8. Cognition
9. Algorithm
10. Inferences

Down

1. Decision Making
4. Judgment
5. Heuristics
6. Mental Set
7. Frame

Chapter 9

Intelligence and Intelligence Assessment

Before you read . . .

This chapter introduces you to intelligence and assessment. It begins with the history of assessment and the origins of intelligence testing. Basic features of assessment including reliability and validity are explored. The derivation of IQ and how we measure it today are discussed at length. From the early Stanford-Binet scales to the modern Wechsler scales, intelligence testing has been a phenomenon of the 20th and 21st centuries. The chapter continues presenting the various theories of intelligence. Psychometric theories, Sternberg's triarchic theory, and Gardner's theory of multiple intelligences and emotional intelligences are compared and contrasted to show the extent to which intelligence theory has affected our lives. Included in the discussion is the politics of intelligence. Can we make judgments about group intelligence differences? To what extent is IQ determined by heredity? How do life circumstances influence IQ? The chapter concludes with a section on creativity. It shows how we assess creativity and poses some questions. Is there a link between creativity and intelligence? Between mental illness and creativity? Finally, issues about assessment and society are covered. How is testing used and misused?

Chapter Objectives

After reading this chapter you should be able to:

- Appreciate the long history of psychological assessment.

- Compare and contrast reliability and validity.

- Define norms and standardization.

- Discuss Binet's influence on the origins of intelligence testing.

- Explain how the concept of IQ was popularized.

- Describe the Wechsler scales.

- Describe the diagnostic criteria for mental retardation and giftedness.

- Define psychometrics.

- Explain how fluid and crystallized intelligence each contribute to IQ scores.

- Discuss Sternberg's triarchic theory and differentiate between analytical, creative, and practical aspects of intelligence.

- Discuss Gardner's eight types of intelligences and his concept of emotional intelligence.

- Explain how intelligence tests have been used to make negative claims about ethnic and racial groups and why environmental disadvantages may be the true cause of lower scores.

- Describe the effects of heredity and environment on IQ.

- Discuss the validity of IQ tests.

- Discuss the qualities of exceptionally creative people.

- Dispute the myth of the link between creativity and mental illness.

As you read . . . Term Identification

Chronological Age	Learning Disorder
Creativity	Mental Age
Construct Validity	Mental Retardation
Criterion Validity	Norms
Crystallized Intelligence	Parallel Forms
Divergent Thinking	Predictive Validity
Emotional Intelligence	Psychosocial Assessment
EQ	Psychometrics
Face Validity	Reliability
Fluid Intelligence	Split-Half Reliability
Formal Assessment	Standardization
G	Stereotype Threat
Heritability Estimate	Test-Retest Reliability
Intelligence	Validity
Intelligence Quotient (IQ)	
Internal Consistency	

As you read . . . Questions and Answers

What Is Assessment?

Why is most assessment concerned with individual differences?

1. What kind of assessment was carried out in ancient China?

2. What four ideas did Sir Francis Galton contribute to the history of assessment?

a)

b)

c)

d)

3. Why did Galton start the eugenics movement?

Define each of these features of formal assessment. Give examples of the different ways of assessing reliability and validity.

1. Reliability

a) Test-retest reliability

b) Parallel forms

c) Internal consistency

d) Split-half reliability

e) Coding schemes

2. Validity

a) Face validity

b) Criterion validity (predictive validity)

c) Construct validity

3. Norms and standardization (give examples)

Intelligence Assessment

Define intelligence.

The Origins of Intelligence Testing

1. What role did Alfred Binet play in the history of intelligence testing?

2. What was Binet's method and how did he define mental age and chronological age?

3. What happened when Binet's ideas were brought to the United States?

IQ Tests

1. Describe Lewis Terman's role in the development of IQ tests. How was the intelligence quotient measured?

2. How has the Stanford—Binet test changed over time?

3. How is IQ calculated today?

4. Why did David Wechsler develop a new intelligence test?

5. What attributes does Wechsler's test measure?

6. How have the Wechsler tests changed over time?

7. How is mental retardation defined?

8. How is giftedness defined?

Critical Thinking In Your Life

1. Why might Web-based assessments of intelligence not be reliable?

2. Why might Web-based assessments of intelligence not be valid?

Psychometric Theories of Intelligence

1. What theoretical tradition uses factor analysis? What is factor analysis and what insights does it yield?

2. Summarize the work of these scholars:

a) Charles Spearman

b) Raymond Cattell

c) J. P. Guilford

Sternberg's Triarchic Theory of Intelligence

1. Explain and give examples of the three components of Robert Sternberg's triarchic theory of intelligence.

a) Analytical intelligence:

b) Creative intelligence:

c) Practical intelligence:

Gardner's Multiple Intelligences and Emotional Intelligence

1. What are Howard Gardner's eight intelligences? What cross-cultural arguments does Gardner make regarding intelligence?

2. What is emotional intelligence? What is EQ?

Psychology in Your Life: Do theories of Intelligence Matter?

1. Do Sternberg's and Gardener's theories of intelligence have practical applications? Give an example.

2. What are the 5 themes embodied in the Practical Intelligence for Schools (PIFS) curriculum?

a)

b)

c)

d)

e)

The History of Group Comparisons

What opinions did Henry Goddard hold? What evidence did he use to bolster those opinions?

Heredity and IQ

1. How do comparisons of monozygotic and dizygotic twins contribute to analyses of the genetic basis of IQ?

2. What is a heritability estimate?

3. Can heritability estimates be applied to comparisons between groups?

4. In what sense is race a social, rather than biological, construct?

5. What has been shown by research on degree of European parentage?

Environments and IQ

1. Summarize evidence on the impact of environments on IQ.

2. What lessons does the Head Start program teach about environments and IQ?

Culture and the Validity of IQ Tests

1. How are minority students affected by testing situations? What is meant by stereotype threat?

2. Why do cultural attitudes toward intelligence matter?

Creativity

How is creativity defined?

Assessing Creativity and the Link to Intelligence

1. What is divergent thinking and how and why have creativity tests measured it?

2. What is the relationship between divergent thinking and IQ?

3. What other measures of creativity have been devised?

Exceptional Creativity and Madness

1. Are there commonalities among "exemplary creators"?

2. What link may there be between madness and creativity?

3. What three patterns predict exceptional creativity?

Summarize the ethical concerns raised by testing practices.

a)

b)

For Group Study

Basic Features of Formal Assessment

As a group, choose some attribute you would like to measure. You can choose any psychological dimension on which you think people differ. Discuss how you would measure the attribute. How would you assure yourself of reliability? How about validity? What would you like to be able to predict from your measure?

Intelligence Assessment

Discuss your experiences with intelligence testing. It's likely that everyone in the group will have been evaluated at some point in his or her schooling. What impact did the testing have on each of your lives? Did you take standardized exams for college entrance? Do you believe those exams really captured your intelligence or potential?

Theories of Intelligence

Do you believe the theories of intelligence presented in the text capture everything that is meant by "intelligence"? Try to develop a definition of intelligence with which everyone in your group is content. Was it easy or hard to do so? Discuss why intelligence so often becomes a subject of public controversy.

Creativity

Have a group discussion about what constitutes creativity. How much agreement can you reach?

Practice Test 1

1. At a job fair, you hear a presentation by a psychologist who is interested in the measurement of psychological functioning. She says that she uses statistical analysis, test construction, and her understanding of psychological processes in her work. Her account best describes the field known as

a. psychometrics.
b. theoretical psychology.
c. optometry.
d. psychodynamics.

2. You take an "intelligence" test on the Web. You are told that you got a 43. In the absence of _____, this number is meaningless.

a. divergent validity
b. componential intelligence
c. parallel forms
d. norms

3. Research demonstrates that a group of racetrack regulars were able to handicap horse races with astonishing accuracy, despite their average IQs. In Robert Sternberg's triarchic theory, this research is most relevant to _____ intelligence.

a. metacognitive
b. practical
c. fluid
d. performance

4. Sir Francis Galton did NOT originate the idea that

a. differences in intelligence could be measured.
b. intelligence is distributed in the form of a bell curve.
c. intelligence could be measured as a ratio of mental to chronological age.
d. the relationship between test scores could be represented as a correlation.

5. Research has shown a _____association between some forms of mental illness and creativity. .

a. weak.
b. strong.
c. causal.
d. direct.

6. You have developed a new test intended to measure a person's emotional stability. After having a large sample of students take the test, you obtain from them lists of their friends. You plan to approach all of these friends and collect their ratings of the original sample students' emotional stability. If you hope that the students' test ratings will be highly correlated with their friends' ratings, you are concerned with

a. test-retest reliability.
b. internal consistency.
c. face validity.
d. predictive validity.

7. Research by Harold Stevenson has demonstrated that Japanese children have much _____ mathematics achievement than U.S. children. People in the United States believe that "innate intelligence" is _____ important than "studying hard."

a. higher; less
b. higher; more
c. lower; less
d. lower; more

8. Mental retardation is defined both with respect to _____ and _____.

a. componential intelligence; experiential intelligence
b. IQ scores; divergent thinking
c. divergent thinking; "g"
d. IQ scores; adaptive skills

9. Mrs. Mines and Mrs. Best are bragging about their children. Mrs. Mines says, "Carlos has the most linguistic intelligence in his class." Mrs. Best says, "Ruth has the most bodily-kinesthetic intelligence in her class." If the mothers are speaking truthfully, Howard Gardner's theory would suggest that Carlos might become a _____, and Ruth might become a(n) _____.

a. journalist; athlete
b. poet; sculptor
c. mathematician; dancer
d. scientist; therapist

10. Jen is able to solve 27 anagrams in five minutes. Jan solves 6 in the same amount of time. From this pattern, you might suggest that Jen possesses more _____ intelligence.

a. experiential
b. analytical
c. practical
d. divergent

Practice Test 2

1. Research on emotional intelligence suggests that

a. having a higher EQ correlates with having higher quality working life.
b. lower level workers generally have higher EQ than their bosses.
c. women and men have roughly the same EQs.
d. women and men's EQs cannot be measured using the same test.

2. Research on the Head Start program suggests that preschool interventions

a. cannot overcome many of the negative effects of poverty.
b. permanently change the IQs of children who participate.
c. have little effect on IQs, even in the short run.
d. cannot overcome genetic deficits in intelligence.

3. Professor Kaskel is doing an analysis of your performance on her midterm. Although each question is meant to be equally hard, you got 91% of the even-numbered questions right but only 23% of the odd-numbered questions. This pattern suggests that the test has low

a. test-retest reliability.
b. split-half reliability.
c. face validity.
d. construct validity.

4. With respect to heritability estimates for IQ, it is NOT true that

a. they are computed by comparing people with different degrees of genetic overlap.
b. the estimate is an average for a population and cannot be used to make predictions for individuals.
c. they allow researchers to make claims about genetic differences between racial groups.
d. they represent the proportion of variability in test scores that can be attributed to genetic factors.

5. Jorge is a Latino student who is about to take an IQ test. Jorge may obtain a lower IQ score than some of his white classmates because

a. he believes that Latinos generally score poorly on IQ tests.
b. his genetic makeup is inferior to that of his classmates.
c. he has less contextual intelligence than his classmates.
d. he has less fluid intelligence than his classmates.

6. When Alfred Binet developed the first intelligence test, his goal was to

a. demonstrate the genetic inferiority of immigrant populations.
b. show that important aspects of intelligence are inherited.
c. prove that mental age is generally higher than chronological age.
d. identify developmentally disabled children for special instruction.

7. If you took the WAIS-III, all of these scores would be reported to you EXCEPT _____ IQ.

a. performance
b. problem-Solving
c. full Scale
d. verbal

8. A psychologist gives you a test in which you are asked to think of all the things you can do with a pencil. This is likely to be a test of

a. crystallized intelligence.
b. convergent thinking.
c. divergent thinking.
d. spatial intelligence.

9. You are visiting a museum show on theories of intelligence. In one case there is a large red sphere marked *g* surrounded by many small yellow spheres marked *s*. It's likely that this display is on the theory of

a. J. P. Guilford.
b. Alfred Binet
c. Charles Spearman.
d. Raymond Cattell.

10. Which of the following is NOT among the primary ethical concerns for psychological assessment discussed in the text?

a. Tests are used unfairly to reject minority job applicants.
b. Teachers spend too much time preparing students for standardized exams.
c. Test creators make large profits from over testing.
d. Students cannot overcome the labels that test scores put on them.

Practice Test 3

1. In Juan's world at home, listening to and respecting authority are the norms. When Juan enters a classroom where Latino norms no longer apply, he may

a. be identified as suffering from mental retardation.
b. be viewed in a negative fashion by the teacher.
c. thrive in classrooms where his respectful behavior is not considered disruptive.
d. have few problems adjusting to this new world.

2. Before Angie begins to take a math test, her professor warns her that she should work extra hard because this is the type of test on which women often do poorly. The professor's warning

a. should allow Angie to overcome the impact of stereotype threat.
b. makes it likely that Angie will be influenced by stereotype threat.
c. should impact the interrater reliability of the math test.
d. illustrates an interaction of heredity and environment in intelligent assessment.

3. Helen was prepared for her history test on ancient Greece. She was therefore surprised when the test she took contained questions on mathematical equations. She should complain that the test had no

a. reliability.
b. criterion validity.
c. predictive validity.
d. face validity.

4. Which of the following is true of Binet's approach?

a. He interpreted scores on his test as a measure of innate intelligence.
b. He wanted to use test scores to identify children who needed special help.
c. He tied the development of his test to a fairly complex theory of intelligence.
d. He chose problems for the test that could only be scored subjectively.

5. Based on recent assessments of the Head Start program, it can be concluded that

a. good programs can have a positive effect on life outcomes.
b. Head Start can negate the effects of poverty.
c. environmental factors are not important determinants of life success.
d. participation in Head Start is more important than adequate nutrition.

6. Suppose you wanted to use a test of fluid intelligence to test your hypothesis that intelligence changes as people grow older. You should probably choose a test of

a. knowledge of vocabulary.
b. arithmetic skills.
c. general information.
d. abstract problem solving.

7. Which of these is NOT a feature of highly creative individuals?

a. risk taking
b. intrinsic motivation
c. mental illness
d. preparation

8. Francois is seven years old. He has just taken a test of intelligence and has been told his mental age is eight. What does this mean?

a. His chronological age must be eight.
b. He is less intelligent than most eight year olds.
c. His score equals the average score of eight year olds.
d. He is in need of remedial education.

9. Which of the following is NOT a type of component of analytical intellingence in Sternberg's triarchic theory of intelligence?

a. metacognitive
b. divergent
c. knowledge acquisition
d. performance

10. Your friend Larry is looking over a sheet full of numbers and figures. When you ask him what he is doing, he says that he is computing the variation in IQ test scores for college students and later he will identify what portion of this total variance is due to genetic factors. Larry is computing what psychologists call

a. a racial index of differences.
b. a heritability estimate.
c. the normal distribution of IQ scores.
d. the nature—nurture controversy.

Comprehensive Test

1. Analyses of the effect of social class on IQ suggest that _____ an impact on IQ scores.

a. heredity alone has
b. both heredity and environment have
c. environment alone has
d. neither heredity nor environment has

2. Which statement best summarizes the state of scientific evidence on the role of genetics in the determination of individual and group IQ scores?

a. Genetics is important in individual IQ scores, but does not explain racial and ethnic group differences.
b. Genetics does not explain individual IQ scores, but it is important in racial and ethnic group differences.
c. Genetics does not seem to play a role in either individual IQ scores or in racial and ethnic group differences.
d. No conclusions can yet be drawn on the role of genetics in either individual or group IQ scores.

3. According to the authors, emotional intelligence is composed of four major components, which include all of the following EXCEPT the ability to

a. perceive, appraise, and express emotions accurately and appropriately.
b. use emotions to facilitate thinking.
c. understand and analyze emotions and to use emotional knowledge effectively.
d. safeguard emotional growth over intellectual growth.

4. Twenty-year-old Lorraine has just finished taking the Block Design test, the Digit Symbol test, and the Picture Arrangement test. She has been working on the

a. nonverbal subtests of the WISC-III.
b. nonverbal subtests of the WAIS-III.
c. verbal subtests of the WISC-III.
d. Stanford—Binet Intelligence Scale.

5. J.P. Guilford has proposed that there are a combination of contents, products, and _____ that combine to make up the structure of intellect.

a. skills
b. technologies
c. abilities
d. operations

6. If you wanted to calculate the test-retest reliability of your bathroom scale, you should

a. weigh several of your friends on it, with and without clothes.
b. weigh yourself on it, then weigh yourself on a scale you know to be accurate.
c. weigh yourself on it several times in succession.
d. ask a friend who is an engineer to look at the schematic drawing of the scale.

7. With which researcher did the idea that intelligence scores follow a normal distribution originate?

a. J. P. Guilford
b. Raymond Cattell
c. Charles Spearman
d. Francis Galton

8. Carol claims that because IQ has been found to be highly heritable, it means that the IQ differences found among different racial groups must be genetic. Is her logic correct?

a. Yes, because whatever is heritable is by definition based on genetic transmission.
b. No, because heritability studies use correlations whereas group differences use IQ test scores.
c. Yes, because the members of the different racial groups are all members of the same society. Therefore, heritability estimates that apply to one group apply to all groups.
d. No, because heritability that is based on an estimate within one group cannot be used to interpret differences between groups.

9. The Cerebral Circumference Index is a measure of intelligence based on the circumference of the head just above the eyebrows. It is most reasonable to assume that the test is

a. reliable but not valid.
b. valid but not reliable.
c. both valid and reliable.
d. neither valid nor reliable.

10. One of the greatest obstacles to using the World Wide Web for accurate assessment would be

a. constructing questions that measure nonverbal skills.
b. maintaining the distinction between fluid and crystallized intelligence.
c. standardization of test-taking circumstances.
d. adjusting tests for the display characteristics of different monitors.

11. The formula for IQ can best be expressed as _____ multiplied by 100.

a. IQ=MA (CA)
b. MA-CA=IQ
c. IQ=MA/CA
d. CA+MA=IQ

12. The degree to which a test produces a similar score is known as

a. validity
b. reliability
c. accuracy
d. correlation

13. All of the following are basic features of formal assessment EXCEPT

a. reliability
b. validity
c. creativity
d. standardization

14. Which of the following is the best description of mental age?

a. the age at which one has a global capacity to profit from experience
b. the average age at which normal children produce a particular score
c. the number of months or years since an individual's birth
d. the age where an individual brings adaptive skills to bear on life's tasks

15. If you were asked, "Name all the things you can think of that are square" or "Think of all the uses for a brick", or "List as many white, edible things you can in three minutes"; you would be engaging in _____ thinking.

a. repetitive
b. exceptional
c. convergent
d. divergent

True/False Questions

1. You could have reliability without validity, but you can't have validity without reliability.   T   F

2. Researchers have found a close association between creativity and madness.   T   F

3. Convergent thinking is the ability to generate a variety of unusual solutions to a problem.   T   F

4. Wealth and social class have little effect on IQ.   T   F

5. Heritability estimates for IQ are around 75%.   T   F

6. Highly creative people generally share the traits of risk taking and intrinsic motivation.   T   F

7. The concept of g refers to the domain specific abilities of intelligence.   T   F

8. The Wechsler scales of intelligence are composed of verbal and performance subtests.   T   F

Essay Questions

1. Describe the 3 theories of intelligence. Pick one and give real life applications of the theory.

2. Explain how divergent thinking can be a measure of creativity. Is there a link between creativity and intelligence?

When you have finished . . . Weblinks

Measurement Tutorial

http://trochim.human.cornell.edu/kb/measure.htm

From the Research Methods Knowledge Base at Cornell University, this site is a tutorial of Measurement. It includes details on reliability and validity.

How to Nurture a Gifted Child

http://www.intuitor.com/Gifted_Children.html

"How to Nurture Gifted Children" contains information about the myths and realities of gifted children with links to other resources.

Mensa International

http://www.mensa.org/workout.html

The "Mensa Workout" is a quiz provided by Mensa International for entertainment only; it is not an IQ test and does not qualify you for Mensa but simulates some of the same features as Intelligence tests. Mensa was started as a society of bright people and welcomes people from every walk of life whose IQ is in the top 2% of the population.

Artificial Intelligence Laboratory

http://www.ai.mit.edu/

The MIT AI lab's mandate is to understand human intelligence at all levels, including reasoning, perception, language, development, learning, and social levels, and to build useful artifacts based on intelligence.

Institute for Research in Cognitive Science

http://www.ircs.upenn.edu/

The IRCS fosters the development of a science of the human mind through the interaction of investigators from the disciplines of linguistics, mathematical logic, philosophy, psychology, computer science, and neuroscience.

After you finish . . . Puzzle it out

Intelligence and Intelligence Assessment

Across
1. does a test measures what is intended to measure
5. emotional quotient
6. standards based on measures of the group
8. the ability to generate novel ideas
9. uniform procedures for gathering testing data
10. general intelligence factor

Down
2. global capacity to profit from experience
3. field that specializes in mental testing
4. stability or consistency of scores
7. Binet's measure of intelligence

Puzzle created with Puzzlemaker at DiscoverySchool.com

Chapter 9 - Answers

Practice Test 1

1. a (p. 282)
2. d (p. 277)
3. b (p. 284)
4. c (p. 274)
5. a (p. 296)
6. d (p. 276)
7. b (p. 294)
8. d (p. 280)
9. a (p. 286)
10. b (p. 284)

Practice Test 2

1. a (p. 286)
2. a (p. 292)
3. b (p. 275)
4. c (p. 289)
5. a (p. 293)
6. d (p. 278)
7. b (p. 279)
8. c (p. 295)
9. c (p. 282)
10. c (p. 274)

Practice Test 3

1. b. (p. 293)
2. b (p. 293)
3. d (p. 276)
4. b (p. 278)
5. a (p. 292)
6. d (p. 282)
7. c (p. 295)
8. c (p. 278)
9. b (p. 284)
10. b (p. 289)

Comprehensive Test

Multiple Choice	True/False

Multiple Choice

1. b (p. 289)
2. a (p. 289)
3. d (p. 285)
4. b (p. 279)
5. d (p. 283)
6. c (p. 275)
7. d (p. 274)
8. d (p. 289)
9. a (p. 275)
10. c (p. 277)
11. c (p. 279)
12. b (p. 275)
13. c (p. 275)
14. b (p. 278)
15. d (p. 295)

True/False

1. T (p. 275)
2. F (p. 295)
3. F (p. 295)
4. F (p. 291)
5. F (p. 289)
6. F (p. 296)
7. T (p. 282)
8. T (p. 279)

Crossword Key

Across

1. Validity
5. EQ
6. Norms
8. Creativity
9. Standardization
10. G

Down

2. Intelligence
3. Psychometrics
4. Reliability
7. Mental Age

 **Chapter 10**

Human Development across the Life Span

Before you read . . .

Human development across the life span can be thought of as the study of growth and development from "womb to tomb". The chapter begins with an overview of how researchers draw conclusions about developmental changes. It then explains physical development in the prenatal period, childhood, adolescence, and finally, the physical changes of adulthood. The chapter goes on to discuss cognitive development across the lifespan. Piaget's stage theory of mental development is explored in detail. Coverage of cognitive development in adulthood includes the topics of intelligence and memory. The chapter continues with language acquisition. What genetic and environmental forces shape early language acquisition? The book suggests how the challenges of acquiring meaning are overcome. Next, social development is explored. Erickson's psychosocial stages, attachment, parenting styles, contact comfort, and human deprivation are all topics included in social development. Social development in adolescence and adulthood are highlighted as well. The chapter goes on to ask how sex and gender are defined. The acquisition of gender roles is explained. The chapter ends with thorough coverage of moral development. Kohlberg's stage theory of moral development is discussed along with criticisms of his theory. Human development truly is a fascinating journey.

Chapter Objectives

After reading this chapter you should be able to:

- Differentiate between longitudinal and cross-sectional research.

- Discuss the environmental factors that can affect a child's development while still in the womb.

- Explain the newborn's remarkable range of capabilities.

- Explain the process of maturation and how it relates to childhood growth.

- Discuss the physical maturation process of adolescence, including the onset of puberty.

- Describe the physical changes of aging in adulthood.

- Compare and contrast assimilation and accommodation.

- Describe Piaget's four stages of cognitive development; sensori-motor, pre-operational, concrete operational, and formal operational periods.

- Discuss current research which suggests that infants and children may be more competent than Piaget thought.

- Discuss cross-cultural research that has questioned the universality of cognitive developmental theories.

- Explain the theories of age-related cognitive decline.

- Describe how interactions with adult speakers are an essential part of the language acquisition process.

- Discuss how the rules of grammar are believed to be constrained by innate principles.

- Explain how social development is dependent on a particular culture.

- Describe Erik Erikson's theory of psychosocial development.

- Discuss socialization in terms of infant attachment.

- Explain the effects of parenting styles and daycare on a child's development.

- Explain the struggles of adolescence which include the search for identity, comfortable social relationships, and choice of future goals.

- Delineate the central concerns of adulthood, according to Erikson.

- Explain why people become less socially active as they age.

- Define ageism.

- Define gender.

- Discuss gender role socialization and gender stereotypes.

- Describe Kohlberg's stages of moral development.

- Discuss the gender and cultural differences in moral reasoning.

As you read . . . Term Identification

Accommodation	Longitudinal Design
Assimilation	Maturation
Attachment	Menarche
Centration	Morality
Child-Directed Speech	Normative Investigations

Chronological Age	Object Permanence
Cognitive Development	Overregularization
Conservation	Parenting Practices
Contact Comfort	Parenting Style
Cross-Sectional Design	Physical Development
Developmental Age	Phonemes
Developmental Psychology	Psychosocial Stages
Egocentrism	Puberty
Foundational Theories	Schemes
Gender	Selective Optimization with Compensation
Gender Identity	Selective Social Interaction Theory
Gender Roles	Sex Differences
Generativity	Social Development
Imprinting	Socialization
Internalization	Temperament
Intimacy	Wisdom
Language-Making Capacity	Zygote

As you read . . . Questions and Answers

Studying and Explaining Development

Think about some of the changes you have undergone over your life span, and try to analyze them as combinations of gains and losses.

1. What is the purpose of normative investigations?

2. What is the difference between chronological age and developmental age?

3. Define these research designs and summarize an example for each:

    a) Longitudinal

    b) Cross-sectional

Prenatal and Childhood Development

1. What is the difference between an embryo and a fetus?

2. What environmental factors can have a negative impact on prenatal development?

3. What is meant by "prewired for survival?"

4. What capabilities are babies born within each of these sensory domains?

    a) Hearing

    b) Vision

    c) Face recognition

    d) Depth perception

5. Give a description of the typical pattern of early childhood growth.

Physical Development in Adolescence

Give a description of the typical pattern of adolescent growth for girls and for boys – including puberty. When do concerns about body image emerge?

    a) Boys

    b) Girls

Physical Changes in Adulthood

1. Explain the motto "Use it or lose it."

2. In each of these domains, what are typical changes across adulthood?

   a) Vision

   b) Hearing

   c) Reproductive and sexual functioning

Cognitive Development across the Life Span

What does cognitive development involve?

Piaget's Insights into Mental Development

1. Define schemes. What role do they play in Piaget's theory?

2. Contrast assimilation and accommodation. Try to understand the distinction in terms of your own experiences with acquiring new information.

3. For each stage in Piaget's theory, list the age range and the major developmental acquisitions.

   a. Sensorimotor (Ages:)

   b. Preoperational (Ages:)

c. Concrete Operations (Ages:)

d. Formal Operations (Ages:)

Contemporary Perspectives on Early Cognitive Development

1. How has the research of Baillargeon and others modified Piaget's views on the sensorimotor child? (Summarize the results.)

2. How has contemporary research modified Piaget's views on the preoperational child? (Summarize the results.)

3. What is meant by children's foundational theories? Summarize research findings for each domain.

4. Why might culture affect cognitive development? What was Vygotsky's view on internalization?

Cognitive Development in Adulthood

1. What are crystallized and fluid intelligence? How are each affected by aging?

2. What are the characteristics of wisdom?

3. Explain each of the components of selective optimization with compensation.

4. What has research revealed about memory changes with aging?

5. What are some of the effects of Alzheimer's disease?

Psychology In Your Life

What plans can you make to keep your brain functioning as well as possible?

Perceiving Speech and Perceiving Words

1. Outline the logic of speech perception research with infants (habituation studies). What has Janet Werker's research revealed?

2. What are the features of child-directed speech?

3. When can children begin to detect the sound patterns of words?

Learning Word Meanings

1. What is the naming explosion?

2. Research on meaning acquisition fits the model of the child as junior scientist. How does each of these concepts fit into that perspective?

   a) Overextensions

   b) Underextensions

   c) Mutual Exclusivity (constraints)

Acquiring Grammar

1. What considerations about input have led researchers to their conclusions about innate structures? What effects can input have?

2. What are some of the features of the child's language-making capacity (Dan Slobin's operating principles)?

3. What is telegraphic speech?

4. What are overregularizations? What do they suggest?

Social Development across the Life Span

1. Define social development.

2. How are individual life courses affected by environments?

Erikson's Psychosocial Stages

To master the material on Erikson's stages, try to relate Erikson's insights to the children and adults in your own life. For each stage, try to understand why the crisis applies to that period of life. Re-create your own table here:

Crisis	Age	Why then?

Social Development in Childhood

1. Define socialization. How does it come about?

2. Define attachment.

3. What is imprinting?

4. How is Mary Ainsworth's Strange Situation Test used to assess attachment? (Summarize the procedure.)

5. What are the three categories of attachment? Focus, in particular, on the distinction between secure and insecure attachment. It should help you to generate a mental picture of how each type of child behaves when his or her mother leaves and returns.

6. What are some consequences of secure and insecure attachment?

7. To master the material on parenting styles, make sure you understand the two dimensions—demanding-ness and responsiveness. How does each parenting style emerge?

8. How do parenting practices interact with parents' goals?

9. How did Harry Harlow's research rule out the cupboard theory?

10. What happened when the monkeys became mothers?

11. How does cross-fostering work?

12. What is known about the costs of human deprivation?

13. What are some consequences of childhood abuse?

Critical Thinking in Your Life

1. What is the best answer to questions about the "dangers" of day care? Why?

2. Summarize the features of quality day care.

   a) Physical:

   b) Education and psychology:

   c) Teacher interaction style:

Social Development in Adolescence

1. Why do researchers believe that adolescent "storm and stress" is a myth?

2. What consequences may adolescent problems bring in later life?

3. What roles do parents and peers play in adolescent lives?

   Parents

   Peers

Social Development in Adulthood

1. How did Erikson define intimacy?

2. Summarize major aspects of adulthood's social relationships. In each case, note any differences that exist for men and women or heterosexuals and homosexuals.

   Marriage (or other long-term relationships)

Parenthood

3. What is selective social interaction?

4. What is generativity? What did George Vaillant learn about the importance of generativity for adjustment?

5. According to Erikson, how do most people feel when looking back on their lives?

Sex and Gender

What is the difference between sex differences and gender differences?

The Acquisition of Gender Roles

1. How do parents influence gender identity and gender roles?

2. How do children participate in their personal construction of gender?

Moral Development

What is morality and why is it important to society?

Kohlberg's Stages of Moral Reasoning

Work to solidify your knowledge of Kohlberg's proposals about moral development. Try to understand why Kohlberg believed that each level was an advance over the previous one. This should help you to memorize the order of the stages.

Stage	Why is this an advance?

1. What was Gilligan's concern about Kohlberg's theory? What did she propose?

2. Has contemporary research revealed consistent differences between men and women?

3. What has cross-cultural research revealed about moral reasoning?

Learning to Age Successfully

Review the concept of selective optimization with compensation.

For Group Study

Explaining Development

For Chapter 3, we suggested that your study group discuss nature and nurture. This would be a good point to renew that discussion. Remind yourselves of the types of conclusions you drew. The goal of this discussion is to help you understand the types of causal hypotheses developmental researchers can formulate. What commonalities among people are dictated by shared genetic inheritance? What differences should be attributed to individual genotypes? Which differences point to different environments?

Cognitive Development across the Life Span

One of the best ways to master the material on children's cognitive development is to spend time with some of them. With the members of your group, see if you can get permission to observe children whose ages range from 0 to 8 years. Before each meeting, review the material in the text. Are there particular tasks you'd like to carry out with each child? Try to develop a model of the types of cognitive activities of which each child is capable. Try to see the way in which even the youngest children are acting like busy little scientists.

Acquiring Language

Once again, you should seek out opportunities to spend time with young children. You should note, in particular, the hypotheses the children develop about word meanings (leading, for example, to overextensions and underextensions) and their overregularizations in grammar.

Social Development in Adolescence

Many of the students who take Introductory Psychology are not at too great a distance from their own period of adolescence. As a group, try to relate the material in this section to your own life experiences. Pay particular attention to the changing roles of family and peers.

Social Development in Adulthood

At several places in this section, the text warns you not to be too dispirited by research results that raise the possibility of negative consequences from marriage and parenthood. Discuss what expectations might be reasonable, given these results. How can this knowledge help you to avoid typical problems?

After you read . . . Practice Tests

Practice Test 1

1. Your friend is making you guess how old her little sister Kara is. Which of these questions will get you off to the best start? Does Kara

a. use assimilation?
b. experience accommodation?
c. use sensorimotor schemes?
d. experience centration?

2. Researchers use the Strange Situation Test to judge whether a child is securely or insecurely attached. The basis of the judgment is the child's behavior when the mother

a. offers the child an unusual toy to play with.
b. leaves the room and then reappears.
c. has a conversation with a stranger.
d. scolds the child for playing too noisily.

3. Which of Erikson's psychosocial stages begins when the child starts to use language and explore the environment?

a. trust vs. mistrust
b. autonomy vs. self-doubt
c. initiative vs. guilt
d. competence vs. inferiority

4. Research on changes in memory performance during adulthood has shown that aging does NOT diminish people's ability to

a. access their general knowledge stores.
b. control their memory processes.
c. cope with Alzheimer's disease.
d. acquire new information.

5. Researchers have demonstrated that infants have acquired some knowledge of the world even before they are born. One research result that supports this claim is that children

a. prefer sweet tastes to salty tastes.
b. prefer their mothers' voices to the voices of other women.
c. turn their eyes in the direction of environmental noises.
d. prefer the unmuffled voices of strangers.

6. What are the consequences of marriage and parenthood for adults?

a. Both men and women typically become depressed when they are left with an "empty nest."
b. After the birth of a child, men find themselves less burdened by traditional sex roles.
c. Marital satisfaction decreases after the birth of a first child.
d. Marital satisfaction is highest when a couple has adolescent children.

7. Laurie and Stan both need to work to support their family. They are somewhat concerned about placing their children in day care. What can you tell them?

a. Children in day care are always at an advantage over children who stay at home.
b. All children respond to day care positively.
c. There is no stigma associated with putting children in day care.
d. Children in day care can benefit from a wider variety of social interactions.

8. When men and women are asked to reason about the same moral dilemmas,

a. women's responses are most similar to Kohlberg's predictions.
b. men put more emphasis on caring than on justice.
c. they give similar patterns of caring responses.
d. they give responses that are consistent with Gilligan's predictions.

9. What conclusion did Janet Werker draw from her studies of the perception of Hindi sound contrasts with adults and infants from English-speaking and Hindi-speaking cultures?

a. Adult speakers of both languages perceive more contrasts in Hindi than in English.
b. English-speaking adults no longer perceive contrasts that would be perceived by their 8-month-old children.
c. Infant learners of both languages perceive fewer Hindi contrasts than all adults.
d. Infant learners of both languages perceive as many Hindi contrasts as all adults.

10. Although the average child can transfer objects from hand to hand at six months, Ismene is unable to do so until about eight months. For this behavior, Ismene's _____ is less than her _____.

a. ability to assimilate; ability to accommodate
b. chronological age; developmental age
c. developmental age; chronological age
d. ability to accommodate; ability to assimilate

Practice Test 2

1. According to Erikson, when earlier crises are left unresolved, people are likely to end life with feelings of

a. stagnation.
b. isolation.
c. self-doubt.
d. despair.

2. To Piaget, an infant's initial collection of schemes is known as

a. sensorimotor intelligence.
b. symbolic representations.
c. preformal intelligence.
d. egocentric representations.

3. Children often suffer negative consequences if their mothers used cocaine while they were pregnant. This finding suggests that

a. the environment has an impact even before the child is born.
b. parents can change some aspects of a child's genetic inheritance.
c. heredity is a more powerful force for some children than for others.
d. the environment has its greatest effect late in life.

4. Each week, starting at age three months, each child in a group of 30 has been given a test of object permanence. This sounds like _____ research.

a. sequential
b. cohort-sequential
c. longitudinal
d. cross-sectional

5. According to Kohlberg, which of these would a person do to be at the highest level of moral reasoning?

a. follow rules
b. gain acceptance
c. avoid disapproval
d. promote society's welfare

6. Which of the following was a result from Harry Harlow's experiments with monkeys who were raised with terry cloth and wire mothers?

a. The monkeys did not know how to be mothers themselves.
b. The monkeys were more likely to become attached to the artificial "mother" who provided food.
c. Once the monkeys were allowed to interact with other monkeys, they showed no adjustment problems.
d. The monkeys were able to have normal sexual relationships.

7. A friend tells you that his grandfather has decided to give up all games except poker. His goal is to read a series of poker books and to play three times a week in a highly competitive game. Which feature of a strategy for successful aging does this plan omit?

a. selection
b. optimization
c. compensation
d. fluidity

8. Research with 10-month-old infants showed that they were more likely to smile when their mothers were watching them. This suggests that the infants are already

a. aware that they shouldn't smile all the time.
b. imprinted on their mother's appearance.
c. insecurely attached to their mothers.
d. using smiles to produce an effect on their mothers.

9. When a parent is centered on the child but makes too few demands to socialize the child, the parenting style is called

a. authoritative.
b. indulgent.
c. authoritarian.
d. uninvolved.

10. A child finds it hard to acquire the word *coat* when she already knows the word *jacket*. What process may be needed here?

a. accommodation
b. bootstrapping
c. assimilation
d. overextension

Practice Test 3

1. Hubert has skipped class again. He gets the lecture notes from Margie, but can't quite read her handwriting, so he makes an error in copying information about Kohlberg's stage model of moral reasoning. Which of the following statements did Hubert copy incorrectly?

a. An individual can be at more than one stage at a given time.
b. Everyone goes through the stages in a fixed order.
c. Each stage is more comprehensive and complex than the preceding one.
d. The same stages occur in every culture.

2. Darryl was abused as a child. Knowing this we can expect

a. past experiences can affect his future social development.
b. future expectations can affect his past experiences.
c. current circumstances can affect his past experiences.
d. future expectations can affect his current circumstances.

3. Robert is 67 years old. Which of the following would NOT be a prediction that you would make about his vision?

a. He will have difficulty seeing things at close range.
b. With corrective lenses he could regain many of his normal visual faculties.
c. His night vision will be as good as always.
d. He will have difficulty discriminating among certain colors.

4. In the Strange Situation Test, a securely attached child will _____ when the parent leaves the room and _____ when the parent returns.

a. seem aloof; actively avoid and ignore the parent
b. show some distress; seek proximity, comfort, and contact
c. become quite upset and anxious; show anger
d. act pleased; act dazed and confused

5. The therapist on television is arguing that "when a person does not develop a coherent sense of self, this may result in a self-image that lacks a central, stable core." Being familiar with Erikson's stages of development, you know that the therapist is talking about the basic crisis that occurs during

a. early childhood.
b. early adulthood.
c. middle adulthood.
d. adolescence.

6. Baby Monte is carried around by his mother in a tightly bound back cradle, common in the Native American culture he was born into. How will this experience affect his ability to walk later?

a. It will delay walking, but not the sequence of locomotion that he goes through.
b. It will change the sequence of locomotion that he goes through.
c. It will delay walking and the sequence of locomotion that he goes through.
d. It will have no impact on walking, but will affect his emotional response to exploring his environment.

7. Based on the information presented in your textbook, which of the following seems to be of LEAST importance among those who want day care to be truly effective?

a. People need to accept the reality that increasing numbers of children will be experiencing day care.
b. Resources must be directed toward the goal of making *all* day care quality day care.
c. People must work to eliminate the stigma associated with "working motherhood" and day care itself.
d. The cost of day care must be reduced or even made free to parents who need it.

8. When psychologists try to understand how individuals' interactions with others and how their expectations change across the life span, they are primarily interested in

a. cognitive development.
b. physical development.
c. social development.
d. maturational development.

9. One implication of the study that compared Indian participants and Westerners on moral issues is that

a. culture determines what is moral and what is immoral.
b. culture does not determine what is moral or what is immoral.
c. there is consensus among most cultures as to what is considered moral and what is considered immoral.
d. Indian participants are considerably more moral than those from the West.

10. Whenever 2-year-old Marnie sees the butterfly-like pattern on her dress shoes, or a moth, or the hair bows that resemble the shape of a butterfly, she proudly exclaims, "Butterfly!" Psychologists refer to this process as

a. the naming explosion.
b. extension.
c. category identification.
d. constraining.

Comprehensive Test

1. A two-year-old's speech is characterized as telegraphic because it is

a. short and simple, using mostly nouns and verbs.
b. used to convey emotional content.
c. intense and surprising, as are most telegrams.
d. made up of single words, linked together with no grammatical structure.

2. Lex is an infant who lives in an orphanage where he receives little attention when he is hungry and thirsty, is rarely picked up and cuddled, and has no particular adult who is in charge of meeting his needs. Erik Erikson would predict that Lex might develop a sense of

a. self-doubt.
b. isolation.
c. mistrust.
d. role confusion.

3. Walking by the school playground, you overhear one child say to another, "My mom and dad expect me to get my homework done, but they usually help me and talk with me whenever I want." This child is most likely being raised by _____ parents.

a. indulgent
b. authoritative
c. authoritarian
d. indifferent

4. Baby Jenny actively searches for a toy that her mother has placed under a blanket. Her behavior leads you to believe that baby Jenny has some degree of _____ and that she is at least _____ old.

a. object permanence; 3 months
b. object permanence; 8 months
c. sensorimotor ability; 3 months
d. sensorimotor ability; 8 months

5. "Imagine that our brains are like blank tablets, on which experience can inscribe all its wisdom and knowledge." The person most likely to have made this statement is

a. Jean-Jacques Rousseau.
b. Victor of Aveyron.
c. Jean Marc Itard.
d. John Locke.

6. Aging seems to diminish elderly individuals' ability to do all of the following EXCEPT_____.

a. retrieve the name of someone they met yesterday.
b. store recently learned facts
c. organize new information.
d. access their personal knowledge store.

7. Contemporary research into the cognitive abilities of young children has found all of the following EXCEPT that children in the sensorimotor stage

a. apparently understand that solid objects cannot pass through other solid objects.
b. are capable of determining object boundaries by perceiving relative motion.
c. are less perceptually and cognitively sophisticated than Piaget claimed.
d. already rely on certain processes to help them organize their perceptual world.

8. Ricky was born 5 years ago, although his language abilities are similar to what one would expect from a 3 year old. Developmental psychologists would say that Ricky's chronological age is _____ and his developmental age for language is _____.

a. 5; 5
b. 3; 3
c. 5; 3
d. 3; 5

9. The 4-year-old child who talks baby talk to her 2-year-old sister, but not to her 7-year-old sister, challenges Piaget's claim that 4-year-old children are

a. animistic.
b. egocentric.
c. decentered.
d. preoperational.

10. Studies of homosexual couples' child rearing practices have shown

a. homosexual couples tend to have shorter, less monogamous relationships.
b. heterosexual couples usually are more committed to child rearing.
c. homosexual couples tend to have increased satisfaction with their relationship once a child is introduced into the family.
d. homosexual couples and heterosexual couples use similar strategies for child rearing and relationships.

11. Vygotsky's theory of cognitive development states that _____ is the most important influence on a child's development.

a. heredity
b. early interactions with the primary caregiver
c. social interactions
d. socioeconomic status

12. We can tell an infant's brain is wired for survival when something touches the newborn's cheek and they turn to seek it. Which type of reflex is working?

a. crying
b. startle
c. rooting
d. sucking

13. Research using an apparatus called the visual cliff was meant to test an infant's

a. depth perception
b. attachment
c. crawling ability
d. temperament

14. Which of the following is NOT one of Piaget's stages of cognitive development?

a. formal operations
b. object permanence
c. sensorimotor stage
d. concrete operations

15. Harry Harlow's research with monkeys was intended to show the importance of _____.

a. nutrition
b. consistency
c. temperament
d. contact comfort

True/False

1. Intimacy is the capacity to make a full commitment, sexual, emotional, and moral, to another person.　　T　　F

2. Gender refers to the biologically based characteristics that distinguish males from females.　　T　　F

3. Kohlberg conceptualized the life span as a series of crises.　　T　　F

4. The *law and order* orientation of morality is considered conventional morality　　T　　F

5. In the Heinz dilemma, Heinz steals a drug for his sick wife.　　T　　F

6. Centration is similar to racism and sexism in its negative stereotypes.　　T　　F

7. A drawback of longitudinal research is the cohort effect.　　T　　F

8. Menarche is the attainment of sexual maturity in women.　　T　　F

Essay Questions

1. Outline Piaget's four stages of cognitive development. Describe the milestone achieved in each stage.

2. Pick one of Kohlberg's stages of morality. Give a real life example of someone functioning in that stage. How would Kohlberg's critics explain it?

When you have finished . . . Weblinks

Parent Soup

http://www.parentsoup.com/

"Parent Soup" brought to you by iVillage is a great site for all kinds of resources about children of all ages. Get parenting tips from toddlers to teens on this long standing website.

Psy Café: Piaget

http://www.psy.pdx.edu/PsiCafe/KeyTheorists/Piaget.htm

Learn more about Piaget at the Psi Café. This site contains history, information, and plenty of links about Piaget and his stages of cognitive development.

Natural Childbirth

http://www.bygpub.com/natural/natural-childbirth.htm

The Natural Family Site has good material on natural childbirth. It has links to information about birth plans, birth assistants, and midwives.

Adult Development and Aging

http://apadiv20.phhp.ufl.edu/

This is the site for the American Psychological Association division 20 – adult development and aging. It has many useful links and information sources.

The Whole Child

http://www.pbs.org/wholechild/

This is a PBS website covering details of child development from birth to age five. There are specific sections for parents and childcare/education providers.

Human Development Across the Life-Span

Across

2. animals follow and form attachments to first moving object
8. cognitive structures
10. start of menstrual cycle
11. commitment beyond one's self to future generations
13. modifying cognitive structures so that new information fits in
14. understanding physical properties do not change even though appearances may
15. fit new elements into existing cognitive structures
16. capacity to commit to another person

Down

1. sperm and egg combines to form single cell
3. age related physical and behavioral changes
4. emotional relationship between child and caregiver
5. inability to take another perspective
6. attainment of sexual maturity
7. child's inability to focus on more than one perceptual factor
9. learned sex related behaviors and attitudes
12. system of beliefs and values

Puzzle created with Puzzlemaker at DiscoverySchool.com

Chapter 10 - Answers

Practice Test 1

1. d (p. 313)
2. b (p. 327)
3. b (p. 325)
4. a (p. 318)
5. b (p. 308)
6. c (p. 334)
7. d (p. 330)
8. c (p. 340)
9. b (p. 321)
10. c (p. 304)

Practice Test 2

1. d (p. 325)
2. a (p. 313)
3. a (p. 307)
4. c (p. 304)
5. d (p. 339)
6. a (p. 329)
7. c (p. 320)
8. d (p. 313)
9. b (p. 328)
10. a (p. 313)

Practice Test 3

1. a (p. 338)
2. a (p. 331)
3. c (p. 311)
4. b (p. 328)
5. d (p. 325)
6. a (p. 309)
7. d (p. 330)
8. c (p. 324)
9. a (p. 340)
10. b (p. 324)

Comprehensive Test

Multiple Choice

1. a (p. 323)
2. c (p. 325)
3. b (p. 328)
4. b (p. 313)
5. d (p. 312)
6. d (p. 319)
7. c (p. 314)
8. c (p. 304)
9. b. (p. 313)
10. d (p. 333)
11. c (p. 317)
12. c (p. 308)
13. a (p. 309)
14. b (p. 313)
15. d (p. 329)

True/False

1. T (p. 333)
2. F (p. 336)
3. F (p. 325)
4. T (p. 338)
5. T (p. 338)
6. F (p. 313)
7. T (p. 304)
8. T (p. 310)

Crossword Key

Across

2. Imprinting
8. Schemes
10. Menarche
11. Generativity
13. Accommodation
14. Conservation
15. Assimilation
16. Intimacy

Down

1. Zygote
3. Maturation
4. Attachment
5. Egocentrism
6. Puberty
7. Centration
9. Gender
12. Morality

Chapter 11

Motivation

Before you read . . .

This chapter is about understanding motivation. What internal and external forces motivate behavior? The chapter begins with a definition of motivational concepts then turns to sources of motivation. Drives and incentives, instinctual behaviors, expectations, and cognitive approaches to motivation are highlighted. The chapter goes on to explore eating and sexual behaviors. What bodily processes guide eating behaviors? What impact do genes have on obesity? How do humans experience sexual arousal? What are the norms for sexual behavior? Next, motivation for personal achievement is explored. Are some people especially motivated to achieve? Attributions for success and failure as well as motivation in the workplace are discussed.

Chapter Objectives

After reading this chapter you should be able to:

- Define motivation.

- Discuss how motivation has been used for five basic purposes.

- Explain how drive theory conceptualizes motivation as tension reduction.

- Describe how people are motivated by incentives.

- Differentiate between reversal theory and instinct theory.

- Discuss how cognitive psychologists explain motivation.

- Describe Maslow's hierarchy of needs.

- Illustrate the body's mechanisms for regulating the initiation and cessation of eating.

- Define restrained eating (dieting) and discuss how this may result in weight gain rather than weight loss.

- Discuss the impact of genetics on weight.

- Discuss eating disorders.

- Present sex from a nonhuman perspective.

- Describe the work of Masters and Johnson in terms of the sexual response cycles of men and women.

- Present sex from an evolutionary perspective.

- Explain how differences in sexual scripts can lead to misunderstandings and even date rape.

- Illustrate how both genes and the environment determine homosexuality and heterosexuality.

- Explain people's varying needs for achievement.

- Relate attributions to success and failure.

- Discuss the influence of optimism and pessimism on people's attitudes toward achievement and motivation.

- Identify what kind of psychologist studies human motivation in the work place.

- Explain how motivation can affect academic achievement.

As you read . . . Term Identification

Anorexia Nervosa	Instincts
Attributions	Motivation
Bulimia Nervosa	Need for Achievement
Date Rape	Organizational Psychologists
Drives	Parental Investment
Equity Theory	Reversal Theory
Expectancy Theory	Sexual Arousal
Hierarchy of Needs	Sexual Scripts
Homeostasis	Social-Learning Theory
Incentives	Thematic Apperception Test

As you read . . . Questions and Answers

Understanding Motivation

How does the origin of the word *motivation* help define the concept?

Functions of Motivational Concepts

For what five basic purposes have psychologists used the concept of motivation?

1.

2.

3.

4.

5.

Sources of Motivation

1. Explain the importance of the distinction between internal and external sources of motivation.

2. Who introduced drive theory? What were his views?

3. What has research shown about the idea that tension reduction can explain all motivated behavior?

4. What are incentives?

5. How did "reversal theory" get its name? What is the importance of metamotivational states?

6. What are instincts? Give examples.

7. What did William James and Sigmund Freud suggest about human instincts?

8. What criticisms have been leveled at instinct theories?

9. After you read the section, "Expectations and Cognitive Approaches to Motivation", go back and review the *Wizard of Oz* example.

   What is meant by a subjective interpretation of reality?

10. Summarize these scholars' ideas:

    Julian Rotter

    Fritz Heider

A Hierarchy of Needs

Use Maslow's hierarchy to connect the themes of the chapter. Make sure you understand why he ordered the needs in the way he did. List and define each class of needs.

1.

2.

3.

4.

5.

6.

7.

8.

The Physiology of Eating

1. What are the four tasks for food regulation?

2. What theory did Cannon & Washburn test about peripheral hunger cues and how did they do so?

3. What has contemporary research shown?

4. What roles do the VMH and LH play in regulating food intake? Make sure you understand why the palatability of the food—good or bad taste—modified early models of eating regulation.

    VMH

    LH

Psychology in Your Life

1. What evidence suggests that obesity has a genetic component?

2. What has been discovered about the genetic mechanisms that may prompt obesity?

1. What are some social and cultural constraints on eating?

2. What distinction did Janet Polivy and Peter Herman originate?

3. What circumstances prompt the disinhibition of eating? Summarize the experimental evidence.

4. Describe these eating disorders:

   a) Anorexia nervosa

   b) Bulimia nervosa

5. What are some of the factors that may trigger eating disorders?

6. What is the impact of culture on body image?

Nonhuman Sexual Behaviors

1. How do hormones control mating in nonhuman animals?

2. What are stereotyped sexual behaviors?

3. What external factors affect mating behavior? (Don't forget pheromones)

Human Sexual Arousal and Response

1. What role do hormones play in human sexual response?

2. What is sexual arousal?

3. What conclusions did Masters and Johnson reach about response to sexual stimulation?

4. Summarize the phases of the human sexual response cycle.

   a) Excitement:

   b) Plateau:

   c) Orgasm:

   d) Resolution:

5. What factors contribute to disruption in sexual function?

The Evolution of Sexual Behaviors

1. What have theorists suggested about men's and women's strategies toward sexual behavior?

2. Why is parental investment relevant to the evolutionary perspective?

3. Why does David Buss make a distinction between short-term and long-term mating? How does research support his ideas?

Sexual Norms

1. How did Alfred Kinsey's work begin to define sexual norms?

2. What are sexual scripts?

3. What psychological factors may lead to sexual risk taking?

4. What social and psychological forces give rise to date rape?

Homosexuality

1. What have researchers theorized regarding causal factors for homosexuality and heterosexuality?

2. Is it possible to determine how many gay men and lesbians there are?

3. What evidence suggests that sexual orientation has a biological component?

4. Summarize Daryl Bem's theory of the development of sexual preference.

5. What are societal attitudes toward homosexuality?

6. What might be one cause of homophobia?

7. How do negative attitudes affect men and women who perceive themselves to be gay or lesbian?

8. How are people's attitudes affected by personal contact with gay men and lesbians?

Need for Achievement

1. How is the TAT used to evaluate need for achievement?

2. What has research shown about people who are high in need for achievement? How does a high need for achievement arise?

Attributions for Success and Failure

1. What is a locus of control orientation? How does it apply to causal attributions?

2. What are two other dimensions along which attributions can vary? Give examples of each.

3. How do attributional styles affect a person's motivation?

4. Summarize the research on the consequences of explanatory style. What outcomes would you predict for optimists and pessimists?

Work and Organizational Psychology

1. What are the activities of organizational psychologists?

2. Summarize equity theory.

3. Summarize expectancy theory.

Critical Thinking in Your Life

What three types of achievement goals can a student have?

For Group Study

Understanding Motivation

To begin group study, you might discuss a question posed toward the beginning of the chapter: Why did you get out of bed this morning? See if you can classify different people's answers in terms of the motivational forces discussed in the chapter.

Eating

Are you ready to have a meal together? It might be easiest to discuss the section on eating in the context of lunch or dinner. Why are some people feeling more hungry than others? How much will you eat of different foods? Can you work through some of the physiology while you eat? (What are your LH and VMH up to?)

You can also have a discussion of issues surrounding dieting and obesity. This will depend to a certain extent on how comfortable the group members are talking about personal matters, but it should be possible for people to relate much of the content of this section to their own experiences. Do members of the group perceive themselves to be restrained eaters? Does the text help them think about escaping that trap? Have you or other people in the group suffered from eating disorders?

Sexual Behaviors

This, again, is a section that can relate directly to different life experiences of members of your group. Try to learn the material by making it relevant to each of your lives. You should be able to have an informed discussion of evolutionary explanations for sex differences in mating strategies as well as sexual scripts and date rape. It will also deepen your understanding of human sexuality if you can discuss the themes of this section with classmates who are lesbian or gay.

Need for Achievement

People show different levels of need for achievement; people have different patterns for explaining events. You should take advantage of the diversity in your group to discuss how these concepts apply.

After you read . . . Practice Tests

Practice Test 1

1. Which of the following is in the right order for Maslow's hierarchy of needs?

a. safety needs, attachment needs, self-actualization
b. biological needs, cognitive needs, attachment needs
c. cognitive needs, esthetic needs, safety needs
d. attachment needs, cognitive needs, esteem needs

2. You pick up a handout on which is printed a list of "metamotivational states." You suspect that the handout was for a lecture on _____ theory.

a. instinct
b. incentive
c. reversal
d. drive

3. Which of these results suggests that tension reduction CANNOT explain all motivated behaviors?

a. Apes copulate for only about 15 seconds.
b. Thirsty rats will drink when they have the opportunity.
c. Food-deprived rats explore a new environment before they eat.
d. Rats will not mate unless hormone levels are appropriate.

4. The concept of sexual scripts explains why

a. men and women have different mating strategies.
b. hormones play such a small role in human sexual response.
c. the plateau phase follows the excitement phase.
d. sexual practices vary between different cultures.

5. You have cooked a big meal for your friend Jacqueline. She is about halfway through a big plate of pasta when she announces that she is full. What peripheral information may have ended Jacqueline's feelings of hunger?

a. Her stomach is distended.
b. Her VMH is being stimulated.
c. Her LH is being stimulated.
d. Her stomach is contracting.

6. Your boss has been doing some reading on expectancy theory. Unfortunately, he doesn't seem to have understood it completely because he ended up setting up a plan with high instrumentality but low valence. Which plan fits that description?

a. Every worker is guaranteed a thousand dollar bonus at the end of the year.
b. Every worker is guaranteed a five dollar bonus at the end of the year.
c. Some workers are guaranteed a thousand dollar bonus at the end of the year.
d. Some workers are guaranteed a five dollar bonus at the end of the year.

7. In Masters and Johnson's description of the human sexual response cycle, the phase in which a maximum level of arousal is reached is called the _____ phase.

a. excitement
b. resolution
c. plateau
d. orgasm

8. You are reading a case study about the sexual behavior of a person who is identified only as S035. S035 reports a long history of one-night stands. Based only on that information, you guess that S035 is a _____ with a _____ mating strategy.

a. female; short-term
b. female; long-term
c. male; short-term
d. male; long-term

9. What is NOT a major source of anxiety for most gay men and lesbians?

a. People's responses to their sexual orientations.
b. The difficulty of establishing a loving relationship.
c. The fact that they are gay or lesbian.
d. Having to decide whether to reveal or conceal their homosexuality.

10. The anthropological work of Ruth Benedict and Margaret Mead undermined instinct theories by showing that

a. collectivist cultures valued instincts more than individualistic cultures.
b. there were large behavior differences between cultures.
c. instincts were different from culture to culture.
d. Freud's ideas only applied to collectivist cultures.

Practice Test 2

1. Which of the following sounds like a situation in which a restrained eater named Dana would be LEAST likely to become disinhibited and go on a binge?

a. Dana's professor announces her failing test score to the class.
b. Dana got lost while driving two friends to a party.
c. Dana's roommate threatens to beat her up.
d. Dana doesn't get a role in a play for which she auditioned.

2. Cross-cultural studies of the prevalence of eating disorders in various ethnic groups has found all of the following EXCEPT that

a. Hispanic females are less likely to suffer from eating disturbances than white females.
b. White females are more likely to suffer from eating disorders than African American females.
c. Eating disturbances are less frequent in Asian Americans than in whites.
d. The precise rates at which African Americans females and white females experience eating disorders are not known.

3. Research by David McClelland and Carol Franz found that the parents of people with a high need for achievement had

a. been easygoing about toilet training.
b. optimistic explanatory styles.
c. pessimistic explanatory styles.
d. been strict about toilet training.

4. Research suggests that a gene called leptin may play an important role in

a. the determination of sexual preference.
b. phases of sexual arousal.
c. career choices.
d. the onset of obesity.

5. For nonhuman animals, _____ provide internal motivation for sexual behavior and _____ provide external motivation.

a. hormones; pheromones
b. hormones; gonads
c. pheromones; gonads
d. pheromones; hormones

6. Joshua was not surprised that he didn't get the job he wanted. The interview was at 9 a.m., and the woman interviewing him seemed to be barely awake. He didn't think she paid attention to him at all. Joshua's attribution for why he didn't get the job was _____ and _____.

a. internal; specific
b. external; specific
c. internal; stable
d. external; stable

7. You have just attended a lecture that discussed the importance of expectations and personal values in explaining motivation. It is likely that the lecture emphasized the theory of

a. Julian Rotter.
b. Clark Hull.
c. Martin Seligman.
d. Fritz Heider.

8. You are watching a demonstration with a rat that has had part of its hypothalamus lesioned. If the rat only refuses to eat food that tastes _____, you will guess that its _____ has been lesioned.

a. bad; VMH
b. good; VMH
c. bad; LH
d. good; LH

9. You notice that your friend Gabrielle watches TV the whole night before a big exam. You decide that she must not be very motivated to pass the course. In this context, you are using the concept of motivation to

a. infer private states from public acts.
b. account for behavioral variability.
c. assign responsibility for actions.
d. explain perseverance despite adversity.

10. Last night, instead of getting a good night's sleep, Jane stayed up until 3 a.m. chatting with friends on the Web. This suggests that Jane's behavior is controlled more by _____ than by _____.

a. instincts; incentives
b. incentives; drives
c. instincts; expectations
d. drives; incentives

Practice Test 3

1. Your friend Ken is excited because the personality test he took shows that he has high *nAch*. You can likely expect that Ken will demonstrate all of the following EXCEPT

a. a desire for efficiency in his work.
b. a willingness to always work harder than others.
c. a tendency to quit when faced with a difficult task.
d. an interest in concrete feedback.

2. Rebecca Stephens's decision to pursue the climb of Mount Everest despite the risk of losing one of her fingers demonstrates the power of

a. previous conditioning.
b. motivation.
c. the athlete's personality.
d. her desire to enjoy life to the fullest.

3. After providing feedback for the first test of the semester, your physics professor wonders out loud what accounted for such a wide range of test scores. This remark reminds you of one of the five purposes of motivation, which is to

a. relate biology to behavior.
b. account for behavioral variability.
c. infer private states from public acts.
d. explain perseverance despite adversity.

4. Your teacher asked the class to read an article on motivation that was written by Julian Rotter. A classmate who was absent and didn't get a chance to read the article asks you what it was about. It would be safe to say that Rotter's theory did NOT place much importance on

a. expectations.
b. instincts.
c. personal value.
d. social learning.

5. The primary reason why instinct theory was rejected was that

a. it was demonstrated that many "instinctive" behaviors are learned.
b. psychologists and others disliked the mechanistic view of humans.
c. instincts cannot be observed and must be inferred from behavior.
d. most researchers agreed that instincts are maladaptive for humans.

6. Cliff is working as a consultant to a large company. He is explaining that workers feel satisfied when they can make favorable comparisons between their own inputs and outcomes and those of other workers. Cliff is applying principles from _____ theory.

a. expectancy
b. equity
c. attribution
d. Maslow's

7. In Heider's approach to motivation, attributing a poor test grade to lack of effort will make it more likely that you will

a. try harder the next time.
b. believe the teacher to be biased.
c. find a poor grade to be reinforcing.
d. attribute good grades to intelligence.

8. Evolutionary psychologists are unclear about whether

a. women have evolved a long-term mating strategy.
b. women have evolved a short-term mating strategy.
c. men have evolved a long-term mating strategy.
d. men have evolved a short-term mating strategy.

9. Your friend comes to you and says, "I told you so! This article says that studies of identical twins reared apart have revealed great similarity in their overall weight." No doubt your friend believes that

a. nurture is more important than nature in determining a person's weight.
b. nature is more important than nurture in determining a person's weight.
c. both nature and nurture are important in determining a person's weight.
d. learning experiences are the most important in determining a person's weight.

10. You overhear one of the competitors at a golf tournament saying that the reason he lost was because his opponent got a lucky break when his ball bounced out of the woods. This golfer is making a(n) _____ attribution.

a. internal
b. external
c. variable
d. stable

Comprehensive Test

1. Women in college are particularly vulnerable to eating disorders. This vulnerability is in part due to

a. the higher levels of stress experienced in college by women when compared to nonstudents.
b. the desire to look attractive yet participate in social eating and drinking with friends.
c. the relationship found between higher level of education and susceptibility to eating disorders.
d. college women's greater acceptance of the ideal body types portrayed in popular women's magazines.

2. In early laboratory studies of the mechanisms underlying eating behavior, animals would appear to stop eating if

a. the lateral hypothalamus was stimulated.
b. the ventromedial hypothalamus was lesioned.
c. either the lateral hypothalamus was stimulated or the ventromedial hypothalamus was lesioned.
d. either the lateral hypothalamus was lesioned or the ventromedial hypothalamus was stimulated.

3. Vanessa is the typical optimist who always seems to see the glass as "half full" rather than "half empty." Vanessa is likely to attribute her successes to _____ causes.

a. internal, unstable, and global
b. internal, stable, and global
c. external, unstable, and specific
d. external, stable, and specific

4. The research of Masters and Johnson described several phases in the human sexual response cycle. The plateau phase occurs

a. during the resolution phase.
b. during the orgasm phase.
c. after the excitement phase.
d. after the orgasm phase.

5. In the study of restrained and unrestrained eaters described in the textbook, participants who were made anxious were given the opportunity to eat good-tasting and bad-tasting cookies. One interesting finding of the study was that anxiety caused the

a. unrestrained eaters to eat fewer of both types of cookies.
b. unrestrained eaters to eat none of the bad-tasting cookies.
c. restrained eaters to eat only the bad-tasting cookies.
d. restrained eaters to eat fewer of both types of cookies.

6. What most sets homosexuality apart from heterosexuality may be that

a. homosexuality is caused whereas heterosexuality is natural.
b. only homosexuality has a genetic basis.
c. there is a continuing hostility toward homosexual behaviors.
d. only homosexuals act on nature's urgings.

7. A cousin of yours tells you that she is a "restrained eater," and yet she is still very heavy. You can conclude most reasonably that she

a. may really be an "unrestrained eater."
b. probably never diets or limits the amount of food she eats.
c. may indulge in high-calorie binges.
d. eats small portions but has too many meals throughout the day.

8. Mary Ellen works at a job where good performances are not rewarded, she does not perceive her work to be fulfilling, and she feels that—no matter how hard she tries—she will not be successful. According to expectancy theory, you would predict that Mary Ellen will

a. continue to make a consistently high work effort.
b. demonstrate low levels of work motivation.
c. restore equity by changing the relevant inputs and outcomes.
d. begin comparing her compensation with those of other workers.

9. According to Daryl Bem, sexual preference

a. is directly caused by biological forces.
b. may be caused by emotional arousal associated with engaging in sex-atypical behavior.
c. is associated with biological factors for heterosexual behavior but emotional arousal factors for homosexual behavior.
d. is based on "exotic becoming non-erotic" activities.

10. Although Grady said that he was "too full to eat another bite of pasta," he happily digs into a slice of chocolate cake. This may be an instance of

a. restrained eating.
b. unrestrained eating.
c. sensory-specific satiety.
d. leptin-induced satiety.

11. Margaret weighs 300 pounds. According to research on restrained eaters, why can't she lose weight?

a. she doesn't have the will power
b. she binge eats under stress
c. she doesn't have the desire
d. it runs in her family

12. Consistently, white, adolescent, American girls tend to rate photographs of large models

a. negatively
b. positively
c. neutrally
d. indifferently

13. All of the following are stages in the human sexual response cycle EXCEPT:

a. arousal
b. orgasm
c. plateau
d. excitement

14. Which personality test has been used to assess the need for achievement?

a. Rorschach
b. MMPI-2
c. TAT
d. 16-PF

15. According to Maslow, which needs are at the lowest level of his hierarchy?

a. safety
b. biological
c. esteem
d. attachment

True/False Questions

1. Researchers have found that 54% of men and 19% of women say they think about sex daily.   T   F

2. College women are more prone to eating disorders than are children.   T   F

3. Maslow created the Hierarchy of Motivation to explain human wants.   T   F

4. The MMPI is a projective test where pictures of ambiguous stimuli are presented to an individual to gauge need for achievement.   T   F

5. Sexual scripts are socially learned programs of sexual responsiveness.   T   F

6. In the human response cycle males tend to reach climax before females.   T   F

7. Physiological processes determine sexual arousal.   T   F

8. Restrained eaters are chronically on diets.   T   F

Essay Questions

1. Describe the psychological forces that determine when and how much a person will eat. Compare and contrast restrained versus unrestrained eaters.

2. Outline the four stages of the human response cycle. How are male versus female patterns different?

When you have finished . . . Weblinks

Need for Achievement

http://www.accel-team.com/human_relations/hrels_06_mcclelland.html

This is a primer on McClelland's Need for Achievement. It also includes links to other theorists such as Maslow's hierarchy of needs. This is presented by the Accel-Team to improve productivity.

Eating Disorders

http://www.eating-disorders.com

This site on eating disorders is sponsored by St. Joseph's hospital in Towson, Maryland. It has information, news and inspiration about all aspects of eating disorders.

APA on Homosexuality

http://www.apa.org/pubinfo/answers.html

APA puts out a good question and answer site aptly called, "Answers to your Questions about Homosexuality". Topics include everything from, "what is sexual orientation" to "how can I find out more information about homosexuality".

Motivation

http://choo.fis.utoronto.ca/FIS/Courses/LIS1230/LIS1230sharma/motive1.htm

This website provides basic concepts and definitions for the various theories of motivation in a clear, easy to read manner.

Maslow's Hierarchy of Needs

http://chiron.valdosta.edu/whuitt/col/regsys/maslow.html

Although this link is to Maslow's theory, the website is designed to encompass the various theories of motivation in a technical manner.

Motivation

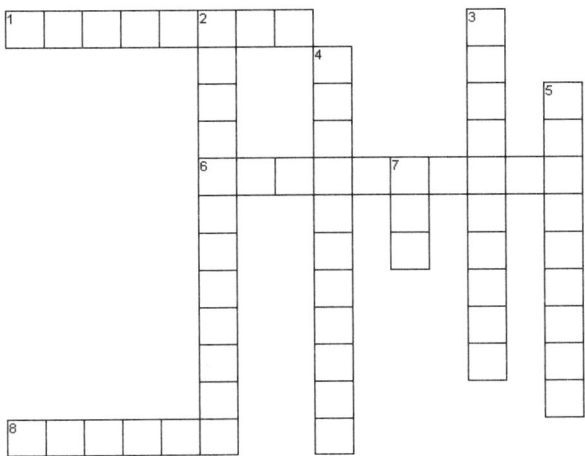

Across
1. unwanted sex by an acquaintance
6. external motivators of behavior
8. physiological needs

Down
2. judgments about causes
3. starting, directing and maintaining behavior
4. equilibrium of the body
5. inborn tendencies for survival
7. projective personality test

Puzzle created with Puzzlemaker at DiscoverySchool.com

Chapter 11 – Answers

Practice Test 1

1. a (p. 352)
2. c (p. 350)
3. c (p. 349)
4. d (p. 365)
5. a (p. 354)
6. b (p. 372)
7. c (p. 362)
8. c (p. 365)
9. c (p. 367)
10. b (p. 351)

Practice Test 2

1. c (p. 358)
2. a (p. 359)
3. d (p. 369)
4. d (p. 357)
5. a (p. 360)
6. b (p. 370)
7. a (p. 352)
8. a (p. 355)
9. b (p. 348)
10. b (p. 350)

Practice Test 3

1. b (p. 369)
2. b (p. 348)
3. b (p. 348)
4. b (p. 352)
5. a (p. 351)
6. b (p. 371)
7. a (p. 352)
8. b (p. 364)
9. b (p. 357)
10. b (p. 349)

Comprehensive Test

Multiple Choice

1. b (p. 358)
2. d (p. 354)
3. b (p. 371)
4. c (p. 362)
5. a (p. 357)
6. c (p. 368)
7. c (p. 357)
8. b (p. 372)
9. b (p. 367)
10. c (p. 354)
11. b (p. 357)
12. a (p. 359)
13. a (p. 362)
14. c (p. 369)
15. b (p. 353)

True/False

1. T (p. 360)
2. T (p. 358)
3. F (p. 352)
4. F (p. 369)
5. T (p. 365)
6. T (p. 362)
7. T (p. 362)
8. T (p. 357)

Crossword Key

Across

1. Date Rape
6. Incentives
8. Drives

Down

2. Attributions
3. Motivation
4. Homeostasis
5. Instincts
7. TAT

Emotion, Stress, and Health

Before you read . . .

This chapter covers emotion, stress, and health. It begins with an exploration of basic emotions and culture. Are some emotional responses innate? Are emotional expressions universal across cultures? Is emotional expression different between individualistic and collectivist cultures? How do cultures constrain emotional expression? This section presents theories of emotion including the contrasting James-Lange and Cannon-Bard theories. The functions of emotion in day-to-day experiences are highlighted as the chapter continues to explore motivation and attention and social-emotional aspects of emotional expression. The chapter moves on to explore the stress of living. Psychological stress reactions and how we cope with those stressors are discussed. What can you do to lessen the impact of stress? The chapter ends with a thorough overview of health psychology. The biopsychosocial model is presented with questions about health promotion. What advice can psychologists give about the structure of the health care system? Is there a way to ensure good health both in the work place and in our daily lives?

Chapter Objectives

After reading this chapter you should be able to:

- Define emotions.

- Explain the difference between evolutionary and cultural causes of emotion.

- Contrast classic theories, which emphasize central neural processes, with contemporary theories, which emphasize the appraisal of arousal in emotions.

- Explain what three functions emotions serve.

- Discuss the root of most stress.

- Explain the interaction of the hypothalamus, hormonal, and nervous systems in stress reactions.

- Describe how the General Adaptation Syndrome shows that stress can be either a mild disruption in health or a health-threatening reaction acquired over time.

- Discuss the variety of psychological stress reactions seen in people.

- Differentiate between traumatic events, chronic stressors, and daily hassles.

- Explain how cognitive appraisal and reappraisal can be used to cope with stress.

- Discuss how social support can be a significant stress moderator.

- Identify the possible positive effects of stress.

- Define health psychology.

- Discuss how the biopsychosocial model explains health and illness.

- Explain what we do to prevent illness in the 21st century.

- Discuss how the psychosocial treatment of illness adds another dimension to patient treatment.

- Compare and contrast Type A, Type B, and optimistic behavior patterns and how they influence a person's likelihood of becoming ill.

- Explain how health-care providers can minimize their risk for burn-out.

As you read . . . Term Identification

Acute Stress	James-Lange Theory of Emotion
AIDS	Job Burnout
Amygdala	Life-Change Units
Anticipatory Coping	Perceived Control
Biofeedback	Posttraumatic Stress Disorder
Biopsychosocial Model	Psychoneuroimmunology
Cannon-Bard Theory of Emotion	Relaxation Response
Cognitive Appraisal Theory of Emotion	Residual Stress Pattern
Coping	Social Support
Emotion	Stress
Fight-or-Flight Response	Stress Moderator Variables
General Adaptation Syndrome	Stressor
Health	Tend-and-Befriend Response
Health Promotion	Type A Behavior Pattern
Health Psychology	Type B Behavior Pattern
HIV	Wellness
Hozho	Yerkes-Dodson Law

As you read . . . Questions and Answers

Emotions

The introductory section defines emotion as a complex pattern of bodily and mental changes. By the end of the emotions section, make sure you understand why that definition is appropriate.

Basic Emotions and Culture

1. What was Darwin's perspective on emotions? How are emotions adaptive?

2. Summarize the evidence that supports the theory that some emotional responses might be innate.

3. What has Paul Ekman's research revealed about the universality of emotional expressions?

4. What is the neuro-cultural theory of emotional expression?

5. Summarize the three examples given in the text of cultural variations in emotional expression.

Theories of Emotion

1. What are the roles of the sympathetic and parasympathetic divisions of the autonomic nervous system in producing emotional responses? (You might want to review the appropriate material in Chapter 3.)

2. What role does the limbic system play in emotional response?

3. Summarize research on the amygdala.

4. What have PET scans contributed to knowledge of the brain bases of emotion?

5. Each of the following questions relates to a theory that specifies the relationship between physiological and psychological experiences of emotions.

   a) What position did William James and Carl Lange originate?

   b) What criticisms did Walter Cannon level against the peripheralist James-Lange theory?

   c) What position did Walter Cannon and Philip Bard originate?

   d) Why is cognitive appraisal central to the theories of Stanley Schachter and Richard Lazarus?

   e) Summarize the research evidence that supports the cognitive appraisal theory.

   f) What two types of criticisms does the book present against the cognitive appraisal theory?

Functions of Emotion

1. In what ways do emotions affect motivation?

2. How do emotions affect communication and social interactions?

3. Define and give an example of mood-congruent processing.

4. Define and give an example of mood-dependent memory.

Psychology in Your Life

Is there a genetic link to happiness? Describe the twin research on the trait of happiness.

Stress of Living

1. What is stress?

2. What are stressors? (Make sure you understand that both positive and negative events are stressors.)

Physiological Stress Reactions

1. How are acute and chronic stress defined? Give an example of each.

2. Define the fight-or-flight response and then summarize its physiology.

3. What is the tend-and-befriend response, and to whom does it apply?

4. Are these responses always adaptive?

5. What reaction pattern did Hans Selye document?

6. What are psychosomatic disorders? How does Selye's work explain them?

Psychological Stress Reactions

1. Summarize the various techniques that are used to measure life changes. What are life-change units?

2. What is some evidence that major life events affect health?

3. What special conditions define catastrophic events? What responses may people suffer as a result of catastrophic and traumatic events?

4. What is posttraumatic stress disorder and what can bring it about?

5. What are chronic stressors? Give examples.

6. What evidence suggests that economic hardship produces negative health consequences?

7. How does chronic stress affect intellectual development?

8. What relationship has been found between day-to-day hassles and health?

Coping with Stress

1. Define coping.

2. What is cognitive appraisal?

3. Define:

   a) Primary appraisal

   b) Secondary appraisal

   c) Stress moderator variables

4. What is anticipatory coping? Give examples.

5. Summarize how these coping strategies are used to manage stress.

   a) Problem-directed coping:

   b) Emotion-focused coping:

4. What are two ways of mentally coping with stress?

5. What is Donald Meichenbaum's stress inoculation technique?

    a)   What are its three phases?

        Phase 1:

        Phase 2:

        Phase 3:

    b)   Describe an application of this technique.

    c)   What is the importance of perceived control?

4. What are the different types of social support?

5. How does the situation determine which forms of social support are most useful?

6. When will social support increase anxiety?

Positive Effects of Stress

What benefits can there be from experiencing stress?

Health Psychology

How is health defined? What are the goals of health psychology?

The Biopsychosocial Model of Health

1. Summarize traditional health practices from non-Western cultures.

2. How does the biopsychosocial model of health embrace the insights of these traditional health practices? Contrast the biopsychosocial model to the biomedical model.

3. Define wellness and health behaviors.

Health Promotion

1. What is the role of psychology in health promotion?

2. What personality and social factors lead people to smoke?

3. What stages do people pass through on their way to quitting smoking?

4. What features are required for successful smoking cessation treatment?

5. What is known about the transmission of AIDS? Who is at risk for AIDS?

6. What are the components of a successful AIDS intervention? Why?

Thinking in Your Life

1. What are the goals of the program *Healthy People 2010*? Why is psychological research relevant to those goals?

2. What have researchers in health psychology discovered about people's willingness to exercise?

Treatment

1. How can psychological interventions improve patient adherence to treatment?

2. Summarize the techniques that have been developed to help the mind heal the body.

   The relaxation response:

   Biofeedback:

3. What has psychoneuroimmunology shown about the effects of stress on the immune system?

4. What are some health benefits of emotional disclosure?

A Toast to Your Health

Try to understand how each of the nine "year-round resolutions" emerges from the research reported in this chapter.

Personality and Health

1. Define Type A and Type B behavior patterns.

2. What is the critical element of Type A behavior that poses a health risk? Can Type A behavior be changed?

3. What are the health consequences of optimism?

Job Burnout and the Health-Care System

1. What is job burnout?

2. What recommendations can be made to change the health-care system?

For Group Study

Basic Emotions and Culture

Are any members of your group from a different culture? You can discuss the different types of emotional responses that are considered appropriate across cultures. Even if you are all from the same culture, you can discuss the reasons why different people feel more or less comfortable with overt emotional expressions.

Functions of Emotion

This may be a good opportunity to focus on the emotional life of your group. What emotions have dominated your group interactions? Does it seem as if the group has a particular emotional tone? Where does it come from? Have there been moments of extreme emotion? If, for example, people got angry at each other, what function did that anger serve? Were you able to diagnose the roots of the anger? As you try to master the material on emotions, treat the group as a laboratory in which you can study the emotions that arise spontaneously.

Coping with Stress

What are the stressors in your life? Are they similar across group members? Can you develop coping strategies as a group? How can the group provide appropriate social support?

Health Promotion

It is likely that every member of your group can acknowledge some behaviors he or she performs that are contrary to good health. Do some of you eat poorly or get no exercise? Do some of you smoke? Do some of you not practice safe sex? You should explore these departures from good health practices. Apply the ideas presented in the chapter to discuss why they occur. Can you use the chapter to improve your own attitudes about health promotion?

After you read . . . Practice Tests

Practice Test 1

1. Darwin believed that emotions were

a) inherited mental states designed to deal with recurring situations.
b. specific situational behaviors that change over time.
c. culturally specific behaviors that are unique to the individual.
d. uniquely individualistic expressions of feelings and affect.

2. Kingston is in a wonderful mood. As he walks down the street with you, he points to all the other people who seem to be having a good time. He may do this as a consequence of

a) mood-congruent processing.
b. cognitive appraisal.
c. mere exposure.
d. mood-dependent memory.

3. Cancer patients benefit most from social support which is primarily

a. informational support—information about the disease.
b. tangible support—money.
c) positive congruent support—consistent with their desires and needs.
d. outcome support—talking about the small impact of the disease.

4. You are participating in an experiment. The researcher has told you to relax and that she will turn on a light on a display in front of you. As you try to relax, you see the light turning on more and more. It's likely that the experiment is concerned with

a) biofeedback.
b. the general adaptation syndrome.
c. stress inoculation.
d. cognitive appraisal.

5. Which of the following hormones does NOT play a role in the fight-or-flight response?

a. epinephrine
b) cortisol
c. thyrotrophic hormone
d. norepinephrine

6. Research on the psychological aftereffects of catastrophe and trauma has shown that

a. few people pass through recognizable stages.
b. people readily ignore the emotional impact of the tragedy.
c) residual stress may persist after the tragedy, or it may subside.
d. people rarely seek social contact after a tragedy.

7. If you want to decrease the likelihood of caretaker burnout in the health-care system, you could

a. increase the number of patients each practitioner sees.
b. ensure that practitioners are in direct contact with patients for long periods of time.
c. avoid the use of teams in health care settings.
d. arrange practitioners' schedules so they get temporary breaks from patient care.

8. You are talking to your friend Carlton about his new romantic interest. Carlton says, "Feel how hard my heart is beating. I guess I must be in love." Carlton's remark comes closest to the _____ theory of emotion.

a. James-Lange
b. Cannon-Bard
c. Tompkins-Plutchik
d. cognitive appraisal

9. The major difference between the biomedical model and the biopsychosocial model of health is that the

a. biopsychosocial model minimizes the importance of physical illness.
b. biopsychosocial model acknowledges the link between the mind and the body.
c. biomedical model draws on traditional health practices.
d. biomedical model is largely concerned with psychosomatic illnesses.

10. Charles Darwin did NOT believe that emotions

a. are vague, unpredictable personal states.
b. serve adaptive functions.
c. deal with recurring situations in the world.
d. evolved alongside other important human functions.

Practice Test 2

1. Paul Ekman's research on the universality of facial expressions revealed that

a. members of Western cultures were unable to recognize most facial expressions produced by people from the Fore culture.
b. one or two facial expressions are universal.
c. people from the Fore culture recognized almost all the Western facial expressions.
d. people from different cultures use the same expressions to convey different meanings.

2. You think that your friend Rudy has a Type A personality. You worry that his personality will put him at risk for disease because he is so _____ all the time.

a. competitive
b. aggressive
c. hostile
d. impatient

3. You are trying to guess if X is from a Western or Syrian culture by watching X's behavior. The most useful information would be to see if X

a. produces a fight-or-flight response.
b. produces a tend-and-befriend response.
c. expresses positive emotions toward another individual.
d. expresses strong emotions, such as wailing at a funeral.

4. Beth has been smoking for several years. She hasn't done anything concrete yet, but she has started to think seriously about quitting. She is most likely at the _____ stage.

a. contemplation
b. preparation
c. precontemplation
d. maintenance

5. With respect to the physiology of emotion, the amygdala plays an especially strong role in

a. the interpretation of emotional tones of voice.
b. attaching meaning to negative experiences.
c. regulating the activities of the parasympathetic nervous system.
d. the interpretation of signals coming from the cortex.

6. All of the following are consequences of chronic stress EXCEPT the

a. increase in illnesses for those in economic hardship.
b. greater rate of smoking among sensation-seeking men.
c. decrease in physical functioning related to basic activities of daily living.
d. impaired intellectual development of underprivileged children.

7. AIDS intervention programs should include training on behavioral skills because people must

a. know which behaviors are safer sex behaviors.
b. be taught how to put safer sex knowledge to use.
c. be motivated to practice AIDS prevention behaviors.
d. avoid situations in which AIDS could be transmitted.

8. How people react to stress relies on interactions between the person, the stressor and _____.

a. available resources
b. the body
c. the brain
d. families

9. You want to give a friend advice on coping with stress that shows an emotion-focus. Which of the following might you say to her?

a. "You have to find ways to fight the threat."
b. "Is there some kind of compromise you can find?"
c. "Can you do anything to get out of the situation?"
d. "You have to plan ways to distract yourself from the situation."

10. You walk into a classroom and see this list of questions on the blackboard:

1. What are your personal resources?
2. What are your social resources?
3. What action options are available?

You decide that the lecture was probably about

a. stress inoculation.
b. secondary appraisal.
c. primary appraisal.
d. perceived control.

Practice Test 3

1. Suppose you wanted to test the cognitive appraisal theory of emotion. You would be most likely to

a. see whether environmental cues are used to help label a participant's arousal.
b. surgically separate the viscera from the central nervous system.
c. measure how long it takes for autonomic nervous system responses to appear.
d. see whether participants experience emotions in familiar situations.

2. After an emergency has passed, the parasympathetic nervous system calms you down by

a. activating the emergency reaction system.
b. instantly shutting down the transmission of information from the peripheral nervous system to the central nervous system.
c. releasing blood sugar in order to inhibit glucose receptors in the brain.
d. inhibiting the release of epinephrine and norepinephrine.

3. While playing the "Trivia Game," you are asked to identify the first modern researcher to investigate the effects of continued severe stress on the body. You should guess that it was

a. Walter Cannon.
b. Donald Meichenbaum.
c. Suzanne Kobasa.
d. Hans Selye.

4. Alan is trying hard to think about his upcoming final exam as not being much different from the other regular semester tests and that, besides, he is well prepared for the exam. Alan is employing _____ to reduce stress.

a. cognitive strategies
b. social approaches
c. controllable stressors technique
d. a problem-directed focus

5. When Grandpa Jones smiles at his granddaughter Emi, she responds with a smile. To psychologists, Emi's response suggests that infants

a. have the capacity to mimic facial expression.
b. may recognize and understand the meaning of an emotion.
c. have an elementary knowledge of what constitutes humor.
d. have an inborn tendency to favor positive emotions.

6. In an extensive series of experiments on the "mere exposure effect," researcher Robert Zajonc demonstrated that

a. the speed with which emotional reactions can occur rules out cognitive interpretation.
b. it is possible to have feelings without knowing why.
c. emotional reactions must be innate, since newborns experience them.
d. people can identify emotions by their unique pattern of physiological changes.

7. Which of the following would NOT be considered part of the basic set of emotions identified by Paul Ekman?

a. fear
b. surprise
c. hate
d. anger

8. You are given a test to determine what personality type you are, with respect to your health. You'd probably be happiest if the test revealed that you are Type

a. A.
b. B.
c. C.
d. D.

9. Randy is lowering his blood pressure in an unusual manner. He is trying to turn a green light on in a box in front of him. Wires lead from the box to a cuff placed around Randy's finger. The technique that Randy is using is probably based on

a. classical conditioning.
b. the relaxation response.
c. biofeedback.
d. socioemotional support.

10. Researchers argue that the _____ evolved to allow women to ensure the safety of their offspring.

a. fight-or-flight response
b. tend-and-befriend response
c. general adaptation syndrome
d. residual stress pattern

Comprehensive Test

1. When you find out that the toy you bought at the store for your child is damaged, you return to the store and angrily demand a refund. This situation illustrates the _____ function of emotion.

a. motivation and arousal
b. social
c. cognitive
d. rival

2. All of the following are stages in stable decision-making EXCEPT

a. appraising the challenge
b. anticipating the outcome
c. surveying the alternatives
d. deliberating about commitment

3. With respect to social support mechanisms, researchers have suggested that

a. additional social support is not always helpful.
b. additional social support is always beneficial.
c. social support from family members is most beneficial.
d. tangible social support is most beneficial.

4. Donna and Debbie are in the same book club. This week, they are reading a romance novel that is filled with happy and sad parts. Donna is in a happy mood when she reads the novel, and Debbie is feeling sad. How will their moods affect their processing of the novel?

a. Donna will pay more attention than Debbie to the happy parts.
b. Donna will pay more attention than Debbie to the sad parts.
c. Both Donna and Debbie will pay more attention to the happy parts.
d. Both Donna and Debbie will pay more attention to the sad parts.

5. Chronic stress differs from acute stress in that chronic stress occurs

a. more severely.
b. over time.
c. more often.
d. frequently.

6. You are watching videotapes of people making requests at a grocery store. All other things being equal, you might conclude that the people making the most polite requests were feeling

a. happy.
b. angry.
c. sad.
d. surprise.

7. Your friend Martha begins to recount all the little hassles that made her day stressful. In keeping with the research on daily hassles, which of the following is she LEAST likely to mention?

a. Losing her keys to the car.
b. Being awakened by a barking dog.
c. Breaking up with her boyfriend.
d. Not finding a parking space at work.

8. Titus didn't get frightened when he passed the graveyard at night unless he started running. When he ran, he got very frightened. Titus's experience best supports the theory of emotion suggested by

a. Cannon-Bard.
b. James-Lange.
c. Lazarus and Schachter.
d. Darwin.

9. The Social Readjustment Rating Scale was developed in order to assess

a. differences in the psychological characteristics of well-adjusted and poorly adjusted people.
b. the relationship between moving one's residence and later social adjustment.
c. the effect of negative stressors on the development of psychosomatic disorders.
d. the degree of adjustment required by pleasant and unpleasant life changes.

10. Stimulus is to response as

a. acute stress is to chronic stress.
b. fight is to flight.
c. stress is to stressor.
d. stressor is to stress.

11. Which brain structure is known as the emotional control center?

a. thalamus
b. hypothalamus
c. amygdala
d. cerebellum

12. Which theory of emotion predicts independence between bodily and psychological processes?

a. James-Lange
b. Cannon-Bard
c. Sapir-Wolf
d. Yerkes-Dodson

13. Which nervous system is activated during a fight-or-flight response?

a. somatic
b. peripheral
c. sympathetic
d. parasympathetic

14. All of the following are stages of the general adaptation syndrome EXCEPT:

a. arousal stage
b. alarm reaction
c. resistance
d. exhaustion

15. The process of dealing with internal or external demands that are perceived to be threatening or overwhelming is known as

a. stress
b. coping
c. hassles
d. emotion

True/False Questions

1. The James-Lange theory is a peripheral feedback theory of emotion.	T	F
2. The part of the limbic system that controls emotion is the thalamus.	T	F
3. Hans Selye originated the general adaptation syndrome.	T	F
4. Psychosomatic disorders are illnesses than cannot be fully explained by physical causes.	T	F
5. The fight or flight response is the tendency for females to protect their offspring or join groups to reduce vulnerability.	T	F
6. The stress response can lead to heightened attentiveness.	T	F
7. Posttraumatic stress disorder is a mood disorder characterized by the persistent re-experiencing of traumatic events.	T	F

8. Hozho is a Navajo concept meaning harmony.   T   F

Essay Questions

1. Compare and contrast the James-Lange theory of emotions with the Cannon-Bard theory. Which one do you think applies to modern living?

2. Outline the three stages of the general adaptation syndrome. What happens in each stage? Give an example of how this applies to your life.

When you have finished . . . Weblinks

Health-Emotions Research Institute

http://www.healthemotions.org

The Health-Emotions Research Institute is sponsored by the University of Wisconsin to understand the biological impact of emotions on physical health. It contains links to research and its own newsletter.

Type A Personality Quiz

http://www.msnbc.com/onair/nbc/nightlynews/stress/stresstypea.asp?cp1=1

Wondering if you are prone to heart attack? Take this Type A personality quiz found at the MSNBC site.

Facial Expression of Emotions

http://www.dushkin.com/connectext/psy/ch10/facex.mhtml

On the Facial Expression of Emotions website you can interact with the figure. Try to select the features that best represent happy, sad, fear and anger. Are these emotional expressions universal?

Ekman on Emotion

http://mambo.ucsc.edu/psl/ekman.html

You have read about the work of Ekman in the area of emotions in your textbook, now see what the work specifically entailed. Site contains links to a Paul Ekman's research articles.

Berkeley Psychophysiology Laboratory

http://ist-socrates.berkeley.edu/~ucbpl/

In addition to providing information regarding work being done at Berkeley, this site provides a number of links to related studies. The BPL studies subjective experiences of emotion, emotional behavior, and physiological reactivity to emotional stimuli.

Emotion, Stress, and Health

Across

2. technique to acquire voluntary control over biological processes
6. continual state of arousal
9. brain structure that controls emotion
11. virus that attacks white blood cells, causes AIDS
12. Navajo harmony

Down

1. optimal health
3. virus that weakens the immune system
4. transient state of arousal
5. demands placed on an organism that tax the ability to cope
7. sound body and mind
8. feelings and cognitive processes
10. dealing with threatening demands

Puzzle created with Puzzlemaker at DiscoverySchool.com

Chapter 12 - Answers

Practice Test 1

1. a. (p. 378)
2. a (p. 386)
3. c (p. 400)
4. a (p. 408)
5. b (p. 390)
6. c (p. 394)
7. d (p. 411)
8. d. (p. 383)
9. b (p. 403)
10. a (p. 379)

Practice Test 2

1. c (p. 380)
2. c (p. 410)
3. d (p. 381)
4. a (p. 405)
5. b (p. 382)
6. b (p. 389)
7. b (p. 406)
8. a (p. 389)
9. d (p. 398)
10. b (p. 397)

Practice Test 3

1. a (p. 383)
2. d (p. 382)
3. d (p. 391)
4. a (p. 399)
5. b (p. 379)
6. b (p. 384)
7. c (p. 379)
8. b (p. 410)
9. c (p. 408)
10. b (p. 390)

Comprehensive Test

Multiple Choice

1. a (p. 385)
2. b (p. 397)
3. a (p. 400)
4. a (p. 386)
5. b (p. 389)
6. c (p. 386)
7. c (p. 396)
8. b (p. 383)
9. d (p. 393)
10. d (p. 389)
11. c (p. 382)
12. b (p. 383)
13. c (p. 382)
14. a (p. 391)
15. b (p. 397)

True/False

1. T (p. 383)
2. F (p. 382)
3. T (p. 391)
4. T (p. 392)
5. F (p. 390)
6. T (p. 401)
7. F (p. 394)
8. T (p. 403)

Crossword Key

Across

2. Biofeedback
6. Chronic Stress
9. Amygdala
11. HIV
12. Hozho

Down

1. Wellness
3. AIDS
4. Acute Stress
5. Stress
7. Health
8. Emotions
10. Coping

## Chapter 13

Understanding Human Personality

Before you read . . .

This chapter covers the many personality theories. It begins with type and trait theories, outlining Allport's trait approach, universal trait dimensions, and the five-factor model. Are there different types of people in the world? Do you inherit personality traits from your parents? Is shyness a personality trait that is inherited? Next psychodynamic theories are explored. Concepts of Freudian psychoanalysis include drives and psychosexual development, psychic determinism, the structure of personality, and ego defense mechanisms. Freud's followers broadened and extended his views. The chapter moves on to humanistic theories. What is the significance of the drive toward self-actualization? Humanists believe that mankind is basically good. Next, social-learning and cognitive theories are covered with particular attention to Mischel's cognitive-affective theory, Bandura's cognitive social-learning theory, and Cantor's social-intelligence theory. The text explores the strengths and weaknesses of each theory. The chapter ends with personality assessment. Assessment is conducted with objective and projective tests. How are personality inventories constructed? How is personality revealed by ambiguous stimuli? This chapter holds the fascinating answers.

Chapter Objectives

After reading this chapter you should be able to:

- Define personality.

- Differentiate between types and traits.

- Discuss the difference between the trait theories of Allport and Cattell.

- Describe the five-factor model.

- Discuss the heritability of certain personality traits using twin and adoption study data.

- Explain the basic concepts of Freudian theory including psychic energy, psychic determination, and unconscious processes.

- Discuss the personality structures: Id, Ego, and Superego.

- Identify ego defense mechanisms.

- Discuss the views of the post-Freudians: Adler, Horney and Jung.

- Define self-actualization.

- Discuss humanistic theory in terms of its holistic, dispositional, and phenomenological base.

- Explain how social-learning theorists understand personality based on different histories of reinforcement.

- Explain how cognitive theorists emphasize individual differences in perception and subjective interpretation of the environment.

- Differentiate Walter Mischel's, Albert Bandura's and Nancy Cantor's cognitive theories.

- Define self-concept.

- Compare independent construals with interdependent construals.

- Compare and contrast the various personality theories and state their strengths and weaknesses.

- Differentiate between objective and projective personality tests.

- Describe the MMPI-2.

- Discuss the newer objective personality tests that measure five personality dimensions.

- Define projective tests and give two examples.

As you read . . . Term Identification

Analytic Psychology	Possible Selves
Anxiety	Projective Test
Archetype	Psychic Determinism
Collective Unconscious	Psychobiography
Consistency Paradox	Psychodynamic Personality Theories
Ego	Reciprocal Determinism
Ego defense Mechanisms	Repression
Five-Factor Model	Self-Actualization
Fixation	Self-Concept
Id	Self-Efficacy

Independent Construals of Self	Self-Esteem
Interdependent Construals of Self	Self-Handicapping
Libido	Shyness
Personality	Social Intelligence
Personality Inventory	Superego
Personality Types	Traits
Unconscious	Unconditional Positive Regard

As you read . . . Questions and Answers

Understanding Human Personality

What two basic concepts do definitions of personality share?

Categorizing by Types

1. What four personality types did Hippocrates propose?

   a.

   b.

   c.

   d.

2. What three personality types did William Sheldon propose?

   a.

   b.

   c.

3. Summarize the evidence in favor of Frank Sulloway's theory of birth order.

1. How are type theories and trait theories different?

2. Based on Gordon Allport's theory, give examples of these kinds of traits:

    a) Cardinal traits:

    b) Central traits:

    c) Secondary traits:

3. What did Allport mean by, "The same fire that melts the butter hardens the egg"?

4. What was the goal of Raymond Cattell's research?

5. What three trait dimensions emerged in Hans Eysenck's analyses of personality?

6. How were the dimensions of the five-factor model derived?

7. What are the dimensions of the five-factor model?

8. How widely applicable are the five factors cross-culturally?

Traits and Heritability

How have researchers demonstrated that personality traits are inherited?

Do Traits Predict Behaviors?

1. What findings led to what is called the "consistency paradox"?

2. How is the paradox resolved, to some extent, by examining psychological features of situations?

3. How do *you* influence your friends' traits?

Psychology in Your Life: Why Are Some People Shy?

1. How is shyness defined?

2. How do nature and nurture interact to produce shyness?

3. What can you do to overcome shyness?

Evaluation of Type and Trait Theories

What are criticisms of type and trait theories?

Psychodynamic Theories

What assumption unifies psychodynamic personality theories?

Freudian Psychoanalysis

1. Why did Freud believe that all behavior was motivated?

2. Summarize Freud's ideas about basic biological drives.

   a) Self-preservation:

   b) Eros (libido):

3. What are erogenous zones? What role do they play in psychosexual development?

4. What is the Oedipus complex?

5. What is fixation and what causes it? What are the consequences of fixation at each stage of psychosexual development?

Stage	Consequences of Fixation

6. Define and illustrate psychic determinism.

7. What role does the unconscious play in guiding behaviors? How do the manifest and latent content of a behavior differ?

8. What is the origin of Freudian slips? Give examples.

9. Summarize the operation of these components of personality structure.

   a) Id:

   b) Superego:

   c) Ego:

10. What is repression and what function does it serve?

11. What function do ego defense mechanisms serve? For each of the defense mechanisms try to generate a concrete example of the mechanism at work. Devise a strategy to link the name of each mechanism to your example.

12. How does anxiety trigger the use of defense mechanisms?

Evaluation of Freudian Theory

1. What are five criticisms of Freud's theory?

   a.

   b.

   c.

   d.

   e.

2. What are important aspects of Freud's theory that have gained acceptance?

   a.

   b.

Extending Psychodynamic Theories

1. What are four general differences between Freud's theory and those of his followers?

   a.

   b.

   c.

   d.

2. In Alfred Adler's personality theory, what do people strive for?

3. What aspects of Freud's theory did Karen Horney challenge?

4. What role did the collective unconscious and archetypes play in Carl Jung's theory?

5. What is analytic psychology?

Humanistic Theories

Why is self-actualization so important in humanistic theories?

Features of Humanistic Theories

1. What is unconditional positive regard? To whom does it apply?

2. Summarize each feature of humanistic theories.

    a) Holistic:

    b) Dispositional:

c) Phenomenological:

4. Why was the humanistic view a "welcome treat"?

Evaluation of Humanistic Theories

1. What criticisms have been leveled at humanistic theories?

2. What is the practice of psychobiography?

3. Why does the analysis of narratives or life stories match particularly well with humanistic concerns?

Social-Learning and Cognitive Theories

Summarize the historical roots of contemporary social-learning theories.

Mischel's Cognitive-Affective Personality Theory

1. What variables affect how you respond to particular situations?

   a)

   b)

   c)

   d)

   e)

2. Why does Mischel view behavior as the interaction of personality and environment? Give examples.

Bandura's Cognitive Social-Learning Theory

1. What is reciprocal determinism and what role does it play in Bandura's theory?

2. What do people learn through observational learning?

3. What is self-efficacy? What are the sources for self-efficacy judgments?

4. How does self-efficacy affect outcomes?

Cantor's Social Intelligence Theory

1. What three types of individual differences does social intelligence theory recognize?

   a)

   b)

   c)

2. What impact do intimacy goals have on relationship satisfaction?

Evaluation of Social-Learning and Cognitive Theories

What are the two main criticisms of social learning and cognitive theories?

1.

2.

Self Theories

Discuss William James' contributions to self-theory.

Dynamic Aspects of Self-Concepts

1. How do self-concepts function as schemas?
2. What is the function of possible selves?

Self-Esteem and Self-Presentation

1. Define self-esteem. What are some consequences of high or low self-esteem?

2. What is self-handicapping?

3. How does self-esteem interact with self-presentation?

The Cultural Construction of Self

1. Define and describe:

   a) Independent construals of self:

   b) Interdependent construals of self:

2. What research results confirm that construals of self differ cross-culturally?

Evaluation of Self Theories

What are two criticisms of self theories?

Critical Thinking in Your Life

1. How does the Internet encourage the exploration of possible selves?

2. What are some benefits of Web-based disclosures?

3. In what ways might the Internet present dangers to the self?

Comparing Personality Theories

Summarize the grounds for similarity and difference among the different types of personality theories.

1.

2.

3.

4.

5.

Objective Tests

1. How are objective tests defined? What is a personality inventory?

2. Summarize the major features of these tests. How are they typically used?

   a) The MMPI

   b) The NEO-PI

   c) The BFQ

Projective Tests

1. How are projective tests defined?

2. How common is the use of projective tests?

3. Summarize the major features of these tests.

   a) The Rorschach

   b) The TAT

For Group Study

Do Traits Predict Behaviors?

Discuss the ways in which people use trait terms loosely in everyday conversation (e.g., "She's very friendly"; "He's not very reliable"). What do people intend when they use these terms? Do they seem to allow for accurate predictions of behavior?

Freudian Psychoanalysis

What did each person in the group know about Freud before you began this psychology class? Did you have an accurate impression of his ideas? How has the description of Freud's theory changed your views?

Humanistic Theories

Discuss the idea of self-actualization. How would you accomplish it in your own lives?

Self Theories

The topic of the self is quite personal, but see if you can discuss as a group the material about different aspects of the self. Are there noticeable differences in the way you each talk about or present your selves? What are your ideas about possible selves? Has your sense of self changed from adolescence into adulthood? If your group includes people from different cultural backgrounds, or if it includes both men and women, discuss how culture may have affected the development of your selves.

Assessing Personality

Have any group members undergone personality testing? What was the purpose of the testing? Did the outcomes reveal useful information?

After you read . . . Practice Tests

Practice Test 1

1. Toby is supposed to build a bird house. You are told that Toby is low in self-efficacy. From this prediction, you are most likely to predict that Toby may NOT

a. have the ability to build the bird house.
b. want to build the bird house.
c. believe that he can build the bird house.
d. understand the plans for the bird house.

2. Jesse has spent most of his life plagued by feelings of inadequacy. No matter how hard he tries, he always ends up feeling inferior to other people. Jesse's life is best understood in terms of the personality theory of _____.

a. Carl Jung
b. Hans Eysenck
c. Joseph Breuer
d. Alfred Adler

3. Research suggests that newsgroup participation on the Web can lead to

a. Internet addiction.
b. decreases in self-efficacy.
c. self-handicapping.
d. greater self-exploration.

4. A major difference between the NEO-PI and the MMPI-2 is that the

a. NEO-PI was designed to be used with non clinical adult samples.
b. NEO-PI was first used as a projective test of intelligence.
c. MMPI-2 has fewer clinical scales than the NEO-PI.
d. NEO-PI has not been found to be reliable.

5. You have built a very lifelike robot whose personality is structured along the lines of Freudian theory. Unfortunately, you forgot to build in the capacity for repression. As a consequence, the robot's

a. id is guided by the reality principle.
b. superego never comes into conflict with its id.
c. ego is overwhelmed by the dangerous impulses coming from its id.
d. ego is not able to strive for its ego ideal.

6. Which of the following statements is NOT consistent with Walter Mischel's theory?

a. People have beliefs about the social world and the likely outcomes for given actions.
b. You cannot tell that much about people by knowing how they behave on average.
c. Most behavior results from the interaction of personality and situations.
d. Most situations overwhelm individual personality differences.

7. When the _____ was constructed, each item had to demonstrate its validity by being answered similarly by members within a group but differently by people between groups.

a. TAT
b. Rorschach
c. WISC-III
d. MMPI

8. According to Freud, it may be difficult to discover the causes of some behaviors because

a. the roots of the behaviors lie in the unconscious.
b. the manifest content of behavior is difficult to uncover.
c. not all people possess libidos.
d. the Thanatos instinct guides psychosexual development.

9. You are attending a lecture on the uses of the Rorschach test. The lecturer is LEAST likely to make the claim that

a. responses are scored for the location on the card that was used.
b. a comprehensive scoring system exists to compare responses.
c. most responses to the inkblots are highly individualistic.
d. Rorschach results can be used to make valid assessments.

10. Suppose you want to use Nancy Cantor's social intelligence theory to make comparisons between two of your friends. You might ask them to describe to you what

a. important behaviors they have acquired by watching other people.
b. situations make them feel most inadequate.
c. life goals or life tasks matter most to them.
d. they consider to be important aspects of their possible selves.

Practice Test 2

1. You are reading a book that describes a new personality theory that divides people into Type D, Type E, and Type F. If this is truly a type theory, which of these sentences should NOT appear in the book?

a. All people who are Type D enjoy late-night snacks.
b. John Wayne was recognizable as a Type E from early childhood onward.
c. More people are Type F than are Type E.
d. Marilyn Monroe was partially Type D and partially Type F.

2. You are reading a case study that describes a patient in therapy as "orderly and obstinate." If you are a follower of Freud, you would guess that this patient is fixated at the _____ stage.

a. anal
b. phallic
c. oral
d. genital

3. Imagine a play in which each character was based on one aspect of Freud's conception of personality structure. The ego would be most likely to say

a. "You've got to wait."
b. "I want it now!"
c. "I don't care what it costs."
d. "That would be wrong."

4. Your friend Elaine has just ended a bad relationship with Larry. His brother Gary has now asked her out on a date. Elaine wonders how likely it is that Gary will share personality traits with Larry. You tell her that it's most likely if they

a. are identical twins.
b. share the same mother.
c. share the same father.
d. are fraternal twins.

5. You have decided to write a psychobiography of the pop star Madonna. Because you take a humanistic perspective on personality, your book is likely to interpret events in her life as

a. the triumph of her id over her superego.
b. the product of archetypes from her collective unconscious.
c. a striving toward self-actualization.
d. the products of reciprocal determinism.

6. Dorothy is playing with a beach ball in the living room of her family's apartment. The ball knocks into her mother's favorite lamp, which falls to the ground and breaks. When Dorothy's mother appears, she punishes Dorothy for playing with the ball inside, but she also reminds Dorothy how much she loves her. This parenting style follows the advice of

a. Carl Jung.
b. Carl Rogers.
c. Rollo May.
d. Abraham Maslow.

7. Which of the following dimensions does NOT appear in the five-factor model?

a. extraversion
b. psychoticism
c. agreeableness
d. neuroticism

8. You'd like to be able to predict how friendly Paul is likely to be if you invite him to your birthday party next month. The best data you could collect to make this prediction would be to

a. ask a large sample of Paul's acquaintances how friendly they think he is.
b. observe how friendly Paul is in other party settings.
c. follow Paul for a day and see how friendly he typically is.
d. ask Paul's mother how friendly he usually is.

9. Although you don't believe there's any one trait that organizes your life, you do believe that you possess several major personality characteristics. In Gordon Allport's terms, you believe that you are better described by _____ traits than by a _____ trait.

a. central; cardinal
b. cardinal; secondary
c. secondary; central
d. cardinal; central

10. Which of these statements might be made by a classmate who is self-handicapping during an exam?

a. "I studied really hard, but I'm still not sure I'm going to do well."
b. "I couldn't study last night because I let my sister come visit."
c. "I think this professor gives really tough tests."
d. "I bet I do better on this test than I did on the last one."

Practice Test 3

1. In terms of the modifiability of personality development, _____ theory has a pessimistic view, and _____ theory holds the most optimistic view.

a. Freudian; humanistic
b. social-learning; trait
c. trait; Freudian
d. humanistic; social-learning

2. Jane's parents describe her as a "born rebel," who seems to always want to do things differently than others. If Frank Sulloway's theory about birth order is valid, you would suspect that Jane is

a. an only child.
b. a firstborn child.
c. a later born child.
d. either a firstborn or a later born child.

3. To illustrate Freud's structures of personality in a theatrical fashion, your psychology professor chooses a few students to play the "roles" of the id, ego, and superego. When Tom begins talking about how much of the society is in moral chaos you know he is playing the part(s) of the

a. ego.
b. id.
c. superego.
d. id and superego.

4. Martha comes home angry after having been reprimanded at work for her lack of motivation. As soon as she sees her two children watching television, she chastises them for being lazy and unproductive, and demands that they complete their chores. Martha's behavior can be considered an outcome of the use of the defense mechanism of

a. denial of reality.
b. regression.
c. reaction formation.
d. displacement.

5. At the end of his job interview, Homer is given the Minnesota Multiphasic Personality Inventory. He wants to make a good impression, so when he sees questions such as "I sometimes worry about things in my life," and "I don't always tell the truth," he answers that these statements are not true. How will the tester evaluate Homer's responses?

a. The tester will not notice anything unusual about Homer's responses.
b. The tester will be impressed with Homer's moral character.
c. Homer will be scored as abnormal and possibly psychopathic.
d. The tester will conclude that the test is not valid.

6. Floyd has just finished reading an interesting article on the famous painter Vincent van Gogh. It tells of van Gogh's troubled childhood, and uses the letters he wrote to his brother in an attempt to produce a coherent explanation of both his artistic creativity and his later mental problems. It sounds as though the author has used the technique of

a. psychobiography.
b. social-learning.
c. self-monitoring.
d. observational learning.

7. All of the following are type categories proposed by William Sheldon EXCEPT

a. ectomorphic.
b. hypomorphic.
c. mesomorphic.
d. endomorphic.

8. Most of Morgan's friends think of him as quiet and shy. Everyone is surprised when he tries out for a part in the school play and wins a major role. This illustrates

a. the defense mechanism of denial.
b. the consistency paradox.
c. self-monitoring.
d. observational learning.

9. Zelda has low self-esteem. When compared to her friend Dobie, who has high self-esteem, Zelda is likely to have

a. stronger levels of motivation.
b. a less precise sense of self.
c. a wider range of life successes.
d. a more positive self-concept.

10. Jules and Jim have different biological parents, but both were adopted in infancy by the Truffaut family. Heredity as a determiner of personality would be supported if the personalities of Jules and Jim are

a. more similar to the personalities of their adoptive parents than to their biological parents.
b. similar to the personality of Jeanne, the Truffaut's biological daughter.
c. more similar to each other than they are to their own biological siblings.
d. less similar to each other than they are to their own biological siblings.

Comprehensive Test

1. In public, Sal seems outgoing and social, but he confesses that, in private, he is actually quite shy. Sal would be described as a(n)

a. introvert.
b. shy extravert.
c. outgoing introvert.
d. extravert.

2. The NEO-PI is LEAST likely to have been used in a study of

a. the differences in the personalities of civil service employees and self-employed people.
b. the differences in the assertive behaviors of people with different forms of schizophrenia.
c. how adult personality traits are related to earlier life events.
d. which individuals are best suited to a special training program for emergency technicians.

3. According to Walter Mischel, how we respond to a specific environmental input depends in part on what we know, what we can do, and our ability to generate certain cognitive and behavioral outcomes. These are examples of what he calls

a. goals and values.
b. competencies and self-regulatory plans.
c. encodings.
d. affects.

4. Little Timmy identifies with his father by trying to be like him in all respects. Within the context of Freud's theory, we can infer that Timmy

a. has not been socialized by those around him to be like his father.
b. has resolved the Oedipus complex.
c. realizes that as a boy he can only identify with his father.
d. expects rewards from his father if he tries to be like him.

5. The weight room in the gym is usually a quiet place until Betsy arrives. She is always cheerful and engages the others in conversation. Soon everyone seems to be talking and laughing. This is a good example of

a. self-efficacy.
b. self-handicapping.
c. the collective unconscious.
d. reciprocal determinism.

6. According to the five-factor model, personality can be classified along the dimensions of

a. egocentrism, reticence, creativity, faithfulness, and energy.
b. honesty, emotional stability, punctuality, hostility, and persistence.
c. agreeableness, extraversion, openness to experience, neuroticism, and conscientiousness.
d. degree of quiescence, egocentrism, introversion, hostility, and emotional instability.

7. "In order for you to really understand how I'm feeling, you would have to be me!" This comment is an example of the characteristic of humanistic theories described as

a. holistic.
b. phenomenological.
c. dispositional.
d. existential.

8. Modern personality theorists suggest that memories about the self, self-schemas, and self-esteem are all components of

a. the self-concept.
b. one's "spiritual me."
c. the "material me."
d. self-verification.

9. You sign up for a research experiment in which you will be given the Thematic Apperception Test. You can expect that you will

a. be asked to add endings to 80 incomplete sentences.
b. make associative responses to 50 nouns.
c. be shown ambiguous scenes and be asked to generate stories about them.
d. be asked to say how you would respond in various uncomfortable social situations.

10. Frank's friends find that he is often sad, brooding, and downcast. According to Hippocrates's theory of personality, Frank has an excess of

a. blood.
b. phlegm.
c. black bile.
d. yellow bile.

11. In objective testing the person must make a forced choice, while in projective testing the person must respond to

a. verbal prompts
b. fixed images
c. random drawings
d. ambiguous stimuli

12. Which of the following is NOT one of Hippocrates' four humors?

a. blood
b. phlegm
c. lymph
d. black bile

13. Boys go through the Oedipal complex in which stage of Freud's psychosexual development?

a. oral
b. anal
c. phallic
d. genital

14. Enduring qualities or attributes that predispose individuals to behave consistently across situations are known as:

a. types
b. traits
c. attributes
d. dimensions

15. All of the following are ego defense mechanisms EXCEPT:

a. denial
b. fixation
c. projection
d. rationalization

True/False

1. Projection is protecting the self from unpleasant reality by refusing to perceive it.   T   F

2. The ego roughly corresponds to the notion of conscience.   T   F

3. Socrates was the Greek physician who believed we could all be categorized into four personality types.   T   F

4. Hans Eysenck's four quadrants of the personality included unstable, stable, introverted and extroverted dimensions.   T   F

5. The five-factor model is a comprehensive personality system known commonly as the Big-Five.   T   F

6. Freud originated the concept of the collective unconscious.   T   F

7. Humanistic theorists believe in self-actualization.   T   F

8. One of the primary criticisms of Freudian theory is that the concepts are vague and not scientifically verifiable.   T   F

Essay Questions

1. Describe eight of Freud's ego defense mechanisms. Taken to the extreme, many defense mechanisms interfere with life. Is there any defense mechanism that is healthy? Explain.

2. Compare and contrast projective versus objective personality testing. Give two examples of each.

When you have finished . . . Weblinks

That's My Theory

http://www.pbs.org/wgbh/aso/mytheory/freud/

Try your luck at the game, "That's My Theory". Join Sigmund Freud and try to guess what other contestants are competing. With the real Dr. Freud please stand up?

Freud's Office

http://www.swt.edu/~rw04/theory-web/freuds-office.htm

On this site you'll see pictures of Freud, his home and office, as well as the famous couch. Freud fled the Nazis in 1938 then died in England in 1939. These pictures put his life in context.

Personality Tests

http://www.queendom.com/tests/

The Queendom site is packed full of tests, tests, and more tests. They claim to have the largest amount of professionally validated tests on the Internet. Beware! Do these tests really measure personality? Take them for entertainment and amusement to get an idea of what personality may be like.

Personality Theories

http://www.ship.edu/~cgboeree/perscontents.html

Great summaries of the many theories of personalities developed by various psychologists, philosophers, and schools of thought.

The Personality Project

http://personality-project.org/personality.html

This is a rather extensive website on the study of personality. Links to recommended readings, academic websites, relevant psychological organizations, and advice for students interested in continuing in the field of personality.

After you finish . . . Puzzle it out

Human Personality

Across

3. enduring personal attributes
5. universal symbolic representation
8. internalization of society's values
10. unconscious part of personality
11. unique psychological individual qualities

Down

1. attachment to object at earlier stage of development
2. exclusion of painful thoughts from awareness
4. emotional response caused by repressed conflict
6. domain of repressed urges
7. discomfort in interpersonal inhibitions
9. sense of self
12. sexual energy life force

Puzzle created with Puzzlemaker at DiscoverySchool.com

Chapter 13 - Answers

Practice Test 1

1. c (p. 437)
2. d (p. 431)
3. d (p. 443)
4. a (p. 445)
5. c (p. 428)
6. d (p. 435)
7. d (p. 444)
8. a (p. 425)
9. c (p. 446)
10. c (p. 438)

Practice Test 2

1. d (p. 419)
2. a (p. 427)
3. a (p. 429)
4. a (p. 423)
5. c (p. 432)
6. b (p. 432)
7. b (p. 422)
8. b (p. 423)
9. a (p. 420)
10. b (p. 440)

Practice Test 3

1. a (p. 433)
2. c (p. 419)
3. c (p. 428)
4. d (p. 429)
5. d (p. 445)
6. a (p. 433)
7. b (p. 419)
8. b (p. 424)
9. b (p. 440)
10. d (p. 423)

Comprehensive Test

Multiple Choice	True/False

Multiple Choice

1. b (p. 426)
2. b (p. 445)
3. b (p. 435)
4. b. (p. 425)
5. d (p. 436)
6. c (p. 421)
7. b (p. 433)
8. a (p. 439)
9. c (p. 447)
10. c (p. 419)
11. d (p. 446)
12. c (p. 419)
13. c (p. 427)
14. b (p. 419)
15. b (p. 429)

True/False

1. F (p. 429)
2. F (p. 428)
3. F (p. 418)
4. T (p. 421)
5. T (p. 421)
6. F (p. 431)
7. T (p. 432)
8. T (p. 430)

Crossword Key

Across

3. Traits
5. Archetype
8. Superego
10. Id
11. Personality

Down

1. Fixation
2. Repression
4. Anxiety
6. Unconscious
7. Shyness
9. Ego
12. Libido

Chapter 14

Psychological Disorders

Before you read . . .

Have you ever wondered about mental illness? Have you ever had the feeling that you or someone you know might be suffering from depression, anxiety, or another form of mental illness? This chapter presents the nature of psychological disorders. It begins with the many definitions of "abnormal". Who gets to decide what is abnormal? It goes on to explore the historical perspectives of abnormality. How have the concepts of abnormality changed over time? When did the medical model and psychological models emerge? The book continues with classification and diagnosis. What are the goals of classification? Are there standards for classification and are they useful? The majority of the chapter is devoted to the major types of psychological disorders. Each section is presented in terms of symptom types and causes. The categories include anxiety disorders, mood disorders, personality disorders, dissociative disorders, disorders of childhood, and schizophrenic disorders. The chapter ends by addressing the stigma of mental illness. This chapter attempts to show how mental illness should be thought of in the same way as physical illness. Patients should be treated with care and compassion without social stigma.

Chapter Objectives

After reading this chapter you should be able to:

- Discuss how psychologists judge abnormality.

- Describe how the mentally ill were treated in earlier times.

- Discuss how contemporary approaches recognize that mental illness can be treated.

- Explain the purpose of classification systems for psychological disorders.

- Describe the DSM-IV-TR and its five axes.

- Compare the biological and psychological approaches to mental illness.

- Identify the five major types of anxiety disorders.

- Describe the four theories regarding anxiety disorders.

- Compare and contrast major depression and bipolar disorder.

- Describe the four theories regarding depression.

- Discuss the biological and psychological explanations for suicide.

- Define personality disorders.

- Discuss the symptoms of somatoform and dissociative disorders.

- Discuss the symptoms of schizophrenia.

- Identify the 5 subtypes of schizophrenia.

- Discuss the biological evidence for the cause of schizophrenia.

- Describe ADHD and autistic disorder in childhood.

- Compare the stigma of mental illness with that of physical illness.

As you read . . . Term Identification

Abnormal Psychology	Major Depressive Disorder
Agoraphobia	Manic Episode
Anxiety Disorders	Mood Disorder
Bipolar disorder	Neurotic Disorders
Comorbidity	Obsessive-Compulsive Disorder
Delusions	Panic Disorder
Diathesis-Stress Hypothesis	Personality Disorder
Dissociative Amnesia	Phobia
Dissociative Disorder	Posttraumatic Stress Disorder (PTSD)
Dissociative Identity Disorder	Psychological Diagnosis
DSM-IV-TR	Psychological Functioning
Etiology	Psychotic Disorders
Fear	Schizophrenic Disorder
Generalized Anxiety Disorder	Social Phobia
Hallucinations	Specific Phobia
Insanity	Stigma
Learned Helplessness	

As you read . . . Questions and Answers

The Nature of Psychological Disorders

1. Define psychopathological functioning.

2. What is the subject matter for the field of abnormal psychology?

Deciding What Is Abnormal

Summarize each of the seven criteria for abnormality.

1.

2.

3.

4.

5.

6.

7.

The Problem of Objectivity

1. Summarize the evidence that supports the statement that the definition of abnormality sometimes depends on the person making the judgment.

2. What did David Rosenhan's research show?

3. What is the view of Thomas Szasz?

Historical Perspectives

1. Summarize the historical interpretation of mental illness.

2. Summarize the roles these scholars played in the emergence of the medical model.

   Philippe Pinel:

   Emil Kraepelin:

The Etiology of Psychopathology

1. Define etiology.

2. What are the main assumptions of each of these approaches?

A. Biological approaches

B. Psychological approaches

   a) Psychodynamic:

   b) Behavioral:

c) Cognitive:

d) Sociocultural:

2. What is an interactionist perspective?

Goals of Classification

What are three goals for a classification system?

1.

2.

3.

DSM-IV-TR

1. Describe the emergence of DSM-IV-TR.

2. What are the five DSM-IV axes?

a.

b.

c.

d.

e.

3. How have diagnostic categories changed over time?

The Etiology of Psychopathology

Review the six etiological approaches to mental disorders.

Anxiety Disorders: Types

Summarize the major symptoms of each anxiety disorder.

1. Generalized anxiety disorder

2. Panic disorder

3. Agoraphobia

4. Phobias

5. Social phobias

6. Specific phobia

7. Obsessive-compulsive disorders

8. Posttraumatic stress disorder

Anxiety Disorders: Causes

How does each of these theoretical perspectives explain the onset of anxiety disorders?

1. Biological

    a) What is the preparedness hypothesis?

    b) What effects do drugs have?

    c) What does genetic evidence suggest?

2. Psychodynamic

3. Behavioral

4. Cognitive

Summarize the major symptoms of each mood disorder.

1. Major depressive disorder

2. Bipolar disorder

How does each of these theoretical perspectives explain the onset of anxiety disorders?

1. Biological

    a) What role do neurotransmitters play?

    b) What does genetic evidence suggest?

    c) What is seasonal affective disorder and what is one way of treating it?

2. Psychodynamic

3. Behavioral

4. Cognitive: Summarize the theories of these scholars.

    a) Aaron Beck:

    b) Martin Seligman (discuss research findings on learned helplessness and explanatory style):

5. What has research shown about self-verification in depressed individuals?

Gender Differences in Depression

Summarize the explanations for sex differences in depression.

Suicide

What factors lead to particularly high suicide rates among adolescents?

Psychology in Your Life

Describe the genetic basis of depression and negative life events.

Personality Disorders

1. What is a personality disorder?

2. What are the main features of each of these disorders?

   a) Borderline personality disorder:

   b) Antisocial personality disorder:

Somatoform and Dissociative Disorders

1. What are somatoform disorders?

2. What is conversion disorder?

3. What are dissociative disorders?

4. What is dissociative amnesia?

5. What are the major features of dissociative identity disorder (DID)?

6. What role might childhood physical and sexual abuse play in the etiology of DID?

7. Why is DID a controversial diagnosis?

Schizophrenic Disorders

What are the major symptoms of schizophrenic disorders?   Distinguish between hallucinations and delusions.

Major Types of Schizophrenia

Summarize the major symptoms of each type of schizophrenia.

1. Disorganized type

2. Catatonic type

3. Paranoid type (mention the different types of delusions)

4. Undifferentiated type

5. Residual type

Causes of Schizophrenia

Summarize what each of these areas of research contributes to understanding the causes of schizophrenia.

1. Genetic approaches (include the diathesis-stress hypothesis)

2. Brain function and biological markers

3. Family interaction as environmental stressor

Critical Thinking in Your Life

What is insanity? How did the insanity defense originate in the legal system?

1. What standard was applied to John Hinckley? Under what circumstances will Hinckley be set free?

2. How often does the insanity defense succeed?

Psychological disorders of Childhood

1. What are some of the hyperactive behaviors in attention deficit hyperactivity disorder?

2. How does the "theory of mind" relate to autistic disorder?

1. Why should mental illness not be considered deviant?

2. What is a stigma? How does the concept apply to mental illness?

3. What consequences does the stigma of mental illness have?

For Group Study

Deciding What Is Abnormal

The text gives a series of different examples of behavior that could be defined as abnormal. For each criterion, discuss examples from your own lives. This exercise should help you better understand what is meant by each criterion. It should also allow you to consider ideas about to what extent abnormal behavior depends on context and who is making the judgment. How do you decide when behavior is abnormal in ways that are problematic or dangerous?

Psychology in Your Life: Is "Insanity" Really a Defense?

Discuss the insanity defense. Do group members think that some criminals really are "insane"? What criteria can be used to make that judgment?

Major Types of Psychological Disorders

To master the material in this chapter, it may be a good idea for each member of the group to become an "expert" on one (or more, depending on the size of your group) of the disorders. Everyone should read the chapter, of course, but then one individual should be responsible for helping the other members learn the symptoms and causes of each major category of psychopathology. An alternative way to structure your study would be to have different group members be "experts" on the different categories of explanation (biological, psychodynamic, etc.). Studying in this way should prompt each of you to find the most efficient way to master a particular portion of the material.

Suicide

Discuss the material in this section as it applies to your own lives. Because depression is so common, and because it can lead to suicide, it is particularly important that you discuss these topics in a context of social support.

Major Types of Schizophrenia

How easy is it for you to understand the symptoms of the different types of schizophrenia? As a group, discuss what it might be like to live with each symptom of the disorder.

After you read . . . Practice Tests

Practice Test 1

1. In the aftermath of tragedies like the Oklahoma City bombing, psychologists are particularly careful to monitor people for symptoms of _____ disorders.

a. generalized anxiety
b. posttraumatic stress
c. obsessive-compulsive
d. panic

2. In _____ type schizophrenia, the patient is free from major positive symptoms but shows minor positive symptoms or negative symptoms such as flat emotion.

a. disorganized
b. paranoid
c. residual
d. catatonic

3. It may be a mistake to label psychological disorders as deviant because

a. many people who suffer from psychological disorders fully recover.
b. about 50% of young and middle-aged adults in the United States have suffered from some mental disorder.
c. many people have family members who are affected by mental illness.
d. personal distress is the most important indication of mental illness.

4. Lisa always has to be the center of attention. When she is not the center of attention, she will often do something overly dramatic or emotional to regain that spot. You might suspect that Lisa suffers from _____ personality disorder.

a. narcissistic
b. antisocial
c. paranoid
d. histrionic

5. Luis will not visit other people's homes because he fears that they may not have searched carefully enough to make sure there are no spiders on the premises. It sounds like Luis suffers from

a. a social phobia.
b. agoraphobia.
c. allurophobia.
d. a specific phobia.

6. You are sent the medical records for a woman who has been admitted to a psychological treatment center. Unfortunately, the record fails to mention the diagnosis. You need to find the patient, so your first guess is to call the unit in which patients with _____ are treated.

a. bipolar disorder
b. schizophrenia
c. depressive disorder
d. dissociate identity disorder

7. The first scholar to create a comprehensive classification system for psychological disorders was

a. Philippe Pinel.
b. Franz Mesmer.
c. Jean Charcot.
d. Emil Kraepelin.

8. _____ theories suggest that phobias are maintained by the reduction in anxiety that occurs when a person withdraws from the feared situation.

a. Behavioral
b. Cognitive
c. Biological
d. Psychodynamic

9. Researchers have found a pattern of bipolar disorder among members of the Amish community in Pennsylvania. This suggests that _____ contribute(s) to the incidence of mood disorders.

a. social isolation
b. alcoholism
c. genetic factors
d. unconscious conflicts

10. Which of the following is NOT an appropriate conclusion from research on biological aspects of schizophrenia?

a. The brain's ventricles are enlarged in many individuals with schizophrenia.
b. Schizophrenia is associated with a relative excess of the neurotransmitter dopamine.
c. Many people with schizophrenia have an eye-movement dysfunction when they scan the visual field.
d. The risk of schizophrenia does not change when more than one parent has suffered from the disorder.

Practice Test 2

1. With respect to the criteria that might be used to label behavior as "abnormal," an individual who "sees" things that do not exist in objective reality would be meeting the criterion of

a. maladaptiveness.
b. irrationality.
c. personal distress.
d. violation of moral and ideal standards.

2. Raphael has been unable to get a job because he is terrified of job interviews. He is able to function just fine in non-interview settings. The criterion for abnormality that Raphael's behavior meets is

a. irrationality.
b. unpredictability.
c. violation of moral standards.
d. maladaptiveness.

3. People who suffer from schizophrenia often experience hallucinations or delusions. Hallucinations are _____, whereas delusions are _____.

a. false sensory experiences; irrational beliefs
b. irrational beliefs; distortions of emotions
c. false sensory experiences; distortions of emotions
d. irrational beliefs; false sensory experiences

4. You have been asked to give a lecture on dissociative identity disorder (DID). One of the facts you are likely to mention is that

a. DID is very similar to schizophrenia.
b. almost all people who experience DID report physical or sexual abuse.
c. multiple personalities serve no known function.
d. sufferers often experience their multiple personalities simultaneously.

5. Aaron Beck's cognitive triad of depression does NOT include negative views of

a. the future.
b. oneself.
c. ongoing experiences.
d. others.

6. After attempting to assassinate U.S. president Ronald Reagan, John Hinckley was found "not guilty by virtue of insanity." The jury believed that Hinckley

a. was incapable of controlling his behavior.
b. did not know that what he was doing was wrong.
c. was unaware that he was shooting a real gun.
d. had been cured by the time of the trial.

7. You have just heard a news story about the rate of suicide among adolescents in the United States. One fact you are likely to have heard is that

a. few adolescents reveal their suicidal feelings before they take their lives.
b. gay and lesbian youths are more likely to commit suicide then are heterosexual youths.
c. men are more likely to attempt suicide than are women.
d. the suicide rate has gone down steadily since the mid-1970s.

8. In ancient times, mental illness was often interpreted as

a. being possessed.
b. a gift from the gods.
c. poisoning by unclean substances.
d. a return to an animal state.

9. You are a clinician using the DSM-IV-TR classification system. If one of your clients were mentally retarded, you would code that on

a. Axis I.
b. Axis II.
c. Axis IV.
d. Axis V.

10. Family studies, twin studies, and adoption studies have shown that persons related to someone who has had schizophrenia are more likely to develop schizophrenia than those who are not related. This evidence highlights the importance of _____ as a possible cause of schizophrenia.

a. the environment
b. genetics
c. brain anomalies
d. thinking patterns

Practice Test 3

1. Dr. Wunsche typifies the viewpoint of current researchers who are attempting to understand psychopathology. It is most likely that Dr. Wunsche's perspective can be classified as

a. only psychodynamic.
b. only behavioral.
c. only cognitive.
d. an interaction of theories.

2. Traveling back once again in your time machine, you find yourself in a lecture hall listening to one of the first presentations by Sigmund Freud on the etiology of psychological disorders. You are one of the few people in the room who anticipates Freud's suggestion that psychological disorders are the result of

a. negative self-attributions.
b. early childhood experiences.
c. interpersonal relationships.
d. social and cultural norms.

3. A person with anxiety sensitivity is more likely to agree with which of the following statements?

a. "I feel the happiest when I am at home relaxing in front of the television."
b. "People that are anxious have been that way since they were born."
c. "When I feel pain in my lower neck, I fear I may be having a heart attack."
d. "The best way to eliminate anxiety is to buckle down, think good thoughts, and take a deep breath."

4. Aware of the importance of explanatory style in predicting depression, you have begun to listen to comments that your classmates make when they receive bad grades on tests. Which of the following explanations would be most likely to be associated with depression?

a. "I'm stupid and I'll never succeed at anything."
b. "These tests are so unfair nobody can expect to do well."
c. "The teacher gave me a bad grade because I ask questions in class."
d. "Next time maybe I'll try studying instead of partying."

5. Oscar suffers from depression. You can surmise that

a. he has periods of mania alternating with depression every six months.
b. he becomes depressed only during the major holidays throughout the year.
c. he finds it difficult to remember anything happy about his life.
d. if he were to move to somewhere that has less snowfall, he would not suffer from depression.

6. Cliff appears not to like people. He won't go to parties, doesn't eat out, refuses to use public transportation, and seems irrationally afraid of all of these situations. If you were to diagnose Cliff's problem, you would say that he has

a. posttraumatic stress disorder.
b. a social phobia.
c. obsessive-compulsive disorder.
d. a mood disorder.

7. Which of these is NOT one of the goals of classification of psychological disorders?

a. Suggesting appropriate treatments.
b. Explaining the stigma of mental illness.
c. Providing a common shorthand language.
d. Describing the causes of disorders.

8. You are a clinician using the DSM-IV-TR classification system. If one of your clients was experiencing a high level of environmental stressors, you would note them on

a. Axis I.
b. Axis II.
c. Axis IV.
d. Axis V.

9. "Mental illness is a myth. In fact, the symptoms used as evidence for mental illness are nothing more than labels used in an attempt to justify and sanction professional intervention." The individual most likely to have made this statement is

a. David Rosenhan.
b. Thomas Szasz.
c. Martin Seligman.
d. Philippe Pinel.

10. According to the theory of _____, depressed people have three types of negative cognitions, called the "cognitive triad" of depression.

a. Aaron Beck
b. Martin Seligman
c. Susan Nolen-Hoeksema
d. Edwin Shneidman

Comprehensive Test

1. People who know Carl say that he can be kind and gentle one moment and fly into a rage in the next. Carl may be considered abnormal when the _____ criterion of abnormality is used.

a. distress
b. disability
c. unpredictability
d. comprehensive

2. Sarah feels she deserves the best that life has to offer and that she is uniquely worthy of living a life of luxury. When her friends chastise her for her opinions, she dismisses them by stating their opinions matter very little. The personality disorder that most closely matches Sarah's pattern of responses is

a. paranoid personality disorder.
b. histrionic personality disorder.
c. narcissistic personality disorder.
d. antisocial personality disorder.

3. Susan Nolen-Hoeksema suggested that sex differences in the incidence of depression are related to

a. the economic and social disadvantages of being female.
b. biological differences between the sexes.
c. differences in the way men and women respond to negative moods.
d. bias in the diagnoses of male therapists.

4. In their explanations of the etiology of psychopathology, behavioral theorists are more likely than psychodynamic theorists to focus on

a. the present rather than the past.
b. internal psychological phenomena.
c. early childhood experiences.
d. hypothetical processes.

5. Although she seemed depressed last week, today Dianne feels unusually elated and believes that she has insider knowledge about financial deals that will make her a billionaire overnight. Additionally, she has little need for sleep. Dianne's symptoms are most similar to those found in

a. histrionic personality disorder.
b. undifferentiated schizophrenia.
c. major depressive disorder.
d. bipolar disorder.

6. When Dr. Flowers, a behavioral therapist, tries to develop an explanation for Jim's adult fear of dogs of all sizes, she is most likely to look for an explanation that focuses on

a. unconscious conflicts that originated in Jim's childhood.
b. the parts of the brain that are active during Jim's phobic responses.
c. a frightening experience that Jim has had involving a dog.
d. the thoughts that lead Jim to be frightened every time he sees a dog.

7. Marnie is suffering from dissociative amnesia. You can surmise that she

a. knows who she is but is pretending not to know.
b. may have experienced some form of psychological trauma.
c. has an organic dysfunction associated with some sort of brain injury.
d. will also be depressed.

8. One of the findings of the National Comorbidity Study was that

a. the number of individuals suffering from a psychological disorder has been steadily declining.
b. people who have experienced one disorder often experience others in their lifetimes.
c. the system of classification of psychological disorders should be revised on an annual basis.
d. there is no available information on the prevalence of different disorders.

9. Because she believes that she is a famous pop star known for her hypersexuality, a patient of Dr. Strange is plagued by uncontrollable sexual thoughts and images. This is an example of a(n)

a. compulsion.
b. hallucination.
c. delusion.
d. obsession.

10. Suppose that someone you know has been talking to you about committing suicide. He seems distressed and has written to his friends about his intentions. It would make most sense if you

a. take him seriously and try to get him immediate professional help.
b. try to determine if he is the "suicidal type."
c. act cheerfully, as though nothing is happening.
d. ignore the person because suicide threats are rarely carried out.

11. Which of the following appears to be responsible for schizophrenia?

a. family interactions
b. genetics
c. brain functioning
d. all of the above

12. Which of the following is NOT an axis of the DSM-IV-TR?

a. Clinical Disorders
b. Major Depression
c. Medical Condition
d. Psychosocial Stress

13. One of the more common symptoms of schizophrenia may be

a. auditory hallucinations.
b. violent behavior.
c. split personality.
d. legal trouble.

14. Marge feels hopeless, helpless and lethargic. She's had these episodes in the past but this time is worse. She can't sleep yet doesn't want to get out of bed. She is likely suffering from

a. hysteria.
b. bipolar disorder.
c. major depression.
d. schizophrenia.

15. A person fears public situations because they are afraid of being judged. This is known as
_____ phobia.

a. specific
b. social
c. anxious
d. public

True/False

1. A major symptom in catatonic schizophrenia is a disruption of motor activity.   T   F

2. Delusions are false perceptions that occur in the absence of objective stimulation.   T   F

3. Schizophrenia of the undifferentiated type is a "grab bag" category.   T   F

4. In the view of psychiatrist Thomas Szasz, mental illness is a myth.   T   F

5. Seligman believed that depression was caused by a disruption in the flow of animal magnetism.   T   F

6. The four axes of the DSM-IV-TR classify abnormal behavior.   T   F

7. Panic disorder occurs with or without agoraphobia.   T   F

8. Almost 30 percent of the adult population has experienced symptoms characteristic of the various anxiety disorders.   T   F

Essay Questions

1. List the five axes of the DSM-IV-TR. State what is measured on each. What does DSM stand for?

2. Pick one anxiety disorder. Explain its symptoms, causes, and treatment according to the behavioral perspective.

When you have finished . . . Weblinks

Mayo Clinic: Anxiety

http://www.mayoclinic.com/findinformation/conditioncenters/subcenters.cfm?objectid=C2CFFA98-7C6C-4FED-8FDA3BB92EDA3B79

Anxiety disorders are the most commonly occurring mental dysfunction in the population. Read all about the signs and symptoms from the Mayo Clinic's excellent information pages.

Internet Mental Health: Schizophrenia

http://www.mentalhealth.com/dis/p20-ps01.html

The Internet Mental Health site contains the signs diagnostic criteria for schizophrenia. It also has many links to outside resources. It contains a wealth of information.

Depression and Bipolar Support Alliance

http://www.dbsalliance.org

This is an excellent clearinghouse from the Depression and Bipolar Support Alliance. At this site you can take a confidential screening for bipolar disorder, join the discussion boards or chat sessions or just immerse yourself in all the information.

Panic Disorder

http://www.apa.org/pubinfo/panic.html

Have questions about panic disorder? This is an APA website that provides answers to many of the commonly asked questions regarding panic.

Research on Schizophrenia and Depression

http://www.narsad.org/

NARSAD is a mental health research association. This site provides information on Schizophrenia and depression as well as some insights into the funding issues behind psychological research.

After you finish . . . Puzzle it out

Psychological Disorders

Across

2. subjective distress, problems in living
4. alternating periods of depression and mania
7. fear of being in public places
8. irrational fear
9. rational reaction to external threat
12. state of being judged legally incompetent
13. state of psychological being
14. negative reactions

Down

1. false beliefs
3. false perceptions
5. diagnostic and statistical manual
6. more than one disorder at the same time
10. causes of a disorder
11. elated, euphoric, unbounded energy

Puzzle created with Puzzlemaker at DiscoverySchool.com

Chapter 14 - Answers

Practice Test 1

1. b (p. 461)
2. c (p. 475)
3. b (p. 452)
4. d (p. 470)
5. d (p. 460)
6. c (p. 464)
7. d (p. 455)
8. a (p. 463)
9. c (p. 465)
10. d (p. 476)

Practice Test 2

1. b (p. 452)
2. d (p. 452)
3. a (p. 475)
4. b (p. 474)
5. d (p. 466)
6. b (p. 480)
7. b (p. 468)
8. a (p. 455)
9. b (p. 455)
10. b (p. 476)

Practice Test 3

1. d (p. 458)
2. b (p. 458)
3. c (p. 463)
4. a (p. 464)
5. c (p. 467)
6. b (p. 460)
7. b (p. 454)
8. c (p. 456)
9. b (p. 454)
10. a (p. 466)

Comprehensive Test

Multiple Choice

1. c (p. 453)
2. c (p. 470)
3. c (p. 467)
4. a (p. 458)
5. d (p. 465)
6. c (p. 458)
7. b (p. 473)
8. b (p. 456)
9. c (p. 475)
10. a (p. 469)
11. d (p. 478)
12. b (p. 456)
13. a (p. 475)
14. c (p. 464)
15. b (p. 460)

True/False

1. T (p. 476)
2. F (p. 475)
3. T (p. 476)
4. T (p. 454)
5. F (p. 466)
6. F (p. 455)
7. T (p. 459)
8. T (p. 459)

Crossword Key

Across

2. Neurotic
4. Bipolar
7. Agoraphobia
8. Phobia
9. Fear
12. Insanity
13. Mood
14. Stigma

Down

1. Delusions
3. Hallucinations
5. DSMIVTR
6. Comorbidity
10. Etiology
11. Manic

Therapies for Psychological Disorders

Before you read . . .

How do we treat mental illness? This chapter outlines the various theories and perspectives psychologists use in therapy. It begins with the goals and categories of the major therapies. In what setting would you find different types of therapists? The text briefly retraces the historical and cultural contexts of the contemporary treatment of mental illness. The chapter follows the perspectives model, outlining psychodynamic, behavioral, cognitive, humanistic, group, and biomedical therapies. The many medications, drug classifications, and biological treatments are covered. The chapter looks at how the brain is affected by psychoactive drugs. It closes with treatment evaluation and prevention strategies. How can researchers determine whether therapies have been successful? How might some mental illnesses be prevented? Perhaps you will be involved in answering the questions of the future.

Chapter Objectives

After reading this chapter you should be able to:

- Describe the goals of therapy, whether medically or psychologically oriented.

- Differentiate between the four major types of therapy: psychodynamic, behavioral, cognitive, and humanistic.

- Contrast the different kinds of professionals who practice therapy.

- Outline how historically harsh and dehumanizing treatments gave way to the disease model, leading to more humane treatments.

- Discuss the interconnection between deinstitutionalization and homelessness.

- Describe Freud's psychoanalytic theory, particularly the role of unconscious conflicts.

- Discuss the importance of free association, catharsis, resistance, dream analysis, transference, and countertransference in psychodynamic theory.

- Explain how post-Freudian psychodynamic theorists place more emphasis on the patient's social situation and interpersonal relationships than Freud did.

- Discuss the possibility of repressed memories.

- Discuss the importance of learning and conditioning in behavior therapy.

- Explain the wide range of behavioral techniques, including: counterconditioning, exposure, contingency management, and social-learning therapy.

- Discuss the focus of cognitive therapy.

- Discuss rational-emotive therapy and how it helps clients recognize their irrational beliefs.

- Explain how cognitive behavior therapy is related to self-efficacy.

- Explain the two major humanistic therapies and how each helps individuals become more fully self-actualized.

- Describe how client-centered therapy can help clients establish a positive self-image.

- Discus the focus of gestalt therapy.

- Describe the purpose of group therapy.

- Explain how couple and family therapy focuses on the group as a system.

- Describe how self-help groups allow individuals to obtain social support.

- Discuss the focus of biomedical therapies.

- Describe drug therapies including antipsychotic, antidepressant, and antianxiety medications.

- Differentiate between psychosurgery, ECT and rTMS.

- Identify some of the research describing what makes therapy effective.

- List some strategies that might prevent mental illness from occurring.

As you read . . . Term Identification

Aversion Therapy	Gestalt Therapy
Behavioral Rehearsal	Human-Potential Movement
Behavior Modification	Insight Therapy
Behavior Therapy	Meta-Analysis

Biomedical Therapies	Participant Modeling
Catharsis	Pastoral Counselor
Client	Patient
Client-Centered Therapy	Placebo Therapy
Clinical Psychologist	Prefrontal Lobotomy
Clinical Social Worker	Psychiatrist
Cognitive Behavioral Therapy	Psychoanalysis
Cognitive Therapy	Psychoanalyst
Contingency Management	Psychopharmacology
Counseling Psychologist	Psychosurgery
Counterconditioning	Psychotherapy
Countertransference	Rational-Emotive Therapy (RET)
Deinstitutionalization	Resistance
Dream Analysis	Social-Learning Therapy
Electroconvulsive Therapy	Spontaneous-Remission Effect
Exposure Therapy	Systematic Desensitization
Free Association	Transference

As you read . . . Questions and Answers

Goals and Major Therapies

1. List and explain the four goals of therapy.

   a)

   b)

   c)

   d)

2. What are the major categories of therapy?

Therapists and Therapeutic Settings

1. Summarize the approaches and settings for each of these types of therapists.

    a) Counseling psychologists:

    b) Clinical social workers:

    c) Pastoral counselors:

    d) Clinical psychologists:

    e) Psychiatrists:

    f) Psychoanalysts:

2. Which of the above therapists use the term "patient" and which use "client" in their practice?

Historical and Cultural Contexts

Summarize the history of the treatment of mental disorders. What role(s) did Dorothea Dix play in the history of how the mentally ill were treated?

Freudian Psychoanalysis

1. Of what importance is repression?

2. Why is psychodynamic therapy called "insight therapy"?

3. Explain free association and catharsis.

4. Why is resistance significant in psychoanalysis?

5. What roles do manifest content and latent content play in dream analysis?

6. What is the significance of transference and countertransference?

Neo-Freudian Therapies

Summarize the ideas of these neo-Freudian thinkers.

1. Harry Stack Sullivan:

2. Melanie Klein:

Psychology in Your Life

1. Who originated the idea of repressed memories? How are they defined?

2. Why does memory research suggest that it may be difficult to identify which reports of repressed memories are accurate?

3. How might the process of psychotherapy produce some "repressed memories"?

Behavior Therapies

Does behavior therapy lead to symptom substitution?

Counterconditioning

1. What is counterconditioning? Summarize Mary Cover Jones's early use of this logic.

2. What was Joseph Wolpe's theory of reciprocal inhibition?

3. What are the three steps of systematic desensitization?

4. What is flooding therapy? Give examples.

5. How can exposure therapy be applied to obsessive-compulsive disorders?

6. How does aversion therapy work? Give an example.

Contingency Management

1. How is positive reinforcement used to change behaviors? Give examples.

2. How is extinction used to change behaviors? Give examples.

Social-Learning Therapy

1. How are models used to bring about behavior change?

2. Contrast participant modeling therapy and symbolic modeling therapy.

3. What is the goal of social-skills training? Why is this an important goal?

4. What is behavioral rehearsal?

5. Has social-skills training been effective?

Generalization Techniques

1. Why is generalization important?

2. Give examples of generalization techniques at work.

Cognitive Therapies

What is the goal of cognitive therapy?

Changing False Beliefs

1. What are three basic patterns of faulty thinking?

2. Summarize the four main tactics of Aaron Beck's cognitive therapy for depression.

3. How does rational-emotive therapy attack faulty thinking?

Cognitive Behavioral Therapy

How does this type of therapy work to build expectations of effectiveness and mastery of self-efficacy?

Humanistic Therapies

1. What are existential crises?

2. What is the human potential movement?

Client-Centered Therapy

1. What are the major assumptions of Carl Rogers's therapy?

2. What are important attributes of the client-centered therapist's approach?

Gestalt Therapy

1. What therapy did Fritz Perls invent? What is its focus?

2. What is one well-known Gestalt therapy technique?

Group Therapies

What are some basic premises of group therapy?

1.

2.

3.

4.

Couple and Family Therapy

1. What makes group therapy effective?

2. What makes family therapy effective?

Community Support Groups

1. How did self-help groups develop? What kinds of problems do they deal with?

2. What features of self-help groups make them effective?

Drug Therapy

1. What is psychopharmacology?

2. Why did psychoactive drugs have such a large effect on the treatment of the mentally ill?

3. For each group, summarize why each type of drug has the effect it does. Are there problems with the treatments?

    a. Antipsychotic drugs

    b.   Antidepressant drugs

    c.   Antianxiety drugs

Psychosurgery

What is the purpose of prefrontal lobotomies? Are they common in contemporary times?

ECT and rTMS

1.   How is electroconvulsive therapy (ECT) administered? What effect does it have?

2.   Why is ECT controversial? What research results answer some of the criticisms?

3.   Describe repetitive transcranial magnetic stimulation (rTMS). How is it similar to ECT?

Evaluating Therapeutic Effectiveness

1.   What did Hans Eysenck declare about the effectiveness of psychotherapy?

2. What is the spontaneous-remission effect? How can it be controlled by using baselines?

3. What is placebo therapy?

4. What is a meta-analysis? What have meta-analyses shown about the effectiveness of psychotherapy?

Prevention Strategies

1. Define these types of prevention.

   a) Primary prevention:

   b) Secondary prevention:

   c) Tertiary prevention:

For Group Study

Goals and Major Therapies

This is another chapter for which it makes sense to have each group member become an expert on one of the major forms of therapy. Try to learn the material in each section, but also challenge your friends to create and analyze new examples.

Psychodynamic and Behavior Therapies

Table 15.3 provides a point-by-point comparison of psychoanalytic and behavioral approaches to psychotherapy. Use this table to have a mini-debate. Choose different types of problems that affect people in real life and try to understand them with respect to both of these programs of therapy. Discuss the merits of each.

Psychology in the 21st Century: Therapies and Brain Activity

How can biomedical and psychological therapies produce the same changes in the brain? Discuss the research within your group that shows the same brain changes for either drug therapy or psychotherapy. What implication does this have for your lives?

Community Support Groups

In what sense is your study group a support group? How can participation in this sort of group enhance your mental health?

After you read . . . Practice Tests

Practice Test 1

1. Generalization procedures are important because they ensure that

a. clients will lose their fear of all members of a phobic category.
b. patients will extend their emotional catharses to other repressed memories.
c. self-statements will be applied to other people as well.
d. behavioral changes will endure after therapy has been terminated.

2. One of the major changes in treatment of mental disorders has been

a. increased use of ritual healing ceremonies.
b. attributing mental illnesses to the stresses of city living.
c. deinstitutionalization of patients.
d. increased use of asylums.

3. Unconditional positive regard is characteristic of what type therapy?

a. client-centered.
b. aversion.
c. conditioning.
d. psychoanalytic.

4. Antipsychotic drugs work by reducing the activity of the neurotransmitter _____ in the brain.

a. serotonin
b. dopamine
c. norepinephrine
d. GABA

5. Benzodiazepines, such as Valium and Xanax, _____ the activity of the neurotransmitter GABA, and are useful in the treatment of _____ .

a. increase; anxiety disorders
b. decrease; anxiety disorders
c. maintain constant levels of; schizophrenia
d. decrease; mood disorders

6. The meta-analysis that compared the effectiveness of different therapies for depression found that

a. the drug therapy was the least effective.
b. the placebo treatment was better than psychodynamic therapy.
c. interpersonal and cognitive therapies were about equally effective.
d. the drug therapy was only better than the psychodynamic therapy.

7. One of the main advantages of electroconvulsive therapy over drug therapies for depression is that

a. treatment only lasts for one day.
b. it works more quickly.
c. the reasons for its effectiveness are well understood.
d. it never produces any memory deficits.

8. Part of the recovery that patients experience when they go into therapy arises from their own expectations of healing. This is known as

a. catharsis.
b. the placebo effect.
c. spontaneous remission.
d. self-efficacy.

9. You have been trained as a family therapist. You are most likely to

a. treat each family member apart from the others.
b. focus on the one individual within the family who is most disruptive.
c. assume that family difficulties are situational rather than dispositional.
d. let family members work out their problems with minimal intervention from you.

10. Suppose you were in therapy with a psychoanalyst and he asked you to free associate. He would treat the free associations as if they were

a. random words, intended only to start you talking.
b. predetermined, with the superego providing most of the content.
c. random words, with the id providing most of the content.
d. predetermined, with important patterns lying below the surface.

Practice Test 2

1. You are setting up a mental health program in a rural community. Your goal is to identify people who are suffering from psychological disorders and try to limit the duration and severity of the disorder. Your program provides _____ prevention services.

a. primary
b. tertiary
c. rational
d. secondary

2. One major problem with trying to verify the validity of repressed memories is

a. the tendency for people to remember only flattering or painful information.
b. distinguishing between the source and the content of the memory.
c. the lack of trained professionals who are engaged in helping patients with repressed memories.
d. controlling for the level of intelligence of the patient.

3. One day in therapy, Willem bursts out with, "Stop treating me like a child! You're always treating me like I'm a little boy!" If the therapist has not, in fact, been treating Willem in this way, you might suspect that this is a case of

a. countertransference.
b. masturbatory thought.
c. transference.
d. resistance.

4. Suzanne is a social worker. When she begins the therapeutic process a new patient, which of the following will she NOT do?

a. identify the possible cause of the disorder.
b. prescribe medication.
c. make a prognosis.
d. makes a determination of the disorder that is affecting the patient.

5. You are introduced to Sonia, who identifies herself as a type of therapist. She goes on to explain that she is particularly sensitive to the social context of people's problems. You guess that Sonia is a

a. clinical social worker.
b. pastoral counselor.
c. psychiatrist.
d. counseling psychologist.

6. In _____ therapy, therapists strive to be nondirective; they do not interpret or instruct the client.

a. insight
b. existential
c. rational-emotive
d. client-centered

7. Luis would like to be cured of his phobia for spiders. Which type of therapy is likely to put him in contact with an actual spider earliest in the course of treatment?

a. systematic desensitization
b. aversion therapy
c. implosion therapy
d. flooding

8. Which of these statements would most likely be the focus of discussion in cognitive behavior therapy?

a. "I'm the worst employee at my company."
b. "I was very close to my mother when I was a child."
c. "When I think about snakes, I start to feel sick."
d. "People should treat me more fairly."

9. People may benefit more from group therapy than from individual therapy for all of the following reasons EXCEPT that group therapy does NOT

a. allow people to practice being an authoritarian figure with respect to the group.
b. allow group processes to be used to influence individual maladaptive behavior.
c. provide people with opportunities to observe and practice interpersonal skills within the therapy session.
d. provide an analogue of the primary family group, which enables corrective emotional experiences to take place.

10. Dr. Rubies uses the "empty chair technique" during your course of treatment. Dr. Rubies is likely to be a _____ therapist.

a. group
b. client-centered
c. Gestalt
d. Freudian

Practice Test 3

1. Teresa's therapist is treating her with antidepressant medication in order to stabilize her moods. Her therapist must be a

a. clinical psychologist.
b. clinical social worker.
c. pastoral counselor.
d. psychiatrist.

2. What was the role of the mental asylum during the mental hygiene movement of the 1900s?

a. Its purpose has always been to offer treatment to those who could not help themselves.
b. It evolved from having the goal of rehabilitation to the more practical goal of containment.
c. Initially, it was looked upon as a money-making instrument of the state.
d. It was developed to contain the poor, criminals, and the mentally disturbed.

3. "Tiny" is seeing a behavior therapist because he feels compelled to eat a gallon of ice cream each night before he goes to sleep. His therapist is likely to describe the problem in terms of Tiny's

a. current relationships with his parents.
b. early childhood experiences.
c. eating behavior.
d. unconscious motivations.

4. Which therapeutic procedure does NOT belong with the others?

a. systematic desensitization
b. theory of reciprocal inhibition
c. flooding
d. free association

5. The theorist who argued that a death instinct preceded sexual awareness was

a. Heinz Kohut
b. Melanie Klein
c. Harry Stack Sullivan
d. Aaron Beck

6. Toby wants to overcome his smoking habit. He has signed up for a course of therapy in which he will be given a drug that will make him violently ill every time he smokes. It sounds like Toby has become involved in

a. systematic desensitization.
b. aversion therapy.
c. contingency management.
d. social-learning therapy.

7. Rational-emotive therapy is similar to humanistic therapy in that its goal is to help clients to

a. learn to use both intrinsic and extrinsic reward systems.
b. learn how to use effective problem-focused coping strategies.
c. develop an extensive social support network.
d. increase self-worth and the potential for self-actualization.

8. Edna recounts a dream to her therapist in which she is being chased by a tall, menacing person whom she cannot identify. The therapist believes the faceless figure could be her father. In this dream, the patient's account of the dream is called the _____ of the dream, and the therapist's interpretation is called the _____ of the dream.

a. manifest content; latent content
b. latent content; manifest content
c. simple level; complex level
d. complex level; simple level

9. Which of the following suggests that catharsis has occurred?

a. Tom remembered how much he liked the little girl who sat next to him in the first grade.
b. Henry didn't want to tell his therapist how he felt about his brother.
c. Sally felt better after she had a good cry.
d. Mary's idea of success is owning lots of jewelry.

10. The Addams family is seeing a family therapist. The therapist is most likely to

a. focus attention on the cognitions of the most maladjusted individuals in the family.
b. focus attention on the behaviors of the most maladjusted individuals in the family.
c. view family problems as being caused by dispositional aspects of family members.
d. view each family member as a part of the whole family system.

Comprehensive Test

1. Mike knows that his friend Rory is shy about asking girls out for a date. He tells Rory to imagine striking up a conversation with a girl, and after spending some time getting to know her, asking her if she would consider going out for a cup of coffee with him. Mike's advice is similar to the technique called

a. counterconditioning.
b. assertiveness training.
c. think-and-act.
d. just do it.

2. Clyde, a patient diagnosed with schizophrenia and who suffers from frequent bouts of agitated behavior, undergoes an operation known as a prefrontal lobotomy. You can expect that after the operation Clyde will

a. be more agitated than before.
b. have difficulties with planning and show emotional flatness.
c. emerge with a new personality with intense emotional arousal and overwhelming anxiety.
d. have no recollection of the surgical procedure.

3. Edgar is terrified of being in a confined space from which he cannot escape. He avoids airplanes and can only ride buses if they stop frequently. Today, he and his therapist will be riding in an elevator that the therapist has arranged to get stuck between floors. This is an example of the technique called

a. flooding.
b. implosion therapy.
c. reciprocal inhibition.
d. eye movement desensitization.

4. Tardive dyskinesia involves

a. two major forms of schizophrenia.
b. recently developed antidepressant drugs.
c. side effects caused by certain antipsychotic drugs.
d. side effects of electroconvulsive therapy.

5. When someone tries to prevent a problem before it begins, he or she is engaging in _____ prevention.

a. primary
b. secondary
c. tertiary
d. spontaneous

6. Someone might choose a clinical psychologist over a psychiatrist if they wanted a therapist who

a. had completed their medical school training.
b. had a broader background in psychology, assessment, and research.
c. was mostly trained in the biomedical base of psychological problems.
d. could prescribe drugs.

7. In a classroom exercise, you are asked to role-play a client-centered therapist. When your client sobs, "My life is so hopeless, what should I do?" you should respond,

a. "Why not get a job and stop moping?"
b. "You sound unhappy and uncertain."
c. "Hopelessness often symbolizes sexual inadequacy."
d. "The reason you feel hopeless is because you feel guilty."

8. The observation that patients who suffered from both schizophrenia and epilepsy showed improvement in their schizophrenic symptoms after epileptic seizures led to the development of

a. electroconvulsive therapy.
b. prefrontal lobotomies.
c. psychosurgery.
d. drug therapy.

9. When researchers have compared drug therapy and psychotherapy, they have obtained all of the following results EXCEPT that

a. both provide relief to patients.
b. only psychotherapy results in changes in brain function.
c. they work best when combined.
d. both work better than placebo treatments.

10. At the end of class, the professor announces that the topic for the next lecture will deal with how principles of conditioning can be applied in a systematic fashion to increase desired behaviors or decrease unwanted behaviors. If the next lecture had a title, it would most likely be called,

a. "The Dynamic Aspects of Self."
b. "The Inner Drive for Positive Behavior."
c. "Principles of Behavior Modification."
d. "Object Relations in the Real World."

11. In _____ therapy, inner conflicts between the unconscious and the internalized social constraints are examined.

a. cognitive
b. biological
c. behavior
d. psychodynamic

12. Which technique is among the best known in Gestalt therapy?

a. free association
b. token economy
c. the empty chair
d. age regression

13. The following are used in the psychopharmacological management of mental disorders EXCEPT:

a. antianxiety drugs
b. antihistamines
c. antipsychotics
d. antidepressants

14. Cognitive therapies have become best known for the treatment of:

a. bipolar disorder
b. schizophrenia
c. depression
d. anxiety

15. Many of the Neo-Freudians placed more emphasis than Freud did on:

a. current social environment.
b. clinical hypnosis.
c. free association.
d. transference.

True/False Questions

1. Psychopharmacology is the branch of psychology that investigates the effect of drugs on behavior.   T   F

2. Prozac is prescribed most commonly for bipolar disorder.   T   F

3. ECT is much more effective at alleviating schizophrenia than depression.   T   F

4. Rational-emotive therapy was developed by Aaron Beck.   T   F

5. Cognitive therapy was developed to deal with the human-potential movement of the 1930s.   T   F

6. Systematic desensitization is a humanistic technique in which a patient imagines fearful stimuli while relaxed.   T   F

7. Behavior therapies use conditioning principles to increase adaptive behavior.   T   F

8. Client-centered therapy is a psychodynamic treatment.   T   F

When you have finished . . . Weblinks

Suicide Prevention Quiz

http://www.sfsuicide.org/html/what.html

Take the suicide prevention quiz. This is from San Francisco's suicide prevention center, America's oldest crisis line. It outlines the steps you can take if someone you know or love is contemplating suicide.

La Chaise Longue: Counseling and Advice

http://www.queendom.com/chaiselongue/index.html

La Chaise Longue is a site where visitors pose questions that are answered by professional counselors. Is it effective? Is it ethical to be giving cyber advice? Read the cyber counselors' responses and judge for yourself.

National Association of Cognitive Behavioral Therapists

http://www.nacbt.org/index.htm

The home of the National Association of Cognitive Behavioral Therapists (NACBT) suggests that Cognitive-behavioral therapy is considered among the "fastest" in terms of results obtained. The average number of sessions is16. The site has multiple links for students and the general public.

REBT Therapy

http://www.threeminutetherapy.com/rebt.html

Everything you ever wanted to know about Rational Emotive Behavior Therapy, developed by Dr. Albert Ellis, is available at this site.

New York Psychoanalytic Institute

http://www.psychoanalysis.org/

Includes links to Sigmund Freud on the internet, news in psychoanalysis, and information on the New York Psychoanalytic Institute and Society programs and activities. Along with this site all you will need is a couch.

Therapies for Psychological Disorders

Across

2. surgery on the brain
5. changing behavior by modifying consequences
7. patient of Carl Rogers
9. blockage to psychoanalysis
10. patient puts feelings onto psychoanalyst
11. rational emotive therapy
12. medical doctor treats mental illness

Down

1. study of drugs on behavior
3. treatment of mental disorders
4. psychiatrist who follows Freud
6. expressing emotion
8. person being treated

Puzzle created with Puzzlemaker at DiscoverySchool.com

Chapter 15 - Answers

Practice Test 1

1. d (p. 499)
2. c (p. 491)
3. a (p. 503)
4. b (p. 506)
5. a (p. 508)
6. c (p. 511)
7. b (p. 509)
8. b (p. 511)
9. c (p. 505)
10. d (p. 492)

Practice Test 2

1. d (p. 513)
2. b (p. 494)
3. c (p. 492)
4. b (p. 488)
5. a (p. 489)
6. d (p. 503)
7. d (p. 496)
8. a (p. 502)
9. a (p. 504)
10. c (p. 504)

Practice Test 3

1. d (p. 489)
2. b (p. 491)
3. c (p. 494)
4. d (p. 495)
5. b (p. 493)
6. b (p. 496)
7. d (p. 501)
8. a (p. 492)
9. c (p. 492)
10. d (p. 504)

Comprehensive Test

Multiple Choice

1. a (p. 495)
2. b (p. 508)
3. a (p. 496)
4. c (p. 506)
5. a (p. 513)
6. b (p. 489)
7. b (p. 503)
8. a (p. 509)
9. b (p. 512)
10. c (p. 495)
11. d (p. 492)
12. c (p. 503)
13. b (p. 507)
14. c (p. 501)
15. a (p. 493)

True/False

1. T (p. 506)
2. F (p. 507)
3. F (p. 509)
4. F (p. 501)
5. F (p. 501)
6. F (p. 495)
7. T (p. 495)
8. F (p. 503)

Crossword Key

Across

2. Psychosurgery
5. Contingency Management
7. Client
9. Resistance
10. Transference
11. RET
12. Psychiatrist

Down

1. Psychopharmacology
3. Psychotherapy
4. Psychoanalyst
6. Catharsis
8. Patient

**Chapter 16**

Social Cognition and Relationships

Before you read . . .

How do people think about their world? This chapter addresses social cognition and relationships. It begins with constructing social reality then goes on to explain how people generate causal explanations. The origins of attribution theory, the fundamental attribution error, and the self-serving bias are highlighted. Next, expectations and self-fulfilling prophecies are explained. The chapter shows how expectations can shape outcomes. The text goes on to discuss attitudes, attitude change, and action. What is the relationship between attitudes and behavior? What is the process of persuasion? Can your own behaviors lead you to modify your attitudes? Coverage continues with compliance. How do you get people to comply with your requests? Next, the topic of prejudice is presented, including the origins of prejudice, effects of stereotypes, and how to reverse prejudice. The chapter ends with the topic of social relationships. What forces lead to liking or loving? After all, we are all social creatures.

Chapter Objectives

After reading this chapter you should be able to:

- Define social reality and social perception.

- Define attribution theory and the covariation principle.

- Explain the fundamental attribution error, self-serving bias, and self-fulfilling prophecy.

- Describe behavioral confirmation.

- Define attitudes.

- Differentiate between the central and peripheral route of persuasion.

- Contrast dissonance theory and self-perception theory.

- Describe the factors that affect compliance.

- Discuss the role of in-group vs. out-group thinking has in prejudice.

- Define stereotypes.

- Describe how the effects of prejudice can be eliminated through jigsaw classrooms.

- Discuss the importance of friendship in eliminating prejudice.

- Discuss the determinants of interpersonal attraction including proximity, physical attractiveness, similarity, and reciprocity.

- Discuss loving relationships in term of passion, intimacy, and commitment.

- Describe the interdependence theory.

As you read . . . Term Identification

Attitude	Persuasion
Attribution Theory	Prejudice
Behavioral Confirmation	Racism
Cognitive Dissonance	Reciprocity Norm
Compliance	Self-fulfilling Prophecy
Contact Hypothesis	Self-perception Theory
Covariation Principle	Self-serving Bias
Elaboration Likelihood Model	Sexism
Fundamental attribution Error	Social Categorization
In-group Bias	Social Cognition
In-groups	Social Perception
Jigsaw Classrooms	Social Psychology
Out-groups	Stereotypes

Constructing Social Reality

How does the Princeton-Dartmouth football game illustrate the construction of social reality?

The Origins of Attribution Theory

Summarize early contributions to attribution theory.

1. Fritz Heider: What did he mean by "intuitive psychologist"? What categories of attributions do people make?

2. Harold Kelley: What is the covariation principle? Define and give examples of distinctiveness, consistency, and consensus.

The Fundamental Attribution Error

1. What is the fundamental attribution error (FAE)? Give examples.

2. Why do people commit the FAE?

3. How do construals of selves affect the FAE?

Self-Serving Biases

What are self-serving biases? How does friendship limit self-serving biases?

Expectations and Self-Fulfilling Prophecies

1. What is a self-fulfilling prophecy? Summarize the experiment on the Pygmalion effect.

2. Under what circumstances are self-fulfilling prophecies most likely to occur? Summarize the Keith/Karen experiment.

Behaviors That Confirm Expectations

1. How did Mark Snyder define behavioral confirmation?

2. When do impressions have their greatest effect?

Attitudes, Attitude Change, and Action

How is attitude defined?

Attitudes and Behaviors

1. Identify the three types of information that produce your attitude:

   a.

   b.

   c.

2. Why does attitude accessibility predict behavior?

3. What makes attitudes accessible?

Processes of Persuasion

1. What is the elaboration likelihood model? Contrast the central and peripheral routes to persuasion.

2. How does time of day affect persuasion?

3. Why is it important to have a match between advertisements and attitudes?

Persuasion by Your Own Actions

1. How did Leon Festinger define cognitive dissonance?

2. What motivation is provided by dissonant beliefs?

3. How can dissonance change attitudes? Summarize the $1/$20 experiment.

4. What impact does culture have on dissonance?

5. According to Daryl Bem, how are attitudes affected by self-perception?

Compliance

1. Define compliance.

2. Summarize these compliance strategies.

   a) Reciprocity:

   b) Commitment:

   c) Scarcity:

Prejudice

Define prejudice. Why have social psychologists studied prejudice?

Origins of Prejudice

1. What is the relationship between social categorization and prejudice?

2. What is an in-group bias?

3. How do feelings of sexism and racism affect how people perceive the world?

4. How is nonprejudice measured?

Effects of Stereotypes

1. Define stereotypes.

2. How do stereotypes generate expectations? What is the effect of those expectations?

3. What is behavioral confirmation?

Reversing Prejudice

1. What experimental procedures have been used to diminish prejudice? Refer to the Robbers Cave experiment and Aronson's use of jigsawing.

2. How can friendship diminish prejudice?

Liking

1. What roles do proximity and mere exposure play in liking?

2. Summarize other factors that contribute to liking.

    a) Physical attractiveness:

    b) Similarity:

    c) Reciprocity:

Loving

1. What are three dimensions of love?

2. What is the difference between loving someone and being "in love"?

3. How does adult attachment style affect loving relationships?

4. What is the difference between passionate and companionate love?

5. What impact do construals of the self have on people's expectations about love?

6. How do the following factors affect the longevity of loving relationships?

   a) The "other" in the "self":

   b) Interdependence:

Psychology in Your Life

1. How often are relationships formed over the Internet?

2. How do relationships begun over the Internet differ from those begun face-to-face?

For Group Study

Constructing Social Reality

People are constantly making causal attributions in everyday conversation. Listen for occasions in which people are explaining the reasons for daily occurences. Have each member of the group collect 5 to 10 everyday causal explanations. Are people making the fundamental attribution error? Do you know enough about the situation to tell? Are people using self-serving biases?

Attitudes, Attitude Change, and Action

Analyze a recent magazine to assess the match between products and advertisements. As you carry out this exercise, also discuss other aspects of the ads. For example, were the ad writers hoping you'd take the central or peripheral route to persuasion?

Prejudice

Take this opportunity for members of the group to explore their own experiences with prejudice. Have they been victims of unfair stereotypes? Are there prejudices they might want to overcome? Can research presented in the text serve as a basis to overcome those prejudices?

Social Relationships

Cut out several pictures of people from a magazine. In your group, rate the pictures 1-attractive, 2-neutral and 3- unattractive. Did you get the same results? Is physical attraction universal? Is physical attraction necessary for love?

Practice Test 1

1. The study of the ways in which thoughts, feelings, perceptions, motives, and behavior are influenced by interactions between people is known as _____ psychology.

a. social
b. cultural
c. clinical.
d. forensic

2. You are working as the campaign manager for Greta Wurz in her congressional race against Polly Badd (who currently holds the position). If you want to get people to shift their support from Badd to Wurz, you might pay Badd supporters _____ to tell you what they _____ about her.

a. $20; like
b. $1; like
c. $20; dislike
d. $1; dislike

3. Just as professional psychologists make causal attributions, Fritz Heider suggested we are all _____ psychologists.

a. intuitive
b. amateur
c. practical
d. practicing.

4. In a social psychology lecture, the professor tells you a story about a time she was invited to a birthday party by a friend. Her car broke down along the way so she never got to the party. Since that time, her ex-friend always tells people that she is "very unreliable." Your professor's story is an example of _____ at work.

a. normative influence processes
b. a total situation
c. a self-fulfilling prophecy
d. the fundamental attribution error

5. You are trying to decide whether to get a $200 VCR or a $300 VCR. While you are trying to make up your mind, the salesperson points to the $300 VCR and says, "If you buy the better model, I'll give you a free three-pack of blank video tapes." This salesperson is acquainted with the use of _____ as a marketing technique.

a. modeling
b. scarcity
c. reciprocity
d. commitment

6. If you'd like to increase the probability of persuading a friend based on cognitive-based arguments, then you should avoid topics

a. for which your friend's attitudes are not accessible.
b. for which your friend has no specific attitudes.
c. that are affect-based.
d. that provide inconsistent norms.

7. You want people to drink a new brand of coffee. You're best off using a _____ based ad.

a. reciprocity
b. commitment
c. elaboration-likelihood
d. emotion

8. Your friend Sadie has invited you to a party. Unknown to you, Sadie has told all the other guests that you are painfully shy and introverted. You stay at the party for about an hour. Is it likely that the other guests will still believe you to be introverted at the end of the hour?

a. Yes—if you have a strong conception of yourself as outgoing.
b. Yes—if you have a weak conception of yourself as outgoing.
c. No—because behavioral confirmation does not affect social judgments.
d. No—because the party setting creates cognitive dissonance.

9. Which of these statements shows the effect of a self-serving bias?

a. "I would've done better on this test if I had studied a couple more hours."
b. "I would've caught that ball if the field hadn't been so muddy."
c. "I wouldn't have won today if I didn't have such a good coach."
d. "I wouldn't have lost so much money if I'd listened to my brother's advice."

10. In determining how best to promote water conservation, we can assume that students will follow the desired pattern of water use

a. when the persuasive statements match the students optimal time of day.
b. when instructions were given on a prominent sign.
c. after they attended discussion sessions about water conservation.
d. after they heard a lecture about environmental issues.

Practice Test 2

1. When Jane is asked her opinion about regulating smoking on campus, she voices an extensive opinion almost immediately. You can predict that her attitude about regulating smoking on campus will be a good predictor of her actual behavior according to the _____ criterion of attitude-behavior consistency.

a. accessibility
b. indirect experience
c. specificity
d. liking

2. Which of the following questions will best allow you to predict whether someone will stay in a loving relationship?

a. Is companionate love more important to you than passionate love?
b. Are your important needs being satisfied?
c. Do you share similar opinions with your partner?
d. Do you consider yourself to be physically attractive?

3. Professor Miles is interested in the process by which people come to understand and categorize the behavior of others. When she is looking for a new job, Professor Miles should probably indicate on her resumé that her field of specialization is

a. social psychology.
b. leadership styles.
c. social perception.
d. social relations.

4. Elliot Aronson and his colleagues developed a program to deal with prejudice in fifth-grade students. Based on the Robbers Cave philosophy, a technique called _____ forces children to _____.

a. compartmentalization; be dependent on one another
b. compartmentalization; compete against one another
c. jigsawing; be dependent on one another
d. jigsawing; compete against one another

5. Social psychology experiments on the nature of prejudice and the process of social categorization have shown that when "in groups" are established,

a. the result is more pleasant relationships with out-group members.
b. bias toward the out-group forms almost instantly.
c. weak in-group solidarity is an immediate consequence.
d. they cannot overcome positive experiences that in-group members have with out-group members.

6. A citizen of the former East Germany believes that Poles and Turks are a financial drain on the society because they take jobs and work away from Germans. This attitude is most likely based on

a. prejudicial attitudes.
b. differences in political ideology between Germans and Poles and Turks.
c. a learned prejudice based on historical conflict between the various groups.
d. threat of competition from Poles and Turks.

7. The definition of prejudice does NOT suggest that prejudice

a. involves negative feelings.
b. has a strong genetic or unlearned component.
c. involves stereotypical beliefs that justify the attitude.
d. includes a behavioral intention to avoid, control, dominate, or eliminate the target group.

8. Someone who scored high on the _____ would endorse the statement "When I meet someone I tend to notice similarities between myself and the other person."

a. universal orientation scale.
b. prejudice/nonprejudice scale.
c. stereotype resistance scale.
d. social categorization scale.

9. Karl believes that if it weren't for illegal immigrants taking work away from American citizens, the American economy would be in much better shape. Ken believes illegal immigrants are part of the

a. tapestry.
b. jigsaw.
c. in-group.
d. out-group.

10. Stereotypes

a. remain an accurate source for making attributions.
b. lead to an attitude of preference toward another human being.
c. produce behavioral confirmations.
d. are based on cultural norms of proper behavior.

Practice Test 3

1. How powerful are the forces of behavioral confirmation?

a. It depends on the strength of the observer's expectations.
b. Not very powerful when there is a scarcity of accurate information from other sources.
c. It depends on the availability of accurate information from the environment and the extent to which the observer finds that information reliable.
d. So powerful that they are very difficult to modify once engaged.

2. When you answer the telephone, you are asked to make a minimal contribution to your school alumni fund. You agree to the requested amount. The next year, the amount that is requested is much larger. This is similar to the sales technique known as

a. commitment.
b. scarcity.
c. reciprocity.
d. entrapment.

3. When Fritz Heider suggested that all people are "intuitive psychologists," he was expressing his belief that people

a. generally do not agree with the Freudian perspective on behavior.
b. try to figure others out and what causes their behavior.
c. prefer inductive reasoning to deductive reasoning.
d. respond on the basis of emotions and "hunches."

4. In the context of adult attachment style, if you are like the majority of people, you are most likely to agree with which of the following statements?

a. I am somewhat uncomfortable being close to others.
b. I often worry that my partner doesn't really love me or won't want to stay with me.
c. I find it relatively easy to get close to others I am in close proximity to, and am comfortable depending on them.
d. I want to get very close to my partner, and this sometimes scares people away.

5. When Sarita scores goals for her soccer team, she takes the credit, saying she did well because she has a "gift" for scoring. When she does not score any goals, however, she blames her teammates for not passing her the ball or the opposition players for dirty tackling. Sarita is demonstrating

a. the fundamental attribution error.
b. the Pygmalion effect.
c. prejudice.
d. a self-serving bias.

6. A group of researchers is interested in people's attitudes about recycling in their region. Which of the following levels of questions that the researchers may ask will yield the highest correlation between people's attitudes and their actual behaviors?

a. Attitudes toward the environment.
b. Attitudes toward recycling.
c. Attitudes toward recycling in general.
d. Attitudes toward recycling in the United States.

7. One can hold attitudes about

a. people and objects.
b. ideas.
c. objects and ideas.
d. people, objects, and ideas.

8. Many of today's critics claim that much of political advertising focuses on style and image, but not on substance and factual information. Social psychologists who conduct research on attitude change would say that today's political ads emphasize the

a. best in politics.
b. worst in politics.
c. central route to persuasion.
d. peripheral route to persuasion.

9. Dick and Didi have been involved in a loving relationship for a few months. Ralph and Alice have been involved for many years. Dick and Didi's relationship is more likely to be characterized as _____ love; Ralph and Alice's relationship is more likely to be called _____ love.

a. positive; negative
b. attached; sad
c. pragmatic; erotic
d. passionate; companionate

10. In the experiment by Robert Rosenthal that was described in the textbook, elementary school teachers were led to believe that some of their pupils were "academic spurters" who would show unusual gains during the academic year. The outcome of this study demonstrated the importance of

a. cognitive dissonance.
b. self-fulfilling prophecies.
c. self-perception theory.
d. interpersonal attraction.

Comprehensive Test

1. Tina likes Ted. If we are like most people, we will infer that Ted has the same feelings for Tina based on the idea of

a. the matching hypothesis.
b. reciprocity.
c. similarity.
d. physical attractiveness.

2. Which of the following people will be most motivated to reduce cognitive dissonance?

a. Edie, who decided at the last minute to go to a movie she initially didn't want to see.
b. Henny, who always gets a warm response to the jokes that he tells.
c. Muriel, who completed a "stop-smoking" program but has started smoking again.
d. Justin, who was a volunteer campaign worker for a successful political candidate.

3. Which of these is NOT one of the dimensions of love?

a. passion
b. commitment
c. intimacy
d. reciprocity

4. "If you ask me, I think liberals are losing touch with the majority of the population." This attitude reflects

a. a vicarious experience.
b. a cognitive experience.
c. an affective experience.
d. a behavioral experience.

5. One day your sister comes home from school very happy. She received an A on her geography test. In applying the covariation principle to understand the cause of her good grade, the "consensus" dimension refers to whether

a. she receives As in most of her courses.
b. she has received As consistently from this teacher in the past.
c. most other people taking the test also received As.
d. she studied especially hard for this test.

6. At your school's basketball game your team loses badly. The other team plays roughly, racking up penalties and injuring your guys. You come to understand and categorize the behavior of others due to

a. covariation
b. social perception
c. polarization
d. consistency

7. Kelly suggested we make judgments according to all of the following principles EXCEPT:

a. distinctiveness
b. consistency
c. perception
d. consensus

8. When given a choice between a situational or dispositional attribution for other's behavior, people tend to assume dispositional causes. This is known as the

a. attribution principle
c. covariation principle
c. social perception error
d. fundamental attribution error

9. Due to the _____, people tend to take credit for their successes and deny responsibility for their failures.

a. fundamental attribution error
b. covariation principle
c. consensus dominance
d. self-serving bias

10. The play *Pygmalion* and later the musical *My Fair Lady* is a great example of the

a. fundamental attribution error
b. social perception theory
c. self-fulfilling prophecy
d. self-serving bias

11. Attitudes consist of the following components EXCEPT:

a. emotional
b. cognitive
c. affective
d. behavioral

12. If you wanted to deliberately change someone's attitude you would use

a. elaboration
b. consensus
c. cognition
d. persuasion

13. Which theory says that it is the tension producing effects of incongruous cognitions that motivates us to reduce tension?

a. tension reduction theory
b. balance theory
c. cognitive dissonance
d. elaboration likelihood

14. One phenomenon that arises from the reciprocity norm is the _____ technique.

a. foot-in-the-door
b. door-the-face
c. commitment
d. scarcity

15. All of the following are elements of social categorization EXCEPT:

a. group think
b. in-groups
c. out-groups
d. in-group bias

True/False Questions

1. Kelly suggested people make judgments about people's actions according to distinctiveness, consistency, and cooperation.　　　　T　　　F

2. People are more likely to choose situational attributions for others' behavior.　　　　T　　　F

3. In the self-serving bias, people tend to take credit for successes and deny responsibility for failures.　　　　T　　　F

4. Expectations can change IQ.　　　　T　　　F

5. Attitudes consist of cognitive, affective, and behavioral components.　　　　T　　　F

6. Cognitive dissonance is the state of conflict someone experiences before developing a relationship with someone.　　　　T　　　F

7. Love can be clustered into three dimensions; passion, intimacy, and credence.　　　　T　　　F

8. Prejudice can be overcome only by indirect contact between hostile groups.　　　　T　　　F

Essay Questions

1. Outline the procedure of the classic "Robber's Cave" experiment. What happened to make competing groups work cooperatively? Will contact alone reduce prejudice?

2. What is the fundamental attribution error? Give an example from your life of the fundamental attribution error and the self-serving bias.

When you have finished . . . Weblinks

Understanding Prejudice

http://www.understandingprejudice.org

"Understanding Prejudice" is a web site for students, teachers, and others interested in the causes and consequences of prejudice. It contains more than 2,000 links to prejudice-related resources.

Attitudes Tutorial

http://sun.science.wayne.edu/~wpoff/cor/grp/attitude.html

This is a brief tutorial on attitudes. Definitions are hyperlinked to more detailed descriptions of attitudes and behavior.

Directory of Attraction, Affection and Love

http://www.allianceforlifelonglearning.org/er/tree.jsp?c=41781

From All Learn, the Alliance for Lifelong Learning comes an extensive directory of attraction, affection and love. They list websites that are reviewed and catalogued by university experts.

The Kinsey Group

http://www.indiana.edu/~kinsey/

Interested in love and sex? The Kinsey Institute promotes interdisciplinary research in the fields of human sexuality, gender, and reproduction. Educational links, publications and related resources are also available through this site.

Media Watch

http://www.mediawatch.com/

Ever think much about racism, sexism, and violence in the media? The Media Watch organizations goal is to challenge stereotypes and other biased images commonly found in the media. Media Watch provides information to help create more informed consumers of mass media.

Social Cognition and Relationships

Across
1. deliberate effort to change attitudes
4. going along with a direct request
6. groups with which people do not identify
8. judgment about the causes of outcomes

Down
2. generalizations
3. group with which people identify
5. evaluative response to people
7. return favors

Puzzle created with Puzzlemaker at DiscoverySchool.com

Chapter 16 - Answers

Practice Test 1

1. a (p. 518)
2. d (p. 528)
3. a (p. 519)
4. d (p. 519)
5. c (p. 537)
6. c (p. 527)
7. c (p. 525)
8. b (p. 523)
9 b (p. 521)
10. a (p. 527)

Practice Test 2

1. a (p. 524)
2. b (p. 539)
3. a (p. 518)
4. c (p. 535)
5. b (p. 531)
6. c (p. 531)
7. c (p. 532)
8. a (p. 531)
9. d (p. 531)
10. c (p. 533)

Practice Test 3

1. c (p. 533)
2. a (p. 529)
3. b (p. 519)
4. c (p. 536)
5. d (p. 521)
6. d (p. 525)
7. d (p. 524)
8. d (p. 525)
9. d (p. 538)
10. b (p. 521)

Comprehensive Test

Multiple Choice

1. b (p. 529)
2. a (p. 528)
3. d (p. 537)
4. b (p. 524)
5. c (p. 519)
6. b (p. 518)
7. c (p. 519)
8. d (p. 519)
9. d (p. 521)
10. c (p. 521)
11. a (p. 524)
12. d (p. 525)
13. c (p. 527)
14. b (p. 529)
15. a (p. 531)

True/False

1. F (p. 519)
2. F (p. 519)
3. T (p. 521)
4. T (p. 522)
5. T (p. 524)
6. F (p. 527)
7. F (p. 537)
8. F (p. 534)

Crossword Key

Across

1. Persuasion
4. Compliance
6. Out group
8. Attribution

Down

2. Stereotypes
3. In group
5. Attitude
7. Reciprocity

Social Processes, Society, and Culture

Before you read . . .

This is the second chapter about social psychology. It begins with the power of the situation and social norms, rules, and roles. This leads to a discussion of conformity. Classic experiments in group conformity are presented. The chapter goes on to discuss altruism and prosocial behavior. Why do people behave altruistically? When will people help others in distress? Next, aggression is presented in terms of evolutionary processes, individual differences, situational differences, and cultural constraints. How do people differ in their level of aggression? How do situations affect the likelihood of aggression? How does culture affect the display of aggression? The classic studies on obedience describe circumstances under which people blindly obey. The chapter then contains a presentation of the psychology of conflict and ends with the psychology of genocide and war, and peace psychology. How can your knowledge of social psychology be applied to help the world?

Chapter Objectives

After reading this chapter you should be able to:

- Describe the consequences of playing a social role.

- Define social norms.

- Describe the classic studies by Sherif and Asch on conformity.

- Explain decision making in groups, including the effects of group polarization and groupthink.

- Explain the motives for prosocial behavior, particularly altruism, egoism, collectivism, and principlism.

- Discuss the bystander intervention studies and what was learned from them.

- Discuss aggressive behavior in terms of the evolutionary perspective.

- Describe individual differences in aggressive behavior in terms of genetic, brain and hormonal function.

- Contrast impulsive and instrumental aggression.

- Describe the role of frustration and ongoing irritation in aggression levels.

- Discuss the effects of temperature, provocation, and culture on aggression.

- Describe Milgram's classic study of obedience.

- Discuss the link between prejudice, mass murder, and genocide.

- Describe the role of peace psychologists.

- Discuss the programs that may pave the way for peace.

As you read . . . Term Identification

Aggression	Impulsive Aggression
Altruism	Informational Influence
Bystander Intervention	Norm Crystallization
Conformity	Normative Influence
Demand Characteristics	Peace Psychology
Diffusion of Responsibility	Prosocial Behaviors
Frustration-Aggression Hypothesis	Reciprocal Altruism
Genocide	Rules
Group Dynamics	Social Categorization
Group Polarization	Social Norms
Groupthink	Social Role

As you read . . . Questions and Answers

Roles and Rules

1. What is a social role? Give examples. How do they affect you?

2. What is a social rule? Give examples. Are they always explicit?

3.   Summarize the methodology of the Stanford Prison Experiment.

4.   Summarize the results of the Stanford Prison Experiment. What does it teach you about roles and rules?

Social Norms

What are social norms? How do people adjust to them? How are they enforced?

Conformity

1.   What two types of influence may lead to conformity?

2.   How did Sherif's research demonstrate norm crystallization? What happened when "new generations" were formed?

3.   Summarize the methodology Solomon Asch used to study conformity.

   a)   What three factors did Asch vary to examine the effect on conformity? What did he discover?

   b)   Describe the individual differences that Asch found.

4.   Summarize the University of Toronto and Indiana University study.

5. Is it possible for a minority to withstand group pressure? What did Moscovici find?

6. Explain the distinction between normative and informational influence in minority influence.

Decision Making In Groups

1. What are the causes and consequences of group polarization?

2. What are the causes and consequences of groupthink?

Altruism and Prosocial Behavior

Define prosocial behavior and altruism.

The Roots of Altruism

1. What is the evolutionary perspective on altruism? How does it apply to helping kin?

2. What is reciprocal altruism? How does it apply to helping non-kin?

Motives for Prosocial Behavior

1. What are four motives for prosocial behavior?

2. How can different motives be in competition with each other?

The Effects of the Situation on Prosocial Behavior

1. What real-life event gave rise to research interest in bystander intervention?

2. Summarize Bibb Latané and John Darley's experiment on bystander intervention. How did it demonstrate the diffusion of responsibility?

3. Summarize the experiments or explanations that are described under each heading.

   a) Bystanders must notice the emergency:

   b) Bystanders must label events as an emergency:

   c) The bystander must feel responsibility:

Describe how you could use social psychology to get people to volunteer.

Aggression

Define aggression.

Evolutionary Perspectives

What claim did Karl Lorenz make about the human species? Was he correct?

Individual Differences

1. What evidence is there that there is a genetic component to individual differences in aggression?

2. Define each type of aggression, and summarize what is known about personality correlates.

    a) Impulsive aggression:

    b) Instrumental aggression:

Summarize research support for each of these situational influences on aggression.

    a) Frustration-aggression hypothesis

    b) Temperature and aggression

    c) Direct provocation and escalation

    1. How do construals of self influence the probability of aggressive acts?

    2. What is the culture of honor? What impact does it have on aggressive behaviors?

    3. What factors lead to different norms for aggressive behavior?

    1. Why does Stanley Milgram's research have so much real-world relevance?

    2. Summarize the basic procedure of Milgram's experiment.

3. How did the experimental participants (the teachers) respond to the request that they continue to give shocks? Did they continue?

4. Why were psychiatrists wrong in their predictions about the outcome of the experiment?

5. Describe the experiment that was cited to rule out the possibility that the Milgram result arose from a flawed cover story.

6. What are demand characteristics? Describe the experiment that ruled out the possibility that the result arose from them.

7. Summarize the explanations for people's willingness to obey authority. What factors influence compliance?

8. What lessons from Milgram's research can you apply in your own life?

The Psychology of Genocide and War

1. What is genocide? What series of events may lead to campaigns of genocide?

   a.

   b.

c.

d.

2. How do groups and governments dehumanize the "enemy"?

3. Describe explanations for why people will go to war.

Peace Psychology

1. Why were early social psychologists interested in the authoritarian personality?

2. Why and how did Kurt Lewin study group dynamics?

3. Summarize the effects of having each type of leader.

   Autocratic leaders:

   Democratic leaders:

   Laissez-faire leaders:

4. What types of governments are most likely to cost people their lives?

5. Explain two examples of situations in which contact can facilitate conflict resolution.

Northern Ireland:

The Middle East:

For Group Study

Social Norms

The time has come to think about your study group as a group. What norms do you think govern behavior in your study group? Discuss how the group became what it is today. Does everything you do make sense? How much did individual people contribute to the formulation of the norms? How do you make decisions? When you make decisions, are minority opinions respected?

You can also ask the same types of questions about the norms that govern life on your campus. How much does each member of your group think he or she has changed by virtue of internalizing social norms?

Conformity

How do you all feel about the results of these experiments? Consider, for example, the Asch experiment. How do the members of your group think they would have behaved as participants? Experiments of this sort teach important lessons about the power of situations. How do the members of the group feel about those lessons?

Aggression

We suggest that you undertake a heredity-versus-environment debate. Some members of the group should be responsible for the evolutionary and genetic approaches to the topic and the other members of the group should master evidence that situations matter. Try to examine particular events—perhaps by taking examples from the day's newspaper—and argue the merits of dispositional versus situational attributions about the roots of aggressive behaviors.

Obedience to Authority

Students are often fascinated and dismayed by this experiment. Your group should discuss whether the information gathered from the experiment was worth the burden put on the participants. (You might review the material on the ethics of research from Chapter 2.) How do group members think they would have behaved had they been "teachers"? Are people willing to acknowledge that the situation could prompt them to behave in ways that would, in retrospect, make them embarrassed or uncomfortable?

Practice Test 1

1. Based on the findings of the experiment cited in the textbook on the roots of altruism, who is most likely to perform altruistic behaviors?

a. Distant friends.
b. Close kin.
c. Acquaintances.
d. Strangers.

2. Reciprocal altruism includes the belief that

a. others will do the same in the future.
b. the world is fair.
c. you must act according to group norms, not your conscience.
d. accepting some deeds, no matter how harmful, is necessary under the right circumstances.

3. The research of Kurt Lewin and his colleagues suggests that an elementary-school teacher who has an autocratic style in the classroom can expect her pupils to be

a. shy and withdrawn.
b. attentive and undemanding.
c. inventive and independent, but also aggressive depending on the task they are working at.
d. hard working, but only when the teacher is watching them.

4. Barney believes that democracy works better than any other political system. When he is challenged to prove his conclusion, he says he bases his statement on

a. historical proof.
b. the behavior of people in small groups.
c. research that samples the behavior of all the people in the country.
d. research involving both small groups and whole countries.

5. The textbook describes the brutal murder of Kitty Genovese to illustrate the social psychology research topic known as

a. bystander intervention.
b. obedience to authority.
c. altruistic contradictions.
d. the self-serving bias.

6. In Stanley Milgram's research, what typically happened when the teacher (the experimental participant) began to protest the experimenter's instructions to continue administering shocks?

a. The participants refused to administer any more shocks.
b. The experimenter allowed the participant to stop.
c. The participants continued to give higher shocks.
d. The experimenter threatened the participants so that they would continue.

7. During lecture, the student next to you asks you what the professor had said about Kurt Lewin's research interests. Because you were paying attention, you inform him that he is most closely associated with the study of

a. the self-serving bias.
b. bystander intervention.
c. the self-fulfilling prophecy.
d. group dynamics.

8. When participants in Milgram's experiments on obedience protested while delivering the shocks, the experimenter

a. verbally ordered the participant to continue.
b. ended the study immediately.
c. shocked the participant.
d. physically forced the participant to continue.

9. A peace psychologist would NOT be likely to try to

a. understand how nations negotiate and make judgments about each others' actions.
b. help military leaders improve techniques for dehumanizing enemies.
c. assist people in reshaping their lives to cope with democratic principles.
d. understand the forces that lead to crises between nations.

10. Your friend Matt is asking you how likely you think it is that he would help out if he were in a bystander situation. One thing you tell him that is NOT very important is whether

a. he notices the emergency.
b. he labels the events as an emergency.
c. he feels a sense of responsibility.
d. he thinks of himself as a nice person.

Practice Test 2

1. Rules that state, "Don't smoke " or Don't eat in class" are known as

a. subjective.
b. objective.
c. explicit.
d. implicit.

2. Sally decides that she will help her friend move. Social psychologists would classify Sally's behavior as

a. altruistic.
b. social.
c. authoritarian.
d. a survival mechanism.

3. Stanley Milgram's research on obedience leads to the conclusion that the blind obedience of the Nazis during the reign of Hitler was due to

a. the German militaristic personality.
b. dispositional characteristics.
c. situational forces.
d. human nature.

4. Which of the following has NOT been found to increase potential for aggression?

a. high temperatures
b. intentional behavior designed to make another person angry
c. escalation of conflict
d. imaginary insults

5. In Kurt Lewin's research on group dynamics, _____ leadership produced groups that were inefficient and did poor-quality work.

a. democratic
b. laissez-faire
c. indulgent
d. autocratic

6. Latané and Darley demonstrated that whether participants would come to the aid of someone in need of help was dependent on

a. the personality of the participants.
b. the gender of the participants.
c. the number of people who were available to help.
d. the appearance of the person who needed help.

7. The major reason that civilians are harmed during war is to

a. produce conformity.
b. indicate dominance.
c. dehumanize the enemy.
d. break the will of the people.

8. The research of Bibb Latané and John Darley points to the importance of _____ as an explanation for bystander "apathy."

a. childhood experiences
b. one's prior experience with authority figures
c. situational forces
d. personality characteristics

9. Kurt Lewin and his colleagues suggested that bullies who identify scapegoats among their classmates to use as targets for their hostility and aggression are likely to be the classes of teachers who use a(n) _____ leadership style.

a. autocratic
b. democratic
c. laissez-faire
d. authoritative

10. In a study, seminarians who were going to deliver a lecture were made to come across a man in obvious need of assistance. We can predict that those most likely to help were those who

a. thought others would take notice of their kindness and reward them financially.
b. had never been in the predicament of the victim themselves.
c. felt empathy-altruism.
d. noticed that others were available to help the victim.

Practice Test 3

1. The classic Asch Experiments studied

a. institutional aggression.
b. bystander apathy.
c. obedience.
d. conformity.

2. The process that Herbert Kelman has used to foster communication among Israelis and Palestinians is

a. jigsawing.
b. diffusion of responsibility.
c. authoritarian cooperation.
d. interactive problem solving.

3. Researchers have found a strong genetic component to aggression. Their research has focused on which neurotransmitter?

a. endorphins.
b. serotonin.
c. dopamine.
d. serotonin

4. The possibility that participants in Milgram's obedience experiment did NOT believe the learner was really getting shocked was ruled out by another study in which participants

a. were tricked into believing they were actually hurting a puppy that they saw jump when shocked.
b. were required to trade places with the learner, so that they could experience the shock themselves.
c. could hear the learner yelling that the shock was painful.
d. were told that a medical doctor would be present and provide feedback at the end of the experiment

5. Why was the Stanford Prison Study stopped?

a. the prisoners rebelled and became uncooperative.
b. many of the participants suffered severe emotional and behavioral effects.
c. administration officials no longer supported faculty.
d. several onlookers reported problems in the scientific method

6. In the field study of obedience that was described in the textbook, groups of hospital nurses were told by an unknown doctor to administer medication to a patient in the doctor's absence. Nurses who were asked said that they would _____ the doctor; nurses who had the opportunity to carry out the order _____ obey the doctor.

a. not obey; did not
b. not obey; did
c. obey; did not
d. obey; did

7. With which of the following statements is a proponent of an evolutionary explanation of war most likely to agree?

a. "People go to war in order to preserve unity in the society."
b. "War may be hell, but sometimes it is the only alternative to preserve the species."
c. "War destroys the most aggressive members of the society, thereby enhancing the probability that the less aggressive members of the society will reproduce."
d. "People may participate in aggressive acts because they believe they are protecting the interests of their own family."

8. Janek comes from a culture that emphasizes interdependence among its members. If you had to guess about his tendency to act aggressively against others, you would say

a. he is more likely to act aggressively.
b. he is more likely to act aggressively, but only verbally.
c. he is less likely to act aggressively.
d. he is less likely to act verbally aggressively, but more physically aggressive.

9. Beau and Merl are arguing over whether politeness and how people respond to insults is related to being a southerner or a northerner. Having just read information on this topic, you inform the two combatants that

a. southerners are more impolite than northerners when not insulted and react more dramatically than northerners to an insult.
b. northerners are more impolite than southerners when not insulted and react more dramatically than southerners to an insult.
c. southerners are more polite than northerners when not insulted and react more dramatically than northerners to an insult.
d. northerners are more polite than southerners when not insulted and react more dramatically than southerners to an insult.

10. The authors of the textbook suggest that one deterrent to behaving in the blindly obedient manner exhibited by many of the participants in Milgram's research is to

a. be willing to be a "team player" if that behavior is required of you.
b. institute psychological training programs to make people less evil.
c. leave the decision making up to those who are in authority.
d. be aware that situational forces are powerful enough to affect you.

Comprehensive Test

1. Instrumental aggression is

a. subtle and easily diffused
b. emotionally fueled.
c. goal directed and cognition based.
d. produced in reaction to situational variables.

2. A group of children expecting to play with a number of attractive toys are frustrated by being kept away from the toys for a period of time. Based on the frustration-aggression hypothesis, how will the children behave once they are allowed to play with the preferred toys?

a. They will act aggressively toward the toys.
b. They will be happy to finally have the opportunity to play with the toys.
c. They will act aggressively toward the other children, but not the toys.
d. It depends on the amount of time they have been kept away from the toys.

3. Which of the following research approaches is LEAST likely to contribute to our understanding of the evolutionary basis of aggression?

a. Meta-analysis studies that combine findings from many studies on the genetic basis of aggression.
b. Comparing monozygotic and dizygotic twins for aggressive tendencies.
c. Analyzing the contribution of nature versus nurture by examining children raised in adoptive homes.
d. Comparing the prevalence of criminal behavior from one generation to the next.

4. You overhear a conversation among a group of students. One of them says something that leads you to believe that he is particularly sensitive to the normative influence of his peer group. He is most likely to have said,

a. "I'm not sure what would be the best way to act in this situation."
b. "I didn't help because I wasn't sure it was an emergency."
c. "I'm not going to the party because I'm sure I won't have a good time."
d. "It's really important to me to be liked and accepted by my friends."

5. Professor Reilly plans to replicate the Stanford Prison Experiment. He wants to reproduce exactly the methodology of the original experiment. It's most important for him to ensure that the students

a. chosen for guard roles be more aggressive.
b. chosen for guard roles be more passive.
c. be assigned to guard and prisoner roles randomly.
d. have the option of choosing to be prisoners or guards.

6. In Solomon Asch's experiments on conformity, he found that

a. the presence of an ally greatly reduced conformity.
b. most participants conformed on a majority of occasions.
c. the discrepancy between the correct and incorrect line did not influence the rate of conformity.
d. all participants conformed on at least one occasion.

7. To be accepted as a "Teen Tiger," you must get a certain type of haircut, wear the right clothes, share the group's attitudes and opinions, and be able to use and understand the "language" of the group. These are examples of what social psychologists refer to as

a. the autokinetic effect.
b. social norms.
c. negative consequences.
d. norm crystallization.

8. Socially defined patterns of behavior that are expected of a person when they are functioning in a given setting or in groups are called _____, and the explicit and implicit behavioral guidelines for specific settings are known as _____.

a. social norms; expectations
b. self-serving biases; social goals
c. demand characteristics; rules
d. social roles; rules

9. Once norms are established in a group, they tend to perpetuate themselves. This is known as

a. law enactment.
b. rule establishment.
c. norm crystallization.
d. group think.

10. In the meeting with the other executives, Arty is focusing attention on the motion that has just been presented. While others simply accept what is said, he consistently brings up important, relevant ideas that contradict the majority view. This is an example of the potential for group members in the minority to

a. have informational influence.
b. create a norm of reciprocity.
c. find allies who also refuse to conform.
d. have normative influence.

11. Shakespeare wrote that "one man in his time may play many parts." Social psychologists refer to these "parts" as

a. social roles.
b. social goals.
c. social norms.
d. demand characteristics.

12. Although she has never been told not to do so, Jasmine is hesitant to disagree with her master music teacher. This is an example of what social psychologists would call a(n)

a. social guideline.
b. implicit rule.
d. explicit rule.
d. behavioral constraint.

13. Asch's experiment is an important demonstration of

a. norm crystallization.
b. normative influence.
c. the door-in-the-face technique.
d. information influence

14. Research on norm crystallization using the autokinetic effect and techniques pioneered by Muzafer Sherif has demonstrated that

a. participants will openly ridicule group members who do not conform to group norms.
b. one participant in each group will take over the leadership role.
c. norms established in groups do not apply when participants are tested individually.
d. group norms persist from generation to generation of participants.

15. When Louie goes on a campus tour with his older brother, he notices that all of the students are wearing turned-around baseball caps. If he asks his brother why they are doing so, his brother should say that this is an example of

a. conformity.
b. obedience.
c. covariation.
d. a demand characteristic.

True/False Questions

1. Some rules are explicitly stated in signs or taught to children.   T   F

2. The classic Stanford Prison study was a surprise because some student guards and inmates adopted their roles so powerfully.   T   F

3. Conformity is the expectation that a group has for its members regarding acceptable and appropriate behavior of other groups.   T   F

4. People sometimes conform because of normative influence.   T   F

5. Prosocial behaviors are behaviors that are carried out with the goal of helping other people.   T   F

6. In the research on aggression there seems to be a stronger environmental component cause than genetic.   T   F

7. Violence increases as temperature increases   T   F.

8. The lessons of history dehumanize the enemy and result in the military's reluctance to wage war.   T   F

Essay Questions

1. Discuss the Milgram's classic study on obedience. What implications does this have for our principle of informed consent today? Could we do the same experiment today?

2. What is the effect of autocratic, democratic, and laissez-faire group leadership on productivity and group cohesion?

When you have finished . . . Weblinks

Prisoner's Dilemma Game

http://serendip.brynmawr.edu/bb/pd.html

The classic Prisoner's Dilemma Game has to do with cooperation versus competition. Try this interactive exercise from Bryn Mawr University.

The Perils of Obedience

http://www.recrea.f9.co.uk/obedience.htm

This is the original article "The Perils of Obedience" as it appeared in *Harper's Magazine*. Abridged and adapted from *Obedience to Authority* by Stanley Milgram. Copyright 1974 by Stanley Milgram. It outlines Milgram's classic study on obedience.

The Stanford Prison Experiment

http://www.prisonexp.org

The Stanford Prison study was a classic experiment in social roles that surprised the psychological community. This site has slides of the study that continues to intrigue us today.

AFF: Cultic Studies

http://www.csj.org

The International Cultic Studies Association (ICSA) is an interdisciplinary network of academicians, professionals, former group members, and families who study and educate the public about social-psychological influence and control, authoritarianism, and zealotry in cultic groups, alternative movements, and other environments.

Group Dynamics

http://www.richmond.edu/~dforsyth/gd/

The group dynamics resource site provides links to studies related to group dynamics.

Social Processes, Society and Culture

Across

1. performed classic study on conformity
3. behaviors that cause harm
6. performed classic study on obedience
8. systematic destruction of a group

Down

2. adopting the behaviors or attitudes of the group
3. prosocial behavior
4. socially defined behavior expected of the group
5. group decision making that filters undesirable input
7. guidelines for action

Puzzle created with Puzzlemaker at DiscoverySchool.com

Chapter 17 - Answers

Practice Test 1

1. b (p. 554)
2. a (p. 554)
3. d (p. 573)
4. d (p. 573)
5. a (p. 556)
6. c (p. 567)
7. d (p. 572)
8. a (p. 567)
9. b (p. 572)
10. d (p. 557)

Practice Test 2

1. c (p. 546)
2. a (p. 553)
3. c (p. 568)
4. d (p. 562)
5. b (p. 572)
6. c (p. 556)
7. d (p. 571)
8. c (p. 556)
9. a (p. 573)
10. c (p. 555)

Practice Test 3

1. d (p. 549)
2. d (p. 574)
3. b (p. 560)
4. a (p. 567)
5. b (p. 547)
6. b (p. 568)
7. d (p. 559)
8. c (p. 563)
9. c (p. 564)
10.d (p. 569)

Comprehensive Test

<table>
<tr><td>

Multiple Choice

1. c (p. 561)
2. a (p. 561)
3. d (p. 559)
4. d (p. 549)
5. c (p. 547)
6. a (p. 550)
7. b (p. 548)
8. d (p. 546)
9. c (p. 549)
10. a (p. 549)
11. a (p. 546)
12. b (p. 546)
13. b (p. 549)
14. d (p. 549)
15. a (p. 549)

</td><td>

True/False

1. T (p. 546)
2. T (p. 547)
3. F (p. 549)
4. T (p. 549)
5. T (p. 553)
6. T (p. 560)
7. T (p. 562)
8. F (p. 570)

</td></tr>
</table>

Crossword Key

Across

1. Asch
3. Aggression
6. Milgram
8. Genocide

Down

2. Conformity
3. Altruism
4. Social Role
5. Groupthink
7. Rules

NOTES

NOTES

NOTES

NOTES

NOTES

NOTES

NOTES